HARVARD THEOLOGICAL STUDIES

HARVARD THEOLOGICAL STUDIES
XVIII

THE
NORMAN ANONYMOUS
OF 1100 A.D.

TOWARD THE IDENTIFICATION AND EVALUATION
OF THE SO-CALLED ANONYMOUS OF YORK

BY

GEORGE HUNTSTON WILLIAMS

ISSUED AS AN EXTRA NUMBER OF THE
HARVARD THEOLOGICAL REVIEW

CAMBRIDGE
HARVARD UNIVERSITY PRESS
LONDON: GEOFFREY CUMBERLEGE
OXFORD UNIVERSITY PRESS
1951

To My Grandparents
DAVID THOMAS WILLIAMS, D.D. (1851–1946)
Churchman

GEORGE W. PEASE (1853–1949)
Citizen

FOREWORD

THE PRESENT STUDY is a reworking of my doctoral dissertation, "The Bearing of Christology on the Relationship between Church and State as Illustrated by the So-Called Anonymous of York," Union Theological Seminary, New York, 1946. A fresh exploration of the field has been made possible by using microfilm (unavailable during the war) of the hitherto unpublished Tractates of MS 415 of Corpus Christi College, Cambridge. I wish to acknowledge my appreciation to Dr. J. P. T. Bury, the Librarian of Corpus Christi, for procuring these microfilms for me and for furthering my research by his many other gracious acts. I wish also to thank the Master and Fellows of Corpus Christi College for their permission to print the hitherto unpublished portions of the Codex in the Appendix of the present study. Virtually all of this unique and important Codex surviving from the eleventh century is now available in print.

My study of the Anonymous began in a seminar under Professor Ernst Kantorowicz, formerly of Frankfurt and now of the University of California. He has been my guide and companion through all phases of the research up to the final revision of the present work. He has given unreservedly of his academic time and treasure and has known precisely the proper proportions of encouragement and criticism which constitute the art of true instruction. In him I have sensed a kindly and sustained concern for personality no less than for factual righteousness. As a would-be subject of the Kingdom, I salute him — a first citizen of the Republic of Letters in presenting my contribution to the subject of liturgical kingship which he has so brilliantly illuminated, especially in Laudes Regiae: A Study in Liturgical Acclamations and Medieval Ruler Worship (Berkeley, 1946).

I wish also to acknowledge my abiding indebtedness to Professor James Luther Adams of the University of Chicago, my beloved teacher in theology and Christian ethics, who, back in 1936, first introduced me to the problem of freedom and power, and to Professor John T. McNeill of Union Theological Seminary, chairman of my doctoral committee, for whose good counsel in the composition of the original dissertation I am profoundly grateful and to whose conception of the rôle of the Church I owe much — in the world, concerned for it, but never entirely of it, free to exercise its corporately prophetic function of constraining or exhorting the rulers of this world, subject to but One.

For assistance in the more recent phases of my research, I wish to thank Madame la Directrice des Bibliothèques de la ville de Rouen, Charles R. Dodwell of Gonville and Caius College and Prof. Ruth J. Dean of Mount Holyoke for advice on the script of Rouen and the Archbishop Robert Benedictional, Professor Bernard M. Peebles of the Catholic University of America for guidance into the palaeographic literature relating to my problem, Director William L. M. Burke of the Princeton Index of Christian Art, Professor George Sarton of Harvard for expert opinion bearing on alchemy, Dr. Arnold Weinberger of Houghton Library for his generous bibliographical assistance, Mr. Ralph Lazzaro, my colleague in Church history, for his expert opinion on difficult places in the MS, Miss Alice Reynolds of Harvard College Library for procuring with speed and resourcefulness the numerous books I have used on inter-library loan, two sometime members of the Kantorowicz Seminar, John Phelan and Harvard Junior Fellow William Chaney, and three of my graduate students in medieval Church history, the Reverend James A. Dailey, Jr., the Reverend Charles J. Speel, II, and Father Frederick Neunert Lang. Finally, I wish to thank Professor Arthur Darby Nock, esteemed senior colleague, for the great encouragement he has given me in preparing my materials for publication.

Dr. Schafer Williams, former member of the Kantorowicz Seminar, read my Study in galley proof in connection with his work on the MSS of Pseudo-Isidore. I am especially grateful to him for his careful checking of my canonical arguments and for the corroborative evidence he has generously placed at my disposal.

A preliminary word is necessary about the numerous Latin quotations. In quoting the Anonymous, I have everywhere purposed to reproduce the edited texts where these are available with one main exception: I have chosen to standardize the MS u ($= v$) as v. (The principal editor, Heinrich Böhmer, used v in Libelli de lite and *u* in the texts he subsequently edited.) Some of the edited texts render the MS *ę* (= *ae* or *oe*) as *ę*, others simply as *e*, others as *ae*. Consistency here is all the more difficult for the reason that the MS itself displays all three forms and a fourth, namely, the syllabic abbreviation. For the last, in my own editing of the texts in the Appendix, I have regularly employed the expanded form. Otherwise I have reproduced the MS or the edited texts exactly as they are. Following Böhmer, I have modernized the punctuation and capitalization. Throughout the study, the thirty-one "Tractates" of the Codex will be commonly referred to by a combination of letters and numbers which indicate the number of the Tractate, the place of publication, and the page and some-times line reference. The names of the Tractates and other data may be found at the beginning of the Appendix.

HARVARD DIVINITY SCHOOL   *July 27, 1949*

TABLE OF CONTENTS

xii CONTENTS

PART I

A SURVEY OF LEARNED OPINION CONCERNING THE "YORK" TRACTATES

IT WAS EXACTLY fifty years ago that Heinrich Böhmer in his Kirche und Staat in England und in der Normandie im XI. und XII. Jahrhundert [1] assigned to a hitherto neglected Codex in the Library of Corpus Christi College, Cambridge [2] an important place in the history of the relations between Church and State, ascribing the bulk of the Tractates of the Codex to the sole authorship of one who has since been known as the "Anonymous of York." Two years previously, Böhmer had edited a selection of five of these Tractates for the Monumenta Germaniae Historica [3] and had tentatively ascribed them to Archbishop Gerard of York, sometime precentor of Rouen cathedral, but now after an exhaustive study of the whole Anglo-Norman Church, Böhmer felt constrained to withdraw his hypothesis concerning Gerard,[4] although he remained convinced that the locale of the later Tractates was York. The earlier Tractates of the Codex were clearly written in Rouen, and Böhmer had indeed already provided them with their Norman historical background in his critical edition of several of them in Libelli de lite, but desiring to give prominence to the corpus as a specimen of the English investiture controversy, he chose to refer to the whole Codex as the "York" Tractates. For fifty years there has been no fresh and comprehensive study of the Codex as a whole.

Before proceeding, however, to a discussion of new elements that may aid in the identification of the Anonymous of "York" and in a re-evaluation of the "York" Tractates, we shall do well to rehearse the findings of scholarship thus far and to trace the history of learned opinion concerning the importance of the Anony-

---

[1] Leipzig, 1899. Hereafter, Kirche.
[2] C.C.C.C. 415.
[3] Libelli de lite imperatorum et pontificum, III (Hannover, 1897).
[4] Kirche, p. 263.

mous allegedly of York. A glance at the Codex itself and the problem of its transmission will help get the matter in focus. Shortly before his death, in 1575, Matthew Parker, Archbishop of Canterbury, promised to present to his old College in Cambridge his treasure in manuscripts. Codex 415 was among these gifts. Unfortunately the provenance of the MS was not indicated. As we are no longer in possession of the original binding which was replaced by a modern one probably in the eighteenth century, we are virtually without indications of the earlier transmission. [5] The Codex contains some thirty-one diverse writings generally referred to as "Tractates." Actually only a portion of them deserve this formal designation. Several are mere sketches and fragments. Occasionally a "Tractate" is really a grouping of loosely related pieces which may have acquired a late title, either in the Table of Contents or within the body of the Codex. [6] Two Tractates are represented by a slightly variant copy or a second version. [7] The range of subject matter is wide: the freedom of metropolitans from the encroachment of primates, the illegitimacy of papally granted monastic exemptions from episcopal jurisdiction, the marriage of the clergy, problems relating to orders, the sacraments, canon law, and the relationship of the *regnum* and the *sacerdotium*. Two long Tractates on this last subject (and a second version of one of them) and in addition several minor pieces have, because of their originality and daring, been considered to give the character to the whole MS which is generally classified as of ecclesio-political significance. All the pieces of the Codex have such marked stylistic and conceptual affinities and so many borrowings and common citations of Scripture and canon law that until recently the homogeneity of the Codex as the literary remains of one writer had not been challenged.[8]

[5] For the problem of transmission, see below, pp. 32 ff. The old binding was lost some time before 1777, when James Nasmith, who comments bitterly on this carelessness, published his Catalogue. See his note on MS 200.

[6] For the discrepancies between the seventeen titles of the Table of Contents and the titles within the Codex, see the Appendix and the discussion pp. 26 ff.

[7] In the one case where the two versions follow each other in the Codex, they are numbered as one Tractate (24 A and B). In the other case where they are separated in the Codex, each has been given a number (22 = 26).

[8] See the discussion of Philipp Funk, "Der fragliche Anonymus von York," below, pp. 14 ff.

In 1621 Bishop Joseph Hall published a tract entitled "The Honour of the Married Clergie Maintained," [9] written against Edmund Coffin while Hall was still Dean of Worcester. At the end of the dissertation he appends the full text of our Tractate, J25/L1, "An liceat sacerdotibus inire matrimonium" [10] and his translation of it into English. Hall apparently attached some importance to the Tractate, for he closed his own tract with a paragraph of introduction to the appended Tractate, the full wording of which follows:

Yet to gratify my reader at the parting, I may not conceal from him an ancient and worthy monument which I had the favour and happiness to see in the inner library of Corpus Christi College in Cambridge: an excellent treatise, written among seventeen [11] other, in a fair set hand, by an author of great learning and antiquity. He would needs suppress his name, but describes himself to be Rotomagensis. The time wherein it was written appears to be amidst the heat of contention which was betwixt the archbishop of Canterbury and York over precedency; which quarrel fell betwixt Rodolph of Canterbury and Thurstin of York in the year 1114, at which time pope Paschalis wrote to king Henry concerning it . . . . The discourse shall speak enough for itself.[12]

It is evident that Hall had looked through the whole Codex when he "had the favour and happiness" to examine this Manuscript of a safely guarded collection. It is not unlikely that he found the royalist Tractates also to his taste, but nothing of their influence in his writings has been traced thus far. Hall was im-

---

[9] Works (London, 1634), I, 687. The circumstances of the composition of this treatise are given by George Lewis, A Life of Joseph Hall (London, 1886), pp. 223–26.

[10] The Tractates of the Anonymous of York will be henceforth referred to in this fashion. "J" stands for the numbering of the Tractates by Montague Rhodes James, A Descriptive Catalogue of the Manuscripts . . . of Corpus Christi College . . . , 2 vols. (Cambridge, 1909). The second reference is to the place where the text is printed, as here in "L," Libelli de lite III, 642–87 in the Monumenta Germaniae Historica where six Tractates have been edited. A complete list of the titles of the Tractates and an indication of where they are printed is given in the Appendix, pp. 206 ff.

[11] Hall has reference to the seventeen titles of the Table of Contents. But he should have said "sixteen other." See below, p. 27. The Codex is considered today as comprising thirty-one Tractates.

[12] Works I, 755; an historical note by Hall omitted; spelling modernized.

pressed by the Norman character of the writings and styled their author the "Anonymous of Rouen." [13]

On a commission from the editors of the Monumenta Germaniae Historica, Karl Hampe traveled in England in search of manuscripts and in his report on the scholarly journey in 1896 [14] published a description of the Codex, giving the late titles, or for want of these, the opening words of the Tractates. He adjudged them to be "kirchenpolitische Traktate, grösstenteils in Rouen um 1100 entstanden." They were assigned to Heinrich Böhmer for detailed examination and editing.

In some haste and with overconfidence in his preliminary conjectures, Böhmer ascribed, as we have already noted, the entire body of Tractates to Gerard, the Norman archbishop of York 1101–1108. In his editing of the most important Tractate, J24/ L4, "De consecratione," he collated the two versions, A and B, and left out a total of forty-seven pages "quae parum ad propositum nostrum facere viderentur." These omissions were perhaps unfortunate because the original contours of the text have been somewhat distorted by his collation.[15] Most of the great generalizations in the past fifty years about the significance of the "Anonymous of York" have been based upon the six Tractates Böhmer edited for the Monumenta. As we have already observed, Böhmer withdrew his ascription of the Tractates to Gerard of York,[16] but compensated for this admission by becoming even more certain about the biography of the author whom he now called simply the "Anonymous of York." The biographical details which he reconstructed and fitted into the historical context constitute a marvelous piece of scholarship which no one since has matched in precisely this area, although not a few have sensed an excess of confidence in his assigning of dates to several of the Tractates in

[13] That Hall's treatise on clerical marriage was translated into French at Geneva in 1685 and that this in turn, along with the appended Tractate of the Anonymous, was partly translated into German by Johann and Augustin Theiner in 1828 has only incidental interest.

[14] "Reise nach England, II," Neues Archiv, XXII (1897), pp. 669 ff.

[15] These omissions are accounted for in the Appendix of this study.

[16] Kirche, p. 261. Not noting Böhmer's revised hypothesis, Henry W. C. Davis in 1905 found a place for Archbishop Gerard as an important publicist of the reign of Henry I: England under the Normans and Angevins: 1066–1272 (London, 1905), II, 126.

terms of specific months and years. Fundamental to Böhmer's reconstructed biography of a hypothetical one-time monk of some St. Stephen's monastery (perhaps that at Caen), a sometime canon of the cathedral of Rouen, a royal chaplain, and a cleric in the circle of Gerard of York, was the assumption that all the Tractates in the Codex (with perhaps one or two exceptions) are from the same writer and that the discussion of the York-Canterbury controversy in a portion of one Tractate (J29/B29) is sufficient demonstration of the residence of the Anonymous in the province of York, defended in the Tractate. As Böhmer's research will remain monumental, even though his conclusions about authorship may be contested, as, for example, by Philipp Funk, we shall nevertheless have ample occasion to refer to his valid findings.

In 1906 Siegmund Hellmann in search of the literary remains of Sedulius Scottus published an excerpt from Tractate J24/L4 which Böhmer had not printed, namely nine axioms from the Proverbia Graecorum.[17] Of these nine, one is found neither in Sedulius Scottus' Collectaneum nor in his Liber de rectoribus Christianis. The establishment of this fact by Hellmann shows that the Anonymous may have had access to the complete body of Proverbia Graecorum. In any event he was not solely, if at all, dependent upon Sedulius. In their Latin form the Proverbs bear the marks of Iro-Scottish transmission.[18] Hellmann notes that the unique inclusion among the Anonymous' set of Proverbs contains the verb *palare* in place of *propalare*.[19] Hellmann says that this usage probably identifies the Anonymous' source as an early Irish version and connects him indirectly, at least, with Sedulius Scottus and Cathwulf. This is of interest because Cathwulf's and Sedulius Scottus' utterances concerning the relationship between the *regnum* and the *sacerdotium* are similar to those of the Anonymous.[20]

[17] Sedulius Scottus, Quellen und Untersuchungen zur lateinischen Philologie des Mittelalters, I (Munich, 1909), pp. 129–131.

[18] Hellmann, op. cit., p. 134.

[19] Ibid., p. 131, n. 5. I note the same verb in the Anonymous' transcription of the Hibernensis. See below, J24/W:App. Item III, 15.

[20] Although Hellmann is only marginally concerned with the Anonymous, who is for him simply a source for the study of Sedulius Scottus, his footnote remarks about Böhmer are worth mentioning: "Dass all 35 [sic] Traktate, die in der Handschrift vereinigt sind, auf ein und denselben Verfasser zurückgehen, ist doch schwer glaub-

In 1908 Anton Scharnagl published Der Begriff der Investitur in den Quellen und der Literatur des Investiturstreits [21] in which he assigned the Anonymous a place as the most extreme proponent of the royal prerogative in investiture. He compared "De consecratione" with the second most important ecclesio-political Tractate of the Codex, J28/L5 "De Romano pontifice," and concluded that despite certain changes in emphasis, "An seinem Investiturbegriff hat der Autor . . . . nichts geändert." This statement is important because some writers have held that "De Romano pontifice," though it copies a section from "De consecratione," nevertheless represents a partial retreat from the extreme views of the earlier treatise.

In 1914 Fritz Kern published his monumental study of kingship [21a] in which he traces the Germanic, the ecclesiastical, the imperial, and Oriental elements in medieval divine right monarchy. Thereupon he discusses the restraints imposed upon kings and the rights and instruments of resisting tyrants on the part of people or clergy. The Anonymous of York is brought in as illustrative of certain points and is very ably summarized in a five-page appended note which is confined to the religio-political theory of "De consecratione." Kern recognizes the quasi-royal character of the bishops as the counterpart of the sacerdotal character of anointed kings. He mentions Continental parallels and notes the kinship of Wyclif and the Anonymous. He expresses regret that Böhmer left out of his edition of the text the section on the meaning of *sanctus*, remarking that it might have thrown light on the extraordinary conviction of the Anonymous concerning the sacrosanct character of the monarch which is nowhere else so strongly advanced, not even by Frederick Barbarossa.

In 1915 A. J. Carlyle introduced to the English-speaking public the Anglo-Norman clerical publicist supposedly of York, who had been for some time attracting attention in German circles. In his

---

lich; die entgegenstehenden Ausführungen Böhmers auf S. 199 sind nicht beweiskräftig" (p. 134, n. 3). Hellmann's views are of course only an opinion, because he never himself leafed through the Codex.

[21] Kirchenpolitische Abhandlungen, edited by G. Stutz, Heft 56, pp. 88–90, 120.

[21a] Gottesgnadentum und Widerstandsrecht im früheren Mittelalter: Zur Entwicklungsgeschichte der Monarchie (Leipzig, 1914); tr. by S. B. Chimes as a part of Kingship and Law in the Middle Ages (Oxford, 1939).

Political Theory of the Roman Lawyers and the Canonists from the Tenth to the Thirteenth Century [22] Carlyle noted the possible dependence of the Anonymous on Hugh of Fleury and this disposed him to underestimate the radical character of the former's royalism, for he observes that the Anonymous too had a conception of an unjust king who could be checked. My own reading of all the Tractates gives me the impression that the Anonymous paid scant attention to the popular right to resist a tyrannous king. He is no more disposed to discuss a tyrant than a biblical writer to discuss the possibility of a wicked Messiah. His acknowledgment of the tyrannous character of one Old Testament king is undercut by his canny observation that nowhere in Chronicles is it mentioned that the king in question, Uzziah, was consecrated with oil, which, operative *ex opere*, would have made the king righteous. Moreover, the Anonymous argues that Jesus and the Apostles taught obedience even to unjust emperors. In the fourth volume of his History [23] published in 1922, Carlyle amplified his earlier treatment of the Anonymous and mentioned again the filiation of thought that runs from Ambrosiaster through Cathwulf to the Anonymous of York and Hugh of Fleury. Carlyle confined his observations to the six Tractates edited in Libelli de lite.

To be mentioned only for the sake of completeness in this chronological survey is the brief reference to the Anonymous by Jean Rivière, who cites him among "des régaliens déterminés" and notes his ascription of the power of the Keys to the king.[24]

In passing to the work of Alois Dempf we encounter the first examination of the Anonymous since that of Böhmer to go beyond purely religio-political observations. Dempf is the first to assign the Anonymous a place in general intellectual history. In his

---

[22] Republished as Volume III of A History of Medieval Political Theory in the West (Edinburgh, 1922). The Anonymous is discussed, pp. 135 f. In the interest of completeness it may be mentioned here that two years later Henry M. Gwatkin perpetuated the older Böhmer hypothesis in speaking of Archbishop Gerard as the English counterpart of the Imperial opponents of the Gregorian Papacy: Church and State in England to the Death of Queen Anne (London, 1917), p. 50.

[23] Entitled: The Theories of the Relation of the Empire and the Papacy from the Tenth Century to the Twelfth, pp. 274–81.

[24] Le problème de l'Église et de l'État au temps de Philippe le Bel: Étude de théologie positive, Spicilegium sacrum Lovaniense, fasc. VIII (Louvain, 1926), pp. 20, 436 f.

Sacrum Imperium [25] he essays to relate theology and history in terms of the Kingdom from St. Paul to Nicholas of Cues. With a never ebbing enthusiasm, he has endeavored to recover for theology its religio-political relevance and for historiography a theological dimension. We have in Dempf's massive synthesis a veritable philosophy of the Kingdom. As the title indicates he has taken as the key to his survey the concept of divine government in history. That occasional errors of fact creep in does not seriously mar a study, the greatness of which lies in the very daring of its self-imposed assignment of embracing, as aspects of one divine compulsion, ideas and events which are usually treated separately as dogmatics, political theory, and history. On a vast canvas which depicts the Christian caravan moving from Antiquity into the Late Middle Ages, Dempf has placed countless figures great and small. Among them the Anonymous bulks larger than Anselm of Canterbury.

Dempf throughout his book, based though it is on a fresh examination of the texts, is nevertheless obliged to depend for textual, chronological, and biographical facts and conjectures upon critical scholarship. As Böhmer is the unrivalled master of Anglo-Norman ecclesiastical institutions, Dempf felt justified in accepting Böhmer's originally only tentative ascription of the Tractates to Gerard of York. Beguiled by the intellectual lure of being able to contrast Gerard and St. Anselm as contemporaneous archbishops, Dempf unfortunately failed to notice that in Kirche und Staat Böhmer himself had withdrawn his hypothesis of Gerard's authorship.

Dempf holds that although "Gerard" remained of necessity anonymous, he was even in the scholastic realm the peer of Anselm. And most certainly the struggle between the two must surely have influenced Anselm, whose ontological Realism was alone possible on the basis of just such an interpenetration of the earthly and the heavenly realms which the thought of "Gerard" represents. For by making the earthly kingdom a counterpart of the heavenly, "Gerard" banished the intellectually paralyzing notion, inherited from Augustine, of the disparateness of the two

---

[25] Sacrum Imperium: Geschichts-und Staatsphilosophie des Mittelalters und der politischen Renaissance (Munich and Berlin, 1929), pp. 199–207.

Cities. In pressing on to an assertion of the metaphysical unity of the two, "Gerard" was "ideeller Gegenspieler Augustins." By making baptismal robes of more honor than the stole, and the hearing of the Word of greater moment than its preachment, and the partaking of the Blood and Body of Christ of more significance than the office of the clerical celebrant, the Anonymous in effect represents the "socio-philosophical" basis of the fusion of the divine and the human, of Church and society, in which setting alone the philosophical Realism of Anselm was possible. Indeed, by understanding the realm of grace as continuously interpenetrating and supplementing the world of nature, as he does in his ideas about marriage and generation, "Gerard" is not only the superior of the "Father of Scholasticism" but also, because of his more radical conclusions, "the first and at the same time orthodox forerunner of Thomas of Aquinas."

Yet even these, as it would seem, excessive ascriptions of importance to the York Tractates do not exhaust Dempf's disposition to compare the Anonymous with the very great. He speaks not only of "Gerard's" "completely Aristotelian realism" but also of his "sovereign mastery of the Epistles of Paul." From Paul, Dempf asserts, "Gerard" took over the tripartite theological periodization of history (period of natural law, Mosaic Law, and Gospel) and transformed it into a royalist theology of history,[26] which makes of the Christian king a messianic figure. The first period, according to this view, is that of the Old Covenant (and natural religion), during which the Kingdom and Royal Priesthood of Christ were merely anticipated, typically, in the priest-kings of pagan antiquity and the Old Testament. The second period extends from the first to the second Advent of Christ, during which a universal priesthood of all believers under the true Priest-King Christ fulfills the expectations of the Old Testament. The third period is without end, the Eternal Jerusalem in which there will be no priesthood, for the priestly office is only for man in his temporal condition. Christ came the first time to make it possible for men to become kings with him, not priests. Dempf goes on to show how, in anticipation of the ultimate conditions of

---

[26] Dempf is quoted on history and philosophy below, n. 522.

mankind as saved, the *sacerdotium* on earth already tends to lose its significance. The subordination of all Christians in body and soul (for both are to be saved) to the king is a natural consequence of the redemptive rôle of earthly sovereigns who perform their task on the model of the Heavenly King. Dempf notes one consequence of the Anonymous' conflation of Church and State, namely, that "there is no right of resistance, that is the sole privilege of kings." In this doctrine of a Spirit-filled Church-Kingdom under an anointed king "Gerard" is, according to Dempf, the creator of a "metaphysics of history comparable to Hegel's idea of the German State."

It is evident even from this bare sketch of the great systems with which that of the Anonymous is compared that Dempf regards our clerical publicist as no secondary figure, taking him as symptomatic of a vast shift of the spirit in the medieval West and as not uninfluential in the process, even though, because of his radicalism, he chose to remain anonymous. Some of the details of Dempf's compact treatment of the thought of the Anonymous will be introduced at appropriate points in the subsequent analysis. Here it is in place to evaluate Dempf's contribution in general. The present writer is in sympathy with Dempf's attempt to treat of ecclesio-political theory in a theological context. One is prepared to tolerate occasional defects of method in so comprehensive an undertaking as his has been. In the few pages of his study, however, which deal with the Anonymous, his errors or manifest excesses are sufficiently numerous to justify our caution in accepting his generalizations. His unquestioned acceptance of Böhmer's assignment of the Tractates to Gerard of York would be a minor point if on it he had not based his confident attribution of widespread influence to the thought of the Anonymous by way of Anselm. If the Anonymous were shown to be a lesser cleric without prominence, much of what Dempf has said about his influence might fall away. Secondly, Dempf has assumed the unity of authorship of all the Tractates and yet has confined his generalizations pretty much to the six printed in Libelli de lite. Thirdly, the royal messianism of the Anonymous is demonstrably dependent upon an obsolescent royal *ordo* of the tenth century. The radicalism of the Anonymous is such only in view of Protestant nationalism centuries ahead. For the period, the thought of the Anonymous is actually "conservative." In any event, it is not symptomatic of a shift of the spirit, creating the matrix and "socio-philosophical basis for the emergence of scholastic Realism." Fourthly, Dempf is mistaken in holding that all the sacraments except the Eucharist are reduced by the Anonymous to symbolism, for he is both a spiritualist and a sacramentalist. Moreover, consecration is clearly an *ex opere* sacrament in both its royal and its episcopal form. Indeed it is the assertion of the indelible character of ordination and coronation that justifies the Anonymous in denying to the people the right to remove their clerical overseers and their rulers, despite the doctrine of the universal priesthood and the royalty of all believers. The sacrament of the altar is, on the other hand, in contrast to Dempf's statement, seriously undercut in its significance in the Anonymous. Lastly, a small point, but an indication of Dempf's disposition to make bold conjectures without due attention even to the facts to which he had access: he observes "that Wyclif must certainly have read the forgotten Codex in Oxford." The Manuscript was, of course, not deposited in Corpus Christi College until after Parker's death, and it was Cambridge, not Oxford. Despite, however, the aforementioned inaccuracies or excesses, Dempf is rich in suggestions. In view of Dempf's study, it is clear that the Anonymous cannot be dismissed as an isolated historical phenomenon, a religio-political sport.

The next to mention the Anonymous is Max Manitius,[27] who assigns our writer the dignity of a paragraph, emphasizing his uniqueness. Gerard of York is taken to be the probable writer of the Tractates.

In the same year, Zachary N. Brooke, who acknowledges a general indebtedness to Heinrich Böhmer, published his study on The English Church and the Papacy from the Conquest to the Reign of John,[28] in which he discusses the Anonymous as a uniquely radical voice on the royal side of the contest with the Pope. Brooke's appraisal of the proper place of the whole body

[27] Geschichte der lateinischen Literatur des Mittelalters, III, in collaboration with P. Lehmann (Munich, 1931), p. 55.
[28] Cambridge, 1931, pp. 157–60.

of Tractates is especially weighty because his discussion of them gives the impression that he has examined the entire original Manuscript, which none of the German scholars thus far, except Hampe, had been able to do.

The Tractates, Brooke says, which deal with papal authority, the primacy of Lyons over Rouen and of Canterbury over York, the episcopal control of the monastery of Fécamp, the marriage of the clergy and the ordination of the sons of clerical concubines, and the consecration of the King "can, I think, possibly be attributed to the same writer; in many cases the same phrases are used." The reserve of this historian in regard to the homogeneity of the Codex is rather marked in contrast to the veritable exuberance of Dempf, but the inference in the one case and the assumption in the other are not far apart, for Dempf's synthesis never actually went beyond the Tractates mentioned. As to their author, Brooke is inclined to accept "as quite likely" the first part of Böhmer's reconstructed biography, but he would leave the Anonymous for the most part in Normandy, although he grants that the latter may well have been a royal chaplain or at least an attendant at the coronation of Henry I. Brooke ascertains the fact that the Anonymous quoted from the Pseudo-Isidorian Decretals in his defense of Rouen and that he had before him the normal Pseudo-Isidorian collection of the canons of the councils when he quoted at length from Chalcedon. This is an important fact to have established because it was Lanfranc's collection which "was apparently the only one current in England at this time." A failure to use Lanfranc's collection would thus point to a Norman provenance even of "De consecratione." In marked contrast to Dempf, Brooke regards the Anonymous as altogether "a peculiar case."

He seems to be so deliberately anonymous, [Brooke continues] for, though he does seem to have particular instances in view, he is very careful to avoid supporting a particular king or attacking a particular Pope. This looks like caution or fear, and it was doubtless justified; for in his generation he is solitary and a unique figure. . . . I do not think that he can be said to represent anyone but himself.

In the following year Charles H. McIlwain in his Growth of Political Thought in the West [29] assigned the Anonymous a place in the development of political theory, freshly and clearly delineating the main arguments whereby the Anonymous "denies two of the most fundamental and most essential points of the papal argument, the superiority of a bishop over a king and the superiority of the Pope over a bishop."

Of more than passing interest is an address of Albert Brackmann delivered before the International Congress of Historians at Warsaw in 1933. In this address, "Die Ursachen der geistigen und politischen Wandlung Europas im 11. und 12. Jahrhundert," [30] inspired in part by Dempf's Sacrum Imperium, Brackmann is at pains to show that it was the *hybris* of Hildebrand, who hurled the epithet of "Antichrist" at Henry IV and made of the Empire (insofar as it was not bound to the Papacy) a *civitas diaboli*, which is ultimately to be blamed for the tragic fact of European civilization, namely, that the prevailing form of the State is national. Brackmann surveys the political development of the eleventh and twelfth centuries and asserts that it was Norman vitality that created the modern national State, joined in creative but fateful conflict with the Gregorian system which had not hesitated to shatter the Gelasian principle of two powers within the *corpus Christianum*. The excesses of Hildebrand called forth a no less extreme assertion of the rights of the natural order within the framework of the national community, the head of which (as the antitype of Hildebrand) was consequently destined to be held supreme both in the spiritual and the temporal spheres. Like Dempf, Brackmann sees in the several Tractates of the Anonymous on clerical marriage and natural fecundity a reassertion on the part of the Anonymous of the goodness of the created world and a repudiation of that debilitating dualism of which the abnormal tensions between marriage and celibacy, *regnum* and *sacerdotium*, earth and heaven were all sorry manifestations. In an address, composed in the founding year of that Third Reich which ascribed to its Leader an absolute religious and political authority, and delivered in the capital of the State destined first

---

[29] New York, 1932, pp. 211–16.
[30] Historische Zeitschrift, CIL (1934), pp. 233 ff.

to be invaded by his ruthless might, Brackmann has assigned to the Anonymous of York a significance which is not only historical but contemporary.

No less enthusiastically than Brackmann, Alois Fauser praised the Anonymous Tractates as "the most significant achievement in all publicist literature." [31] In the author of these Tractates he beheld a man of the Enlightenment, a Renaissance type of the early twelfth century. In him, reason was used not simply to defend tradition, but to break with it if it violated natural law. Fauser rejoiced in the historical relativism of the Anonymous and was particularly impressed by the Anonymous' sense of providence and the divine will experienced as man's fate and eternal election. Fauser noted the Anonymous' application of Paul's freedom from the law to a Northern Christian's freedom from canon law.

The next writer to take up the problem presented by our Tractates was Philipp Funk in his, for us, very important article, "Der fragliche Anonymus von York." [32] It was the sober work of a Catholic scholar who threw into question the entire sequence of scholarship from Böhmer to Dempf, Brackmann, and Fauser.[33] He was distrustful of the inordinate claims made for the Anonymous by the latter three and critical of the scholarly procedure and overconfident conjectures of Böhmer himself, though not of course of the relevant facts unearthed by the latter in an admittedly masterful way.

Funk's criticism of Böhmer comes under four points. He charges the overeager *privatdozent* with undue haste in editing the Tractates, in order to get them into Libelli de lite before the date line. Haste involved carelessness. Funk is particularly critical of the arbitrary character of Böhmer's selections and especially of his editing of "De consecratione." In the latter, he says, Versions A and B are combined to fit the editor's taste, while whole sections which might have detracted from the composition as an appropriate one for publication among the *libelli de lite* are

---

[31] Die Publizisten des Investiturstreites: Persönlichkeiten und Ideen: Inaugural-Dissertation . . . der Universität zu München (Würzburg, 1935), pp. 131–36.

[32] Historisches Jahrbuch, LV (1935), 251 ff.

[33] Fauser himself reckoned with Funk's criticisms in a footnote appended to his already completed manuscript where he insists, despite Funk's allegations, "dass die Traktate durch ihre geistige Haltung doch eine innere Einheit besitzen."

left out. In view of the Appendix of Version A and the very bulk of the Tractate itself, Funk is not inclined to consider the "De consecratione" a true *streitschrift*. Funk's charge of capriciousness in editing is based in part upon the seemingly altered pagination which gives Böhmer's text the appearance of being a much more radically conceived conflation of the two versions than is actually the case. A misplaced quire in the Codex happens to fall within the "De consecratione." Apart from this quite desirable correction, the only "tendentious" editing is by way of omissions.[34]

The second criticism, and one which must be taken seriously, is that Böhmer has given the faulty impression of a homogeneous collection of Tractates by one author. Funk assails Böhmer's assumption of a single author for the major pieces of the Codex and sets out to show the disparate character of the entire collection of Tractates, insofar as they had been published. Funk is thus the first scholar since Böhmer himself seriously to bring under consideration the Tractates of both the Libelli and the "Beilagen" of Kirche und Staat. The greater part of his article is taken up with an examination of each of these Tractates. At the end he is confident that he has sufficiently thrown into question their homogeneity and exposed the mock seriousness of enough of them to forestall any further Dempf-like flights into speculation until a fresh critical edition has been made of *all* the Tractates. In an effort to demonstrate the lack of homogeneity, Funk seems to be motivated by a desire to show that the Anonymous deserved less attention than he received from the editors of the Monumenta because the Codex as a whole cannot be classified as publicistic. But as he takes up one Tractate after another, it is not at all clear that his assignment of the pieces to different literary *genres* necessarily argues for multiple authorship. The Codex could well be the varied literary remains of one man in different phases of his vital concerns. From internal evidence based upon an examination of all the Tractates it seems clear to the present writer that enough of the Tractates are from the same radical spirit to warrant their consideration together. A number of the Tractates Funk calls simply *lehrstücke*, but these, when they deal with

---

[34] The nature of the omissions is clearly indicated in M. R. James, Descriptive Catalogue, II, pp. 306 f. And see Appendix below.

the nature of the Church and the sacraments, are surely not utterly irrelevant (as Dempf has rightly perceived) to ecclesiopolitical theory.

Under a third heading one may bring a number of technical points. Funk says "it is a complete misunderstanding of the general moral, biblical and liturgical argumentation [of the Anonymous] when Böhmer reads into the Tractate the assertion of a genuine ecclesiastical sovereignty, that is, a power over the *spiritualia.*" "Of ecclesiastical supremacy there is nothing at all in him." The solemn ascriptions of power to the king with which the Tractate "De consecratione" abounds are, according to Funk, purely formal or they are "grotesquely misunderstood commonplaces of the author."

Funk's fourth criticism of Böhmer is that his ascription of the Tractates to a cleric in the entourage of Gerard is "a pure conjecture," as are also his precise dating of the Tractates and the biographical reconstruction. Böhmer himself admits the paucity of specific references in the texts to places and events. Böhmer's reconstructions are, however, not without their value. They are surely informative and can be assimilated, as long as the unity of the collection is not seriously called in question. And that, for all his long article, Funk has not succeeded in doing.

The next treatment of the Anonymous is that of Lotte Knabe in her study of the history of the Gelasian formula.[35] She notes the sensitivity to the nuances of language which characterize the original Gelasian distinction between the priestly *authority* and the regal *power.* She traces the manner in which the ninth century disengaged the two powers from the actual political context and replaced them with the two orders, priesthood and the laity. While both powers were recognized as divine, there was always a contest between them for the place of superior dignity. After the Hildebrandine policy of extending the sacerdotal competence became generally felt, three types of religio-political reaction were possible. Miss Knabe takes Hugo of Fleury and the author of Liber de unitate as representative of the attempt to recover the older Gelasian position of coördinate responsibilities. She takes

[35] Die gelasianische Zweigewaltentheorie bis zum Ende des Investiturstreites, Historische Studien, edited by Ebering, Heft CCLXXXXII (1936), pp. 145–53.

Honorius of Autun as the representative of papal supremacy and the Anonymous as the representative royalist. Her several pages on him constitute a good summary of the "De consecratione" and the related religio-political elements of the other Tractates published in Libelli de lite. There is nothing particularly new in this exposition.

In the same year Gerd Tellenbach in his Libertas cited the Anonymous as a radical thinker of his age.[36] He drew attention to the fact that the Anonymous claimed for the Archbishop of Rouen the papal formula, "servus servorum Dei." The following year, John T. McNeill acquainted a larger circle with the Anonymous by assigning him a place in his Christian Hope for World Society.[37]

With the monograph of Jean François Lemarignier on monastic exemptions,[38] a hitherto neglected aspect of the Anonymous Tractates is brought under consideration. In discussing the place of the Anonymous in the history of the exemption of Fécamp, Lemarignier accepts at least that part of the chronology of the Tractates to which Böhmer assigned a Norman background. Lemarignier's contribution, quite incidental to his primary concern, relates to the struggle of Fécamp to maintain its exemption from the control of the metropolitanate which the Anonymous defends on several counts in several Tractates. In Tractate J27, published here for the first time, the Anonymous argues that Fécamp should be subject to Rouen, as a daughter to her mother, for had not the famous monastery received her faith from the metropolitan see? Now Lemarignier shows that this argument from priority of foundation could not, before 1090, have been countered by the monks of Fécamp. But sometime shortly after the Anonymous' composition of "Tractate" J27 — actually it is no more

[36] Libertas: Kirche und Weltordnung im Zeitalter des Investiturstreites, Forschungen zur Kirchen-und Geistesgeschichte, VII (Stuttgart, 1936); translated by R. E. Bennett as Church, State and Christian Society at the Time of the Investiture Contest (Oxford, 1940); references to the Anonymous: pp. 136, 142, 146, 158 n.

[37] Chicago and New York, 1937, pp. 53 f.

[38] Étude sur les privilèges d'exemption et de juridiction ecclésiastique des abbayes normandes depuis les origines jusqu'en 1140, Archives de la France monastique, XLIV (1937), Paris. He discusses the Anonymous pp. 196–200 and prints for the first time, as Pièce justificative IV, Tractate J27, entitled "Fragment de l' 'Anonyme d'York' concernant l'exemption de Fécamp."

than a sketch or fragment — a new legend concerning the miraculous foundation of Fécamp sprang up which provided the embattled monastery with the credentials of superior antiquity. According to this new legend, Joseph of Arimathaea was aided in the entombment of Christ by Nicodemus who saw to the gathering up of the blood from the wounds. Before his death he confided this precious relic to his nephew Isaac who was thereafter bidden by God to enclose it in a leaden vial which was to be placed inside a fig log and set free upon the waters. In due time the winds carried the log to the shores of Fécamp, *Ficus campus*, the field of the fig tree. On the site of the fig log miraculously revealed by a stag, St. Vaninge constructed the first church of Fécamp. Thus the monastery antedated by its possession of Christ's blood the beginnings of the faith in Rouen and the argument of the Anonymous was henceforth deprived of its cogency. Lemarignier points out that Fécamp's Liber de revelatione, composed between 1079 and 1108, and probably shortly after 1090, knew nothing of the legend of the sacred blood in the foregoing form. The Tractate of the Anonymous, dated by Böhmer c. 1090, thus provides Lemarignier with a *terminus a quo* for the dating of the new Fécamp legend, while the legend itself provides us with possible evidence of the Anonymous' contemporary influence. In any event Lemarignier's research brings the earlier activities of the Anonymous into sharper focus.

Such is also the value of another French study of a selected Tractate of the "York" Codex, Augustin Fliche's analysis of J25/L1, "An liceat sacerdotibus inire matrimonium," in his account of the opposition to the Gregorian Reform.[39] Fliche characterizes this document as a third Norman version of the Rescript of Ulrich [40] and shows, on the basis of technical terms employed, that its author belonged to the school of Anselm at Bec even though his views on clerical marriage differed markedly from Anselm's. Fliche's research is very important for filling in the Norman background of our Tractates.

[39] La réforme grégorienne, III, L'opposition antigrégorienne, Spicilegium sacrum Lovaniense, fasc. 16 (Louvain, 1937), pp. 34–8.
[40] Hitherto Ulrich was commonly thought by critics to be bishop of Augsburg. Fliche has identified him as the bishop of Imola who resisted the introduction of Gregorian regulations concerning clerical marriage in his diocese.

With three studies of coronation orders by Percy Schramm we return to the *chef d'oeuvre* of MS 415, "De consecratione," and to the problem of the relationship of Church and State which it poses in terms of the coronation liturgy used by the Anonymous to support royal authority as divine. In 1938 at the appropriate place in his exhaustive study of the filiation of royal orders,[41] Schramm identified the *ordo* quoted in Tractate J24/L4 and copied in its entirety in the unpublished "Appendix" thereto as the Edgar Ordo composed by St. Dunstan in 973. In his History of the English Coronation,[42] Schramm had already summarized in a lapidary way the significance of this Ordo which had been first used by St. Dunstan to secure through King Edgar the reform of the English Church. "If in the tenth century," he says, "the clergy had thoroughly clericalized the coronation, the wheel had now come full circle and the argument of the Anonymous showed how the coronation service supplied the legal title for the regalization of the Church."

In 1934[43] Schramm had already shown that the Edgar Ordo was an expression of the new monastic reform movement, stemming from the Continent and led in England by Dunstan of Canterbury. By assigning a new and quasi-sacerdotal dignity to Edgar, Dunstan had sought to extend the influence of Edgar (who had been won to the cause of ecclesiastical reform) to the entirety of the hitherto divided Isle. Dunstan, mindful only of the contemporary woes of political divisiveness and ecclesiastical decay, thus contributed to the enhancement of royal power which his successors, St. Anselm and St. Thomas, were destined to check, only at the cost of exhausting vigilance, exile, and martyrdom. In this earlier study Schramm had traced the history of the components of this Edgar Ordo which includes elements from an earlier *ordo* inspired by St. Dunstan and from the German Ordo of 960. Back of these elements lie more ancient materials which are to

---

[41] "Ordines — Studien III: Die Krönung in England," Archiv für Urkundenforschung, XV (1938), pp. 314, 325 f.

[42] Geschichte des englischen Königtums im Lichte der Krönung (Weimar, 1937); translated by Leopold G. Wickham Legg (Oxford, 1937). Discusses the Anonymous, pp. 33 f., 120.

[43] "Die Krönung bei den Westfranken und Angelsachsen von 878 bis um 1000," Zeitschrift der Savigny-Stiftung, kanonistische Abteilung, XXII (1934), pp. 117 ff.

be assigned to Hincmar and others of Frankland. The remarkable designation of the king as *presul princeps*, which the Anonymous uses to great advantage in Tractate J24/L4, "De consecratione," seems to come from the Coronation Ordo of Louis II for whom Pope John VIII performed the rite.[44] By a strange coincidence, the Anonymous was enabled to defend a king against the Pope by exploiting a phrase unwarily bestowed upon an earlier king by an earlier Pope.

Following close upon the researches of Schramm, P. L. Ward in a valuable article, "The Coronation Ceremony," [45] advanced our knowledge of the sources of the "York" Tractates in a footnote reference incidental to his main discussion.[46] Here he states that upon examining the text of the Codex he found "very few points at which the variants peculiar to the [Archbishop] Robert text [of the Edgar Ordo] do not appear. Therefore the writer [the Anonymous] made his relatively careless copy either from a manuscript extraordinarily like the Robert document, *or else from the Robert book itself*, which had evidently gone to Rouen at least half a century before." The italics are mine. The significance of this identification was not followed up by Ward. It will prove basic to our task of identifying the Anonymous.

With the publication in 1938 of Joseph Funkenstein's doctoral dissertation on the use of the Old Testament in publicist literature,[47] we resume the discussion of the Anonymous in terms of the investiture controversy. Funkenstein traces the use of the key royal and priestly passages of the Old Testament and shows how the Anonymous was the culmination of the royalist exegesis.

In the same year Wilhelm Berges in his survey and analysis of medieval mirrors of princes,[48] expressly distinguishes between God-

[44] For another example of an appeal to John against the ruling Pope, see below, p. 57.

[45] Speculum, XIV (1939), pp. 160 ff.

[46] Op. cit., p. 168, n. 1.

[47] Das Alte Testament im Kampf von regnum und sacerdotium zur Zeit des Investiturstreits, Inaugural-Dissertation at Basel, 1933 (Dortmund, 1938), pp. 28–33. At this point may be mentioned a similar dissertation, that of Max Hackelsperger, Bibel und mittelalterlicher Reichsgedanke (Munich, 1934). He discusses the York Tractates briefly.

[48] Die Fürstenspiegel des hohen und späten Mittelalters, Reichsinstitut für ältere deutsche Geschichtskunde, Schriften, II (Leipzig, 1938), p. 28.

kingship and Christ-kingship, contrasting concepts basic to the present study, and he regards the Anonymous as the culmination of "Christocentric" political theory as distinguished from "Theocentric" political theory which became characteristic of the later Middle Ages. Berges, with a theological discernment akin to Dempf's at this point, observes in the Tractates the importance of a hitherto unnoticed anthropology based upon the conception of Christ as the New Adam, who restored to humanity the possibility of rejoining that which had been separated by the Fall, the spiritual and the temporal. Berges shows how the Anonymous regarded baptism as the act of personal rebirth and coronation as the vicarious rebirth of a whole generation, for the anointment of a king was the reënactment of the scene at Jordan which was at once Christ's Ordination as the Suffering Servant and his Consecration as the Royal Son of God. The other valuable insights of Berges will be noted at appropriate places.[49]

Also in 1938,[50] Frank Gavin sympathetically presented in some detail the "York Anonymous" as a lone survivor of what must have been not a few representatives in the earlier Middle Ages of what he calls "the peculiar ethos of the Anglican communion."

In 1939 Harald Scherrinsky published his Berlin doctoral dissertation, the first full-length study of the Anonymous since Böhmer's.[51] Indeed it was based upon an examination of the unpublished literary remains of Heinrich Böhmer including the full texts of five hitherto unedited Tractates. These (except for J27/A) were printed for the first time in Scherrinsky's "Anlage." [52] The contours of Scherrinsky's book were shaped by his resolve to come to terms with Funk's challenge to the Böhmer hypothesis of the unity of the "York" Corpus. After a fruitless inquiry into the transmission of the MS and an examination of the notations of the older catalogues of the Corpus Christi College Library,

---

[49] Below, pp. 79, 163, 176; n. 622.
[50] Seven Centuries of the Problem of Church and State (Princeton, 1938), pp. 50–62.
[51] Untersuchungen zum sogenannten Anonymus von York (Würzburg-Anmühle, 1939). Scherrinsky lists a number of incidental bibliographical references to the Anonymous on p. 10, n. 20.
[52] Tractates 6, 9, 15, 21, 27. In addition to these texts, Scherrinsky was able, on the basis of Böhmer's notes, to discuss the contents of still other unpublished Tractates.

with the thought that the Codex might have been enlarged in the process of rebinding in the eighteenth century, Scherrinsky took up one Tractate after another, analyzing its style and contents with a view to finding out whether they could all have been written by the same person. In a concluding Table (p. 116) he brought together all the parallel and allied thoughts, stylistic peculiarities and allusions proving incontestably that a net of interrelationships binds all the Tractates together as the work of one writer.[53] In his demonstration of a single authorship, Scherrinsky regarded the hitherto unpublished Tractate J9 as a key document. Scherrinsky did not question the alleged English origin of the "later" Tractates and accepted Böhmer's chronology for the "earlier" Tractates composed in Rouen, but here he insisted that none of them yielded enough certain data to warrant Böhmer's confident assignment of dates in terms of months and years. Scherrinsky expressed the view that Böhmer's abandonment of the Gerard hypothesis was perhaps unnecessary. Böhmer had at first dated Tractate J4/L3 as of 1081 and subsequently found reasons to assign it to the year 1096, which thus made the ascription to the Bishop of Hereford (later Archbishop of York) impossible. But Scherrinsky felt that the reasons adduced by Böhmer for redating the Tractate were not compelling. Scherrinsky himself has presented no new theory concerning the identity of the Anonymous, but has pointed out that it would have been better to style the author the Anonymous of Rouen, since most of his Tractates are connected with the affairs of the metropolitan see of Normandy. Unfortunately Scherrinsky's study remained generally unnoticed outside of Germany because of the outbreak of war.[54]

By 1940, more than forty years after his discovery by Böhmer, the Anonymous was at last accorded a place in a general history of the Church. This was in Augustin Fliche's Réforme

---

[53] "Auf Grund der . . . gewonnenen Einzelfeststellungen kommen wir zu dem Ergebnis, dass — trotz der Funkischen Gegenmeinung — die von Böhmer vertretene Ansicht zutrifft, dass *alle* Traktate unseres Kodex von *einem* Verfasser stammen" (p. 114).

[54] The book is briefly reviewed by H. Klewitz, Deutsches Archiv, V (1941), p. 212. Scherrinsky stood at the West Front at the time of the publication of his dissertation. Unaware of his work, the present writer in 1946 completed his independent analysis of the Tractates with a view to establishing the homogeneity of the Corpus and refuting the claims of Funk.

grégorienne et la reconquête chrétienne (1057–1125)[55] where the Anonymous is discussed in connection both with the struggle of Rouen against the primatial authority of Lyons and with the struggle of Henry I against the Pope.

The Anonymous is several times called in as witness in Edward Eichmann's Die Kaiserkrönung im Abendland.[56] In 1944 František Dvorník mentions the Anonymous as a representative of national Christianity.[57] In a collaborative study in a war camp, M. Brémond and J. Gaudemet had found the Anonymous sufficiently important to be discussed in their analysis of universalism and particularism in the High Middle Ages.[58] In connection with the Anonymous' assertion that Jerusalem rather than Rome is the mother of all churches, these writers observe that in the same period, indeed in 1100, Daimbert, elected patriarch of Jerusalem, made the same claim.

What appears to be the most recent study of the Anonymous is that of Pierre de Lapparent,[59] who, like Gavin (but without the latter's enthusiasm), interpreted the Anonymous as a representative of pre-Reformation Anglicanism. The chief merit of Lapparent's study was his independent witness to the homogeneity of the "York" Tractates. Unaware of the previous labors of Scherrinsky, Lapparent set out to refute Funk's thesis that the "York" Tractates are not a unity and not by a single author. Like Scherrinsky, he adduced numerous stylistic and theological parallels and borrowings within the Codex, examining the Tractates of Böhmer's "Beilage" no less than the six principal Tractates in Libelli de lite.

Having reviewed a half century of research and interpretation we may conclude with the following points. Doubt concerning a sole authorship of the Codex has not been entirely eliminated.

[55] Histoire de l'Église depuis les origines jusqu'à nos jours, VIII (Paris, 1940).

[56] Ein Beitrag zur Geistesgeschichte des Mittelalters mit besonderer Berücksichtigung des kirchlichen Rechts, der Liturgie und der Kirchenpolitik, 2 vols. (Würzburg, 1942), I, 118, 208; II, 95, 125.

[57] National Churches and the Universal Church (London, 1944), p. 57.

[58] L'Empire chrétien et ses destinées en occident du xie au xiiie siècle: Essai sur les forces d'universalisme et de particularisme dans l'Europe du Moyen Âge, Travaux de l'Oflag VIII F (Paris, 1944), pp. 164–166.

[59] "Un precurseur de la Réforme anglaise: l'Anonyme d'York," Archives d'histoire doctrinale et littéraire du Moyen Âge, XV (1946), pp. 149 ff.

No new evidence has come forward to connect any of the Tractates with York. On the contrary, some new evidence has been assembled to connect even one of the supposedly English Tractates with Rouen. The originality, if not the representative character of the Tractates, is widely, if not unanimously, recognized. Thus far the research and evaluation have been based almost entirely on Böhmer's selection and editing of twenty-one of the thirty-one Tractates, fragments, and sketches. To the new findings based upon the whole Codex we may now turn.

PART II

BEHIND ANONYMITY: CLUES AND SOURCES

The new facts and conjectures based thereon have been assembled under eleven headings. Not all of these inquiries yield certainties, but a fresh exploration of the clues bearing on the localization of the Codex and the identification of its author is in order. Part Three will bring these findings together with conjectures concerning the authorship of the entire Codex. Part Four will systematize the thought of the Anonymous, particularly in respect to the relationship of the *regnum* and *sacerdotium*.

1. Transmission, Textual Criticism, Palaeographic Clues

Pretty much all that can be said concerning transmission is contained in The Sources of Archbishop Parker's Collection of MSS at Corpus Christi College Cambridge [60] by M. R. James and in the same writer's Introduction in A Descriptive Catalogue of C.C.C.C. In the latter James observes that the largest contributors to the Parker manuscripts were the two Canterbury libraries of Christ Church Priory and St. Augustine's Abbey. Of the entire collection of 433, James assigns forty-seven volumes to the former library and twenty-six to the latter. A striking feature

---

[60] Cambridge Antiquarian Society, Octavo Publications, XXXII (Cambridge, 1899).

in Parker's collection, according to James' analysis, is the rarity of books from northern abbeys.[61]

MS 415 may well have come to Parker from John Bale (1495–1563), former Carmelite monk and sometime bishop of Ossory, who ended his stormy career as prebendary of Canterbury under Parker. As one who had broken his monastic vows to take a wife, Bale was much concerned to seek out historical precedent for clerical marriage. His rare collection of MSS gathered in England, Ireland, Germany, and Switzerland was coveted by Parker. John Strype believed that the Bale collection came into "the Archbishop's hands by purchase" on the canon's death,[62] but James holds that only a few of the known Bale MSS can be traced in the present C.C.C.C. collection.[63] However this may be, Bale is known to have given at least one MS relating to clerical marriage to the "Prelate for his use, in compiling his vindication of Priest's marriage."[64] It contained the Rescript of Ulrich, ascribed here to Volusianus of Carthage and a second tract which John Foxe also ascribed, by contagion, to Volusianus [65] but which is regarded

[61] In the first volume of his Descriptive Catalogue, where the sources and circumstances of the Parker collection are discussed, James brings in some general facts perhaps unknown to Böhmer. He states that Parker's secretary and chaplain was an industrious collector of manuscripts relating to Anglo-Saxon antiquities. As this man held the deanship of York and the treasurership of Exeter as well as the two positions at Cambridge, he was strategically well placed for the advancement of his hobby. He is credited with securing for the Archbishop a number of manuscripts bearing on the history of York, including chronicles of the archbishops of York covering the period in which our Anonymous was active. James in his Catalogue as in his Sources of Archbishop Parker's MSS never seems to have been attracted to Codex 415 as an especially intriguing problem of transmission and provenance. James makes mention of a distressing feature of the Archbishop's fondness for manuscripts. It seems that he employed a scribe adept in simulating ancient hands to fill out manuscripts that were defective or incomplete. Our Codex does not seem to have suffered from this imposture.

[62] Life and Acts of Matthew Parker . . . (Oxford, new ed. 1821), II, 520.

[63] Descriptive Catalogue of C.C.C.C., I, xvii. His strictures are based upon Parker's letter No. 221 to Illyricus "which proves conclusively that we must not expect to find any large proportion of Bale's collection at Corpus Christi." Parker's references to the Bale MSS are to be found in his Correspondence, ed. for the Parker Society by John Bruce (Cambridge, 1853), pp. 140, 198, 287.

[64] A Defence of Priests' Mariages . . . against a civilian naming himself Thomas Martin (London, n.d.). See below, n. 70.

[65] Foxe gives the Latin and a translation, Acts and Monuments of the Church Historians of England (London, 1857), V, I, 314 ff. There is an omission which is filled in in the more authoritative edition of the text by Ernst Dümmler. "Eine Streitschrift für Priesterehe," S.B., Berliner Akademie der Wissenschaften, I (1902), pp. 418 ff. The basis of Dümmler's text is the sixteenth century C.C.C.C. MS 101 which

by A. Fliche as the work of a Norman cleric composed between 1074 and 1080, for Fliche shows that its theological vocabulary betrays clear connections with the school of Bec under Anselm.[66] Dümmler believed that Bale procured his copy of this tract and the Rescript from the Amerbach collection in Basel.[67] In any event, the archiepiscopal redactor of A Defence of Priests' Mariages was in possession of one Continental MS dealing with this subject and we may not be far off in conjecturing that he also prized MS 415 with its several Tractates on the marital theme for the same reason and that it came to him from Bale who may well have obtained it from the same Continental source whence he had obtained the allied Norman tract.

The internal evidence for transmission is minimal. In addition to the several twelfth century hands of the Tractates themselves there are two more, the late hand of the superscriptions over twenty-one of the Tractates and another late hand of the titles in the Table of Contents. The former is thought to be that of Archbishop Parker himself and the latter, that of a secretary probably Joscelin. The Table of Contents is on the verso of the fourth of four separate leaves bound in with the Codex. Here the twenty-one superscriptions are combined or slightly altered to make seven-

---

is the one he supposed Foxe to have used. The tract is also found in Gonville and Caius College MS 427 given by William Moore (1590–1659). It is this twelfth century MS on which Foxe based his edition according to M. James. A Descriptive Catalogue of the Manuscripts in the Library of Gonville and Caius College (Cambridge, 1908), II, 498 f.

[66] L'opposition antigrégorienne, p. 21. Dümmler, op. cit., had regarded the work as German or French, more probably German.

[67] Op. cit., p. 722. Dümmler supposed that Bale had procured only a copy of the original for which, to be sure, Dümmler sought in vain, basing his edition on the sixteenth century C.C.C. MS 101. But Foxe seems to have used not a copy but the original, for he writes:

it appeareth by the copy, which I have seen and received, of the above-named Matthew, archbishop of Canterbury, to be of an old and ancient writing, both by the form of the characters and by the wearing of the parchment, almost consumed by length of years and time (pp. 313 f.).

To be sure, he is here describing the Rescript (of Ulrich), but this was by all accounts connected with the second tract. The Bale gift to Parker, which was thereafter used by Foxe, must have been G. & C. MS 427 as M. James says. But how it got from Parker or Foxe to William Moore is not explained or even noticed by M. James. I have not been able to consult the MS Catalogus Librorum quos Magister G. More . . . listed in A Catalogue of the Manuscripts . . . of Cambridge (Cambridge, 1856) I, p. 237, No. 211.

teen titles fitting into seventeen ruled spaces. This crowding and spacing explains Hall's reference to only seventeen treatises.[68]

In the top two spaces on the page above the "Contenta" Archbishop Parker, presumably (for the hand seems to be that of the superscriptions) has written these words: "Hic Author fuit Normannus quidam et multus est in defensione Rhotomagensis ecclesie." This notice has specific reference to one Tractate, indicated as beginning on p. 39, namely, J4/L3, wherein the connection with Rouen is quite evident. Only by contagion does this notice apply to the other Tractates, but the large clear "print," in marked contrast to the wretched script of the following titles, could indicate that the one who conceived the title page intended this notice to serve as a kind of caption for the whole Codex.[69] Though it may be the casual observation of a collector it nevertheless clearly testifies to the fact that there was nothing known to the learned collector-donor himself about the source of his MS which made its ascription to a Norman anything out of the ordinary. This is all the more significant for the reason that the man who prepared the "Contenta" was apparently aware of the "regnum Anglorum sive Saxonum" (in the royal *Ordo*), which he must have had in mind when he drew attention to p. 171 in "De consecratione" (Appendix). Parker, it would thus appear, regarded all the pieces of his MS as composed by one man, and that author a Norman.[70]

[68] These seventeen titles of the "Contenta" are given in the Appendix, pp. 206 ff. They were first printed by T. James, op. cit., p. 856, where the reading is slightly different from that of the present MS. These differences may be explained by the difficulty of transcribing accurately the miserable hand of the "Contenta."

[69] Old catalogues draw the same inference. Nasmith (1777), p. 388, William Stanley (1772), p. 50. Writes Thomas James, Ecloga Oxono-Cantabrigiensis (London, 1600), p. 856: "Auctor *huius libri* Normannus fuit quidam et multus est in defensione Rhotomagensis Ecclesiae."

[70] There is a further bit of negative evidence on this head. Parker's supplement (pp. 276–351) to the Defence of Priests' Mariages, commonly ascribed to John Ponet, yields no certain references to the several Tractates on the subject of clerical marriage in MS 415, although Parker deals extensively and learnedly with the very period covered by the Tractates. He discusses Gerard of York, William Giffard (falsely connected with York), Anselm, and Henry I. Here if ever, amid numerous other quotations from the ancient and medieval MSS he had proudly garnered, was the place to bring in the "York" Tractates on marriage if indeed they were in his possession at the time. Now Joseph Beale has dated the enlarged edition of the anonymously published Defence as 1565, only ten years before the Prelate's death and two years after Bale's. A Bibliography of Early English Law Books (Cam-

The ineptness of several of the titles and page references is evidence of hastiness in the perusal of the Tractates. The Table refers, for example, to J10/W, "De potestate sacerdotali et regia," as beginning on p. 85 and then indicates in an additional page reference (p. 219) that the same subject is discussed here and this is true, but the reference is to a place midway in J24B/L4, "De consecratione,"[71] which despite its liturgical title is entirely taken up with sacerdotal and royal power and not on this page alone. The present numbering in gross Arabic numerals by pages (but recto only) rather than by folio seems to have been done by the same person who prepared the Table of Contents. The present pagination ignores a misplaced quire falling within Tractate J24/L4. It was apparently after this pagination that Tractate J15(I)/S, "De nuptiis," was mutilated by the cutting off of the lower two-thirds of page 109 which is pasted on a new sheet, and by the removal of the next leaf and the replacement thereof with new vellum left blank to constitute pages 111 and 112. This replacement with a blank leaf would have been unnecessary except to preserve the full complement of pages safeguarded by the

---

bridge, Mass., 1926), p. 294. My explanation for the want of specific reference to Codex 415 is that Parker himself knew that it was of Continental provenance and therefore not directly relevant to his argument, for the Archbishop's concern was to show the continuity of clerical marriage in England and for this reason deals at length with the importation of Gregorian ideas under his predecessors Lanfranc and Anselm but does not adduce the related Tractates of MS 415 because, though apposite to his general position, they do not provide precedents *for England*. They were for him, who knew better than anybody else the ultimate source of his MS, solely *Norman* documents.

I have not been able to consult John Ponet's original A Defence for Mariage of Priestes (Zurich, 1555/6), which first called forth Thomas Martin's (Stephen Gardiner's) "blasphemose book" to ascertain the sources of the Bishop of Winchester's work.

An attempt to draw from Parker's Register of MSS further clues regarding transmission has proved fruitless. This Register (M. James, Descriptive Catalogue, I, xxxiii ff.) groups the Parker MSS under classes A to W with from four to forty-one articles in each class. Size rather than date of accession or subject matter seems to be largely determinative in this classification. Cf. James, ibid., xxii. Our MS 415 comes under Class O in the Register with twenty-eight articles. Since one *incipit* only was given for MSS 442, 453, and 415, it appears that these three items may have been acquired as a unit. Three lines have been erased from the Register at this point. MS 453 contains epistles of Grosseteste, many of them bearing on the rights of the English episcopate against undue papal encroachment. MS 442 has this in common with MS 415: it was copied in the eleventh or twelfth century in a hand not unlike that of Christ Church, Canterbury.

[71] The place indicated comes at l. 18, p. 671 in the edited text.

terms of Parker's bequest.[72] What survives of the mutilated Tractate argues for the invalidity of marriage with an infidel, Jewess, criminal, adulteress, or member of Satan. No true sacrament of marriage has been performed and any marital relationship of such a character should be dissolved as though it had not been. It is possible that some learned member of the Henrician or Elizabethan Church found satisfaction in these views and then saw fit to remove from the Codex certain less acceptable contentions of the ancient cleric of Rouen.

Although there is no clearly discernible sequence of subject matter in the Codex,[73] there is no evidence of any other misplacements of quires or leaves within the Codex as now bound. Tractates, quires, and hands are so interconnected that we must assume that, with the aforementioned exception, the contents were copied in the present sequence in one scriptorium. The fact that the last hand in the Codex is the same as the first confirms this view.[74]

Where the Codex was assembled and the Tractates copied remains uncertain.[75] There were some seven or eight scribes at

[72] The verso of the first of the four folios of the Codex has the following words: "Hic liber continens paginas–312" in a sixteenth century hand.

M. James in his Descriptive Catalogue describes the stringent precautions Parker took against the loss or mutilation of the MSS he bestowed on his college (I, xii f.). An annual inspection of the library by the Masters and Parker scholars of Gonville and Caius and of Trinity Hall was instituted by the donor. The inspectors were empowered to fine Corpus Christi College 4 d. for every leaf found to be missing in the MSS. We may have here a clue as to the time when MS 415 lost one leaf and suffered the mutilation of a second, namely, *after* the acquisition of the Codex by the College when the replacement of a lost or excised folio would be felt necessary. The fact that the "Contenta" of the Codex groups "De nuptiis" and "De depositione" together under one compounded title may be some confirmation of this view, for had the blank leaf now separating these two Tractates been present at the time of the listing of the contents of the Codex, it would have been more natural to list these two Tractates separately rather than as parts of a single Tractate, numbered 11(=J15 & 16).

[73] There is, however, a faint trace of earlier groupings surviving in the present larger collection. J6–J11 all bear on the necessity of modifying canon law in the interests of true evangelical justice (except J10); J13–J19 deal with problems of the sacraments. J24A, B, C, D may once have constituted a single *libellus*. Cf. Scherrinsky, op. cit., p. 26. See also below, p. 32 on J1–4 and 31.

[74] M. James, in his Descriptive Catalogue, II, 308.

[75] The most recent survey of the original homes of English MSS fails to identify the source of C.C.C.C. 415. N. R. Ker, Medieval Libraries of Great Britain: A List of Surviving Books, Royal Historical Society Guides and Handbooks, No. 3 (London, 1941).

work.[76] Some of these hands, so James observed, resemble those of Christ Church in Canterbury, whence Parker, directly or indirectly derived a large number of his MSS. The scribes were not always alert to the significance of what they were copying. The best instance of what seems to be uninstructed copying occurs in connection with Tractate J24/L4, "De consecratione." There are two versions of the Tractate here, written in the same scribal hand. Version A concludes with the insertion of a long "Appendix" of *pièces justificatives*, principal among which are the orders of episcopal and royal consecration *in extenso* and excerpts from canons. The ornate capitals of the orders and the *tituli* are conscientiously reproduced in the scribal copy. Then, two-thirds down on the final page of this documentation, in the same hand, with neither an ornate capital nor a space between it and the foregoing, begins the second version of the Tractate with its distinctive opening section "Sancta ecclesia sponsa Christi est" not found in Version A.[77] At the top of the next page and for four pages the hand (IVb) is unusually large.[78] The unique material of this section is verbally spliced with the larger section of Version B which differs from Version A in certain omissions.[79]

[76] Hampe (op. cit., pp. 670 ff.) distinguished eight, suggesting the probability of the identification of the first and eighth hands. James (Descriptive Catalogue) notes somewhat fewer. My own examination of portions of the Codex by means of microfilm yields seven but not exactly the same seven noted by Hampe. Hand I, according to my reckoning, extends from Tractate J1 to the end of J4; Hand II, to the end of J23, interrupted on p. 120 by Hand III in the small piece of Hand IVa, to the end of J24D (with four pp. within J24B written in unusually large letters — Hand IVb); Hand V, from the beginning of J25 part way through J26 (p. 255); Hand IVa resumes from the middle of J26 through one page of J29 (but interrupted from the middle of p. 265 to the middle of p. 266 by Hand VI); Hand VII, through the remainder of J29 (pp. 280 to the middle of p. 284); Hand VIII, J30; Hand I, J31. The hands are here numbered the same as by Hampe except for my Hand VIII which he does not mention. Hampe uses this numeral instead for the last, saying that his VIII is probably the same as I. Since M. James leaves no doubt of the identity, I have simply indicated that the first and last hands of the Codex are the same, i.e., Hand I.

[77] See below, p. 75.

[78] The large hand is hard to explain. It appears on the later leaves of quire 13 and on the first leaf of quire 14 and thus cannot be regarded as a later reworking and insertion.

[79] Böhmer assumed that B was a copy of A, but this is not at all certain. For example, at the point where the royal and episcopal *ordines* are quoted and compared (J24/L4:674, 34), the quotation from the *ordo* is cut short by A. But B has additional words quoted from the royal *ordo*; thus B could not be copied from A as it stands. There is also evidence that the "Exordium" unique to version B was

At the end of Version B follow two addenda (J24c and d), unique to the latter version. The Tractates in their present form have apparently come to us from scribes who were bidden to copy material which they themselves had not completely understood.[80] Most of the hands within the Codex display a mixture of Insular and Caroline abbreviations.[81] The Tractates which are demon-

---

known by A. Version A begins at the top of page 143 in the Codex with the sentence:

Duę in veteri testamento *persone*, pontificis scilicet et *regis*, olei sancti unctione consecratę et divina benedictione sanctificatę leguntur ad hoc, ut in *regendo* populo Christi Domini *figuram* vicemque tenerent et in sacramento preferrent *imaginem*.

There is no doubt but what a Tractate might begin just this way, although it is a little abrupt. The five words italicized, however, are, in B, found in the two preceding sentences (wanting, of course, in A). One of these sentences is a quotation from a sermon falsely ascribed to St. Augustine. It would therefore appear that A was aware of this sentence with its key words and doubtless the whole of the "Exordium" of B, although A chose not to copy it as no longer apposite to the immediate purpose for which the adapted, and for the most part amplified, transcript was made. See below, pp. 75 f. Version B reads as follows:

In hoc igitur istę duę personę, sacerdos videlicet et rex, vices Christi tenere videntur et imaginem. Sicut enim beatus Augustinus asserit. . . . Dominus noster Iesus Christus unus verus rex et unus verus sacerdos, illud ad regendos nos, illud ad expiandos, has duas personas apud patres si[n]gillatim commendatas suam figuram egisse declaravit. Quoniam et istę duę personę in veteri testamento olei sancti unctione consecratę et divina benedictione sanctificatę leguntur ad hoc ut in regendo populo *vel expiando* Christi Domini figuram vicemque tenerent et in sacramento preferrent imaginem.

In Version B, *sacerdos* and *rex* are the image and the figure of Christ and take His places in ruling and making expiation for the people. In A we note a shift: it is now the *pontifex* and the *rex* who are the image and the figure of Christ and take His place in *ruling* the people. It is clear from this that A follows and adapts B. We may have here a clue to the changed status of the author or occasion of his adapted composition. On pages 665, 34 to 666, 1, we take note of an insertion into an abstract discussion of the relationship between the *sacerdos* and the *rex* in the Old Testament, of contemporaneous material concerning the relationship of the *episcopus* and the *rex*. To give the preceding sentences an air of contemporaneity A changed the opening verb of the paragraph, line 21 from *habebat* (B) to *habet*. It will be observed that at the end of the insertion, page 666, 1, *episcopus* gives way to the *sacerdos* of what may be the older textual stratum and that the verbs are again in the past, as is appropriate for the discussion of relationships under the Old Covenant. In A and B both, there is evidence of reworking, and perhaps of the expansion of an originally smaller study with new, or previously composed, materials.

[80] Other evidence that our Codex was assembled by someone other than the original author is the want of order in the arrangement of the Tractates and the fact that while Versions A and B of J24 follow one another, the two versions of "Apologia pro filiis sacerdotum," J22 and J26 are separated in the Codex as though they were distinct Tractates rather than two copies of the same.

[81] The Insular abbreviations for *est, enim, et, quia, etcetera* are found alongside other contractions and the full forms. Cf. S. Hellmann, op. cit., pp. 192 f.

strably Norman in origin do not differ in regard to palaeographic peculiarities from the Tractates which Böhmer believed to have been composed in England. In the quest of criteria for distinguishing English and Norman scripts [82] we are at a disadvantage in that we are poorly informed concerning the scriptorium of Rouen at the turn of the eleventh century.[83] I have, however, secured photographs of certain parts of the Benedictional of Archbishop Robert (the formularies of the supplementary Ordinatio episcopi) which were written in Rouen cathedral in the second half of the eleventh century. The hand of these formularies and that of several of our Tractates are similar.[84]

The photographs of the supplementary formularies were made available to me by Mr. Charles R. Dodwell of Gonville and Caius College who took them while in Rouen in connection with his work on Canterbury manuscripts. Mr. Dodwell has very graciously responded to my subsequent inquiries concerning the provenance of MS 415. On examining the Codex he felt sure that it was not a Canterbury manuscript and that James' notation of a resemblance between several of the scribal hands contained therein and the style of Christ Church is no longer a valid clue. He is of the opinion that the whole manuscript is Norman — possibly from Bec. He notes that the script of J4/L3, "Apologia archiepiscopi Rotomagensis," is similar to that of Bib. Nat. lat. 2342, of the Anonymus Beccensis. The initials of pp. 285 to 293 in J31/B30 are filled with red and green, a feature he connects with Trinity MS 405, a Bec book brought by Lanfranc from Bec to Canterbury.[85] Tractate J5/B3, which opposes papal exemptions of monasteries from episcopal jurisdiction, is written in a hand similar

---

[82] Doris Bains has been helpful: A Supplement to Notae Latinae: Abbreviations in Latin MSS from 850 to 1050 A.D. (Cambridge, England, 1936). But nothing conclusive has emerged from an application of her criteria for localization, since by the time of the Norman Conquest, as Edward Maunde Thompson points out, "the Saxon scribes had learned to write quite efficiently in the style used on the other side of the Channel." An Introduction to Greek and Latin Palaeography (Oxford, 1912), p. 436.

[83] Émile Lesne, Histoire de la propriété ecclésiastique en France, IV: Les Livres, Mémoires et Traxaux des Facultés Catholiques; XLVI (Lille, 1938), p. 199.

[84] On the transmission of the Benedictional, the dating of its several parts, and other important connections between it and our Codex, see below, pp. 44 ff.

[85] This is the former B. 16. 44 described by M. James, The Western Manuscripts in the Library of Trinity College, Cambridge (Cambridge, 1900), I, 405 f.

to that of Rouen MS 456 which is from Saint-Evroult by way of St. Ouen.

2. The Question of Sole Authorship of the Tractates

Not until Funk's article [86] in 1935 had anyone seriously questioned Böhmer's assumption that all the Tractates of Codex 415, with one or two exceptions, are from the same author. Up to this time almost all who made use of the Tractates bore witness to the homogeneity of the collection.

Working independently of each other, Scherrinsky in Germany (1939), Lapparent in France (1946), and the present writer (doctoral dissertation, [87] 1946), took up Funk's challenge and refuted his thesis. Scherrinsky's study was the earliest and, by reason of the author's access to the Böhmer notes and the hitherto unpublished transcripts of several of the Tractates, the most significant of the three demonstrations. Because of the war-time unavailability of the Codex for the purpose of microfilming, Lapparent's and my own efforts had less significance. But thanks to the isolation of these three independently conducted inquiries, they triply reinforce the original contention of Böhmer against Funk. In view of this threefold confirmation, it is scarcely necessary to repeat here my earlier statistical and stylistic tables of comparison. It will suffice to state the general nature of the evidence for a single authorship of the Tractates accompanied by a few illustrative details and an occasional bit of fresh evidence from the Tractates of which also Scherrinsky had no transcript.

The key Tractate of the Codex for the purpose of ascertaining the interrelationship and interdependence of the several pieces in it is J28/L5, "De Romano pontifice." This Tractate brings together many themes found disparately in the Codex: the want of Apostolic virtue in the Pope, monastic exemption from episcopal control, the onerous visits to Rome to receive the pallium, the excummunication of bishops, the encroachment of legates, the ecclesiastical authority of the consecrated king. Moreover, this

[86] Discussed above, pp. 14 ff.
[87] "The Bearing of Christology on the Relationship of Church and State as Illustrated by the So-Called Anonymous of York," Union Theological Seminary (New York, 1946).

Tractate quotes from J24/L4, "De consecratione," *in extenso* and is related verbally to J29–30/B29+L6,[88] "De obediendo Romano pontifice." Tractates J28 and J29(II) both quote the Epistle of Ivo of Chartres to Hugh of Lyons, dated 1097, which, incidentally, provides us with a *terminus a quo* for the two pieces. Both these Tractates dwell on the meaning of *apostolus* as *missus a Christo*. Tractate J28, in which the cathedral Church or the bishop himself is considered the mother or the father of the monasteries of the diocese,[89] is connected by this concept and image not only with J24, but also with two of the Tractates which were presumably composed in Rouen, J5 and J27.[90] Parallels in mood, thought, and sentence construction are common. Equally important parallels between J28 and Tractates 2, 4, 6, 9, 11, 12, and 31 are also observable. The correspondence between the "De Romano pontifice" and other members of the Corpus is thus so clear that we may assume that the author thereof must even have had a certain number of them before him as he wrote.

J24, "De consecratione," is likewise clearly related to the other Tractates of the Codex, in respect to numerous points of style, vocabulary, and characteristic concepts. From these examples of conceptual and stylistic parallels [91] — the massiveness of which evidence rules out the possibility of mere coincidence — it appears that "De consecratione" has palpable affinities with Tractates 1, 4, 5, 6, 8, 9, 11, 12, 13a, 14, 16, 18, 22(26), 25, 30, 31 as well as with the "English" Tractates 28 and 29. Correspondence will be most frequent, of course, among Tractates dealing with similar subject matter. The fact that not all of them are bound together by obvious and palpable similarities does not exclude the unmentioned Tractates from consideration as likewise belonging to the same author.[92] These stylistic parallels are merely

---

[88] The latter is really three loosely related pieces which might be referred to respectively as 29 (I) and 30 (III), both edited in Libelli de lite, and 29 (II) which was left out by Böhmer to appear among the "Beilagen" of Kirche.

[89] J28/L5: 682, 27; 683, 12.

[90] J24/L4: 680, 35; 683, 13; J5/B3: 452 (last sentence); J27 A.

[91] Tables of correspondence of such key phrases as *ecclesia sponsa Christi, per naturam — per gratiam, conregnare Christo* are to be found in the author's unpublished doctoral dissertation, op. cit., Tables 6–8. Cf. Scherrinsky, op. cit., p. 116.

[92] But I do not follow Scherrinsky, who holds that since a very large majority of the Tractates are palpably from one author, therefore all the others must be his *ipso facto*.

readily available criteria for establishing the homogeneity of the Codex as regards authorship. The skein of interrelating strands among the Tractates scarcely needed formal demonstration had it not been for Funk's argument from a diversity of subject matter in the Tractates (not all of them publicist!) to a diversity of authorship. We are certainly justified in using clues provided by any of the Tractates, save J10/W, to throw light on the origins and authorship of the Codex as a whole.

Lest the presence of this one alien item call into question the foregoing demonstration of a unity of authorship for the other pieces of the Codex, we shall examine this Tractate as a special case. Unfinished as it stands, J10/W, "De potestate sacerdotali et regia," argues for the complete subordination of the *regnum* to the international *sacerdotium*, appealing to, or rather simply explicating, the familiar Gelasian formula. The contention is entirely out of keeping with everything else said on this head in the other Tractates. Böhmer conjectured either that J10 represented the abandonment of "Gerard's" extreme royalism (which was indeed the case in 1105 when he sided with Anselm) or that the Anonymous intended to state the position of his opponents in order to tear it down. The incompleteness of the piece disposed Böhmer to favor the latter explanation.[93]

My own view is that J10 is an extraneous leaf that was perhaps mistakenly copied into our Codex. First of all, the sacerdotal side of the argument is taken so emphatically, that it cannot be put down as our author's objective statement of the position of his foe, made in preparation for an assault upon it. This is not the way of the Anonymous. Moreover, the grammar and vocabulary of the piece seem to be a little different from what we find in the other Tractates.[94] This and the fact that the piece comes to an end with a period even though the line and the page are not filled out and the additional fact that in the present Codex this "Tractate" takes almost two pages (85 f.) support the conjecture that we have in J10 a leaf from an extraneous work which strayed in among the literary remains of our author and was mistakenly copied along with his authentic writings.

[93] Kirche, pp. 197 f. Cf. Scherrinsky who agrees, op. cit., pp. 61 ff.
[94] Appendix, n. 738.

But perhaps not mistakenly. It is quite possible that this piece was the crucial section of a Gregorian tract which had set the Anonymous off in composing "De consecratione." This conjecture is supported by the fact that J10 contains an extraordinary number of propositions which are dealt with and refuted in "De consecratione," notably that the royal power is inferior to the sacerdotal since it deals only with earthly things, that it cannot remit sins, nor open the gates of heaven and paradise, nor break the gates of hell, nor change bread and wine and perform other sacraments, nor save both bodies and souls, nor propitiate the divine wrath and liberate from perdition, changing the sons of perdition into adoptive sons of God. In sum, *rex filius est, non presul*, for only the *sacerdos* may be called an *angelus Dei* and *christus*.[95] Of every one of these Gregorian asseverations, "De consecratione" is a would-be refutation. If J10 was indeed a portion of the tract which called forth the Anonymous' vigorous defense of royal and episcopal dignity, it is not surprising that it was preserved among his papers.

The presence of J10 in our Codex may well be the exception that proves the rule, indirectly substantiating the claim for a unity of authorship.

3. The Dependence of "De Consecratione" on the Archbishop Robert Benedictional

Böhmer ascribed Codex 415 to a cleric of York on the strength of three points: 1) two of the Tractates deal with the English investiture problem, 2) one of these quotes from an English coronation order, and 3) a third Tractate deals with the primatial controversy between York and Canterbury. Convinced that all but J10 of the some thirty Tractates came from a single author, Böhmer after abandoning Gerard was moved to hypothesize an anonymous Rouen cleric who later went to York to serve under Gerard.[96] Böhmer even thought that this devoted cleric would have felt obliged to leave York on the death of the unpopular

---

[95] These terms can be seen in context below, p. 224. That it is the king who is a *christus* and as such the *summus presul* of his people rather than the Pope is the theme of "De consecratione."

[96] See above p. 4.

Archbishop. On so slender an argument rests the famous appellation "Anonymous of York."

Böhmer's arguments for a York authorship may be countered thus. Against his first, that two of the Tractates deal with English investiture, it should be pointed out that the theorist finally responsible for the solution of the English problem was a Frenchman, not even a Norman, Ivo of Chartres. We may suppose that a Norman cleric could have been as much concerned about Henry I as was Ivo or Hugh of Fleury.[97] As to Böhmer's second inference, from the cited coronation order, it will be shown that the pontifical from which the Anonymous quotes the *ordo* was that of Archbishop Robert which, though it was English in origin, was in Rouen cathedral when "De consecratione" was composed. As to Böhmer's third contention, it can be argued that an espousal of the side of York against Canterbury could have been prompted by the author's desire, a) to support the king favoring York rather than the Archbishop of York as such, which would be in keeping with the royalism of the other Tractates and no clear argument for localizing the Tractate in York, or b) to support one metropolitan (York) as such, against the primatial intrusions of another (Canterbury) which would be consonant with the author's repeated defense of the metropolitan dignity of Rouen against the primatial claims of Lyons, fostered by the Pope. The Anonymous' interest in York in one portion of one Tractate is surely not sufficient justification to style the whole Codex the Tractatus Eboracenses.[98]

Evidence in support of the second point, concerning the dependence on a Rouen *ordo*, must now be submitted. Schramm [99] first identified the royal *ordo* cited and quoted in "De consecratione" as the Edgar Coronation Order. Ward [100] followed this up by a footnote observation that the Anonymous might well have been using the Archbishop Robert Benedictional, one of the seven

---

[97] On Ivo and Hugh see below, Section 6.
[98] This third point will be more fully developed in Section 8.
[99] "Ordines-Studien III," pp. 325 f.
[100] Op. cit., p. 168, n. 1.

extant MSS [101] (apart from "De consecratione" itself) containing the Edgar Ordo. An examination of a microfilm of the unpublished Appendix of "De consecratione" leaves scarcely any doubt concerning derivation.

The royal Ordo from the Robert Benedictional covers seven printed pages. The points at which the Anonymous varies from this long text are very few. Most of the instances fall under the head of slight omissions, slight transpositions, and changes in

[101] Schramm ("Ordines-Studien III," pp. 313 f.) finds the Edgar Ordo contained in the following MSS:
1. The Benedictional of Archbishop Robert, Rouen, Bibliothèque Municipale 369. Though by long usage called a "benedictional," the Codex is properly speaking a pontifical. Composed at Winchester towards the end of the tenth century, it contains additional materials adapted for its use in Normandy, notably a ducal *ordo* modeled on the therein contained royal *ordo*. Edited by H. W. Wilson as The Benedictional of Archbishop Robert, Henry Bradshaw Society, XXIV (London, 1903).
2. The misnamed "Aethelred" Ordo, London, British Museum, Cotton, Claudius A iii. It was composed at Winchester or at least in the Province of Canterbury at the end of the tenth century or the beginning of the eleventh. Printed (with emendations) by Arthur Taylor, The Glory of Regality (London, 1820).
3. The Pontifical of Bishop Sampson of Worcester, Cambridge, Corpus Christi College 146. The original portion of the Pontifical, the part containing the royal *ordo*, came from Winchester and probably from the Old Minster and was composed toward the end of the tenth century. Edited and translated by L. G. W. Legg, English Coronation Records (Westminster, 1901); re-edited to show the sources by Percy Schramm, "Krönung bei den Franken und den Angelsachsen," pp. 117 ff.
4. The St. Dunstan or Sherborne Pontifical, Paris, Bibliothèque Nationale lat. 943. It seems to have been composed and illuminated for the bishop of Sherborne at the end of the tenth century. It has not been edited in full. It is described by Victor Leroquais, Les Pontificaux manuscrits des bibliothèques publiques de France (Paris, 1937), II, 6 ff. The episcopal *ordo* and the *ordines* of the lesser clergy are published by Edmond Martène, De antiquis Ecclesiae ritibus libri tres (Antwerp, 1763), I, viii, 11, *ordo* 3; II, pp. 40 ff. A facsimile of one p. in F. Steffens, Lateinische Palaeographie (2 ed.; Berlin, 1929), pl. 71.
5. The St. Thomas Pontifical, Douai, Bibliothèque Municipale 67 (formerly 94). A pontifical of the twelfth century, it came to Douai from the monastery of Marchiennes. It is said to have been a gift of Thomas à Becket.
6. The Lanalet Pontifical, Rouen, Bibliothèque Municipale 368. Composed in Cornwall or France on a Winchester model. Only the coronation service for the queen belongs to the Edgar Ordo. Edited by G. W. Doble as Pontificale Lanaletense, Henry Bradshaw Society, LXXIV (London, 1937).
7. Codex, London, British Museum, Cotton, Vitellius A vii. This copy of the Ordo was largely destroyed by fire in the eighteenth century.
Of these seven copies of the Edgar Ordo, only Nos. 1 through 4 are of significance for our purpose, since the St. Thomas Pontifical was composed after the composition of "De consecratione" and the Lanalet Pontifical does not contain the kingly portion of the Edgar Ordo, while No. 7 has been too seriously mutilated by fire to enter into any kind of textual comparison.

spelling. Examples will suffice.[102] The Anonymous, near the opening of the Ordo drops *dei* in the phrase *ecclesia dei*; he transposes *nostrae* in the phrase *ad preces nostrae humilitatis*; he adds a *c* to Robert's *eclesia*; converts *sanxisti* into *sancxisti*; *annexis* into *adnexis*. The some thirty-five variations of this kind can be explained as hasty transcriptions, the persistence of the scribes' peculiar spellings, or as corrections of the original. The remaining variations number six. The Anonymous writes *a gyon* for Robert's *in gyon, operatistis* for *operati st(= o. sunt)*. He at one place adds *valeat* for lucidity, and converts the mood of two rubrics into the indicative, for example, *Hic datur anulus*; and he mistakes *super* for *semper*. None of these is a key variant reading in differentiating the extant texts of the Edgar Ordo.[103]

Especially impressive therefore are the instances of the Anonymous' transcription of key variant readings which mark off one MS of the Edgar Ordo from another. For example, the crucial royal appellation, *presul princeps*, in "De consecratione" is a variant reading unique to Robert's Benedictional among the extant MSS of the Edgar Ordo. *Preelectum principem* is the reading both in the Dunstan and the Sampson pontificals.[104] Robert also has the following unique reading (p. 142): ". . . . et instruat contraque omnes visibiles et invisibiles hostes idem potenter regaliterque tuę virtutis [regimen] amministret. . . ." The *regimen*, essential to the sense, is wanting in Robert, though found, for example, in Sampson. The Anonymous, in the Appendix to "De consecratione," is content to copy Robert without emendation, but in the body of the Tractate he feels the need of some grammatical accommodation to make sense of his excerpt and drops the *s* of *virtutis* converting the latter into the dative case. Surely this *virtuti* in the body and the unaltered *virtutis* in the Appendix betray an understandable perplexity on the part of the Anonymous

---

[102] Complete Tables of correspondence (based on the edited portion of the Tractate) are given in my original Dissertation, pp. 47–57.

[103] J. Wickham Legg, Three Coronation Orders, Henry Bradshaw Society, XIX (London, 1900) gives the variant readings in the as yet unpublished MSS of the Edgar and allied orders in his "Notes on the consecration of the Anglo-Saxon King [the William Ordo]," pp. 162 ff.

[104] For the Bishop Sampson text: Leopold G. W. Legg, English Coronation Records (Westminster, 1901), p. 20; for the Dunstan Pontifical: J. W. Legg, op. cit., p. 169, s.v. *Deinde*. Cf. Robert, p. 146: *Benedic domine hunc presulem principem*.

as he came upon what must be a lacuna unique to the Robert
Benedictional.

Equally impressive are the points at which the Anonymous
follows Robert where the text of the latter has been modified by
later hands. It would appear that the Anonymous assimilated
all emendations made up to the time of his transcription. Where
a late hand has added *-lia* above *tempora*, the Anonymous absorbs
the emendation and writes *temporalia*, dropping the *bona*. And
there are other instances.[105]

The evidence provided by the transcription of the episcopal
order of consecration in the Appendix of "De consecratione" is
especially eloquent testimony to the Anonymous' dependence on
Robert's Benedictional. At first sight, the copy appears quite
erratic, for the sequence of its several parts differs from that in
the main part of the Robert Benedictional. The seeming disorder,
however, becomes at once almost certain proof that the Anonymous used Archbishop Robert's Benedictional the moment it is
realized that certain parts of his transcribed *Ordo* are taken *from
the eleventh century Supplement to the Benedictional, intended
to adapt this Anglo-Saxon pontifical*[106] *for use in the Province of
Rouen.*[107]

To make clear the sequence of prayers and rubrics in the
Appendix to "De consecratione" we shall assign Arabic numbers
to each of the parts of the Ordinatio episcopi in the edited Benedictional,[108] from 1, *Oremus dilectissimi* to 17, *Populus te*. For
the sake of distinction we shall letter in sequence the several parts
of the Supplement to the Benedictional, from *a, Adesto deus* to *i,
omnipotens sempiterne*. In his Appendix the Anonymous adheres

---

[105] In the Bishop Sampson Pontifical, by way of comparison, the *tempora bona*
original in the Edgar Ordo stands untouched. Where a later hand in the Robert
Benedictional has corrected *regna* to *regni*, the Anonymous follows, although Sampson also has the corrected *regni*. A faultily spelled *renocerotis* becomes *rinocerotis*
in the Anonymous with a superscribed *e*. In two instances where later hands have
made changes in the MS, the Anonymous does not follow them: *vuarum pomo-
rumque* is not changed to *vuluae*, and at another place an inserted *et* does not
reappear in the Anonymous. These may well have been changes wrought in the
Robert MS after the Anonymous made use of it.

[106] Robert's Benedictional is properly speaking a pontifical.

[107] Beginning on p. 162. For the date of this Supplement, see below, p. 45.

[108] Beginning on p. 125.

to the following sequence: 4(p. 164),[109] 5(165), 8(166), f(166), h(166), 13(166), g(167), 12(167), 11(167), *Accipe evangelium* (167 not found in Robert), 17(167f.), *i*(168), 15(168f.), 16(169). Here we have almost certain evidence that the Anonymous was copying from the Rouen pontifical the prayers and rubrics of the episcopal consecration in the form and *sequence* observed in Rouen cathedral, as he must have known from first hand acquaintance. We cannot otherwise account for his weaving back and forth between the older *Ordo* of the Pontifical and the Rouen Supplement. The sequence of prayers resulting from his selections is a perfectly viable order and not a miscellany.[110] The variations of the Anonymous from Robert's text remain to be noted. While they are more numerous than those observed in his transcription of the royal *Ordo*, nevertheless the fact that several marginal and interlinear emendations of the Robert Benedictional show up in "De consecratione" confirms the position taken that the Anonymous had before him the Robert Benedictional.

We shall mention these coincidences first. In formulary 4, Robert has *affectu* altered to *affatu*, and the Anonymous has *affactu* as a hybrid compromise between the two readings; Robert has *exemplo* altered to *exemplis* and the Anonymous has *exemplis*. In 5, Robert has a mistaken *mysterium* for *ministerium*, and the Anonymous perpetuates it; in Robert a later hand has interlined *vel oportuno* which the Anonymous copies; in Robert a later hand has underlined *lassitudinem* for deletion and substituted *laudibus* which is taken over by the Anonymous; a whole sentence added in the margin of Robert is reproduced in its proper place by the Anonymous.[111] In 17, Robert has a grammatically faulty *apostolatum* which the Anonymous perpetuates.

---

[109] The reference in parentheses is to the p. in the Codex. See Conspectus in my Appendix, pp. 229 ff.

[110] The Rouen rite, according to the Anonymous, touches upon the following matters in the following sequence: 4 (prayer with the Evangel held behind the ordinand's head) ; 5 (oil on the head); 8 (hands) ; f (thumb) ; h (ring) ; 13 (ring) ; g (staff); 12 (staff); 11 (staff); *Accipe evangelium*; 17 (benediction of the ordinand) ; *i* (benediction of the episcopal throne); 15 (enthronement); 16 (final prayer).

[111] The significance of these coincidences is felt when a comparison is made with the episcopal *ordo* from the Dunstan Pontifical published by Edmond Martène, op. cit., II, 40. Only two of these readings that might be thought peculiar to the Robert MS appear here, *exemplis* and *affactu*, and this might be due to Martène himself, for his text is not a critical edition of the *ordo*.

As to the readings of the Anonymous varying from Robert, twenty-five fall under the heading of omissions, spelling, and transposition. A few are slight additions or substitutions of words; for example, the Anonymous begins formulary 4 as *Domine sancte pater omnipotens eterne* where Robert has *Deus honorum omnium*; in 5, Robert has *diligat veritatem*, and the Anonymous has *humilitatem diligat*. All of these more important variants can be easily accounted for. We may suppose that the Anonymous was more or less familiar with the hallowed words of episcopal consecration and might have been writing from memory with occasional glances at the pages of the Benedictional in which case slight changes would have been introduced. By way of comparison, the Anonymous quotes most of the smaller passages of Scripture from memory as is evidenced from the frequent substitution and displacement of words in his biblical quotations. Or again, he might have incorporated into the prayers slight modifications which had become customary in using the Benedictional in Rouen.

This appears all the more likely in that no important variants appear in the prayers taken from the Rouen Supplement. They all appear in connection with the older *Ordo* of the Benedictional. Leroquais notes, for example, the general trend to replace the *Deus honorum* (as in prayer 4 above) with the *Domine sancte*, as in the Anonymous.[112] Moreover, this is the very first formulary with which the Anonymous begins his quotation from the *ordo*. Unlike the subsequent formularies, it is introduced without an initial in the middle of the line.[113] It is quite possible that the Anonymous is quoting here from memory before getting out the Benedictional for the task of transcribing and that in consequence the customary opening phrase is given rather than the *Deus honorum* of the Benedictional. Where we are able to control the Anonymous' transcriptions, namely in connection with the formularies which are both quoted in the body of the Tractate and also transcribed in the Appendix, we have good evidence that our author depends partly upon memory, for surely he has the same *ordo* in mind. A good example of discrepancy between body and Appendix occurs in formularies 11 and 12 of the episcopal *Ordo*.

[112] Op. cit., I, lxxxvii.
[113] See below, p. 229, I, 1.

In the body these two formularies beginning *Accipe baculum* are conflated. In the Appendix the two are given as in Robert's Benedictional.[114] Occasional variations from the Robert Benedictional may thus be explained by the partial dependence of the author upon his memory, by the incorporation of slight adaptations which had become customary in Rouen without their having been written into the Benedictional, and by the inaccuracies of the copyist.

It remains to explain, however, the presence of a formulary in the Anonymous' "transcription" not found in the Robert MS itself: *Accipe evangelium*.[115] The liturgical bestowal of the Evangel (or Missal) does not go back beyond the end of the ninth century.[116] It is attested only once for the tenth century. In the eleventh century it appears in the form recorded by the Anonymous in a pontifical of Rheims. By the middle of the twelfth

[114] In the Tractate proper (J24/L4: 674, 33 ff.), the Anonymous has the following:
Accipe baculum signum regiminis
ut inbecilles consolides [Version B, *im*becilles.]
titubantes confirmes,
pravos corrigas,
errantes dirigas in viam salutis ęternę,
et in corrigendis viciis sis sęviens et,
cum iratus fueris, misericordię recordaberis.
But in the Appendix (MS p. 167) the Anonymous has the following:
Accipe baculum sacri regiminis signum.
ut inbecilles [–os, in R.] consolides.
titubantes confirmes.
prauos corrigas.
errantes [rectos, in R.] dirigas [er. dir., in margin] in uiam salutis ęternę.
[habeasque potestatem erigendi dignos
et corrigendi indignos, in R.] cooperante domino nostro ihesu christo.
cui [qui, in R.] cum patre in unitate spiritus sancti est.
[et spiritu sancto vivit et, in R.]
virtus et imperium per omnia secula seculorum [lacking in R.].
From the foregoing it would appear that the Anonymous was quoting from memory in the body of the Tractate, for here he combines elements from the two formularies which begin *Accipe baculum*. Incidentally, we have here the only instance in the entire *ordo* of a double *Accipe* and it is possible that in the practice which had grown up in Rouen cathedral in the time of the Anonymous these two formularies were actually conflated.
[115] Formulary given in full below, p. 229, I, 10.
[116] V. Leroquais, op. cit., I, xc. It occurs with the following words in a pontifical of Aurillac:
Accipe hoc evangelium,
et ita doce populum tibi commissum,
docens eos servare. . .

century its use is attested in Rouen.[117] While we might expect the *Accipe evangelium* to have already found its place in the Supplement to the Robert Benedictional, nevertheless if the practice was just beginning to be observed in Rouen at the time the Anonymous was writing, it is understandable that this addendum to the living and growing rite had not yet found its way into the Supplement,[118] assembled some time before.

Since the evidence of the quotations from the royal and the episcopal *ordines* points rather clearly to the employment of the Benedictional of Archbishop Robert by the Anonymous, it is now the occasion to inquire briefly into the history of the transmission of this MS and to make certain of its presence in the cathedral library of Rouen at the beginning of the twelfth century.

We are fortunate in having an ancient reference to the Benedictional in *Le livre d'ivoire* [119] of Geoffry, Archbishop of Rouen (1111–1128). The list contained therein of the possessions of the cathedral library mentions under items 9–13 the "Benedictionarius Roberti archiepiscopi." [120] All the contestants in the controversy over the transmission of the Benedictional before it came to Rouen agree that the entry in the ancient list refers to the present volume, now transferred to the Municipal Library of Rouen where it lies side by side with the Missal of Robert of Jumièges.

There is no doubt that the Missal belonged to Robert of Jumièges, Archbishop of Canterbury for the one year, 1051.[121] Some scholars have also assigned the Benedictional to the same Robert of Jumièges. Others have argued that the Benedictional

---

[117] Paris; Bibliothèque nationale, ms. lat., nouv. acq., 306. The presence of the *Accipe evangelium* is noted by V. Leroquais, op. cit., II, 223. I have also found the *Accipe evangelium* in two unidentified pontifical MSS said to be from Bec. These are significant attestations because within the *ordo* professions of loyalty to the Church of Rouen are given. E. Martène, op. cit., II, viii, art. 11, *ordo* 12, p. 67.

[118] In the Supplement itself there is evidence of intended elasticity here. The last prayer, *i*, is found on the verso of folio 191. Between it and formulary *h* on the recto of 190 are two blank pages.

[119] Rouen, Bibliothèque Municipale, MS Y 27.

[120] "Hi sunt libri qui reperti sunt in aecclesia Rothomagi tempore Gaudfridi archiepiscopi: . . . 9–13 Benedictionarius Roberti archiepiscopi." Quoted by H. Omont, Catalogue général des manuscrits des bibliothèques publiques de France, Vol. I (Paris, 1886), p. x.

[121] The opposition of Stigand caused him to take flight. He had previously been bishop of London.

belonged rather to Robert, Archbishop of Rouen from 990 to 1037.[122]

The contest between the proponents of Robert of Canterbury (Jumièges) and Robert of Normandy (Rouen) goes back to the eighteenth century when Dom Tassin of St. Ouen in Rouen accused Abbé Saas of the cathedral of having made erasures and substitutions in the Benedictional in favor of Archbishop Robert of Canterbury.[123] Recently, the whole question was decided in favor of Abbé Saas. With the application of an acid, the effaced letters have been restored: *Cantuariensis*. The Benedictional belonged to Robert of Jumièges, Archbishop of Canterbury.[124]

Gerald Ellard supports a very early date for the transmission of the Benedictional from Winchester to Rouen, because France was everywhere following the lead of the Dunstan liturgical movement, especially as it heightened the dignity of episcopal and priestly orders.[125] We have already taken note of the rapidity with which the Benedictional was adapted to the needs of Rouen, by means of the Supplement to the episcopal *ordo*, Wilson having stated indeed that this section of the MS is an addition probably

[122] This Robert of Normandy was a brother of Emma, the Queen successively of Aethelred II and Canute, and the mother of Edward the Confessor. According to this view of the transmission, Robert of Normandy received the Benedictional from his sister at the death of Archbishop Aethelgar of Canterbury in 990, the same year in which he was raised to the archiepiscopal throne of Rouen. The Benedictional would have been a fitting enthronement gift from his queenly sister. The book, it is conjectured, was made for Aethelgar, who had formerly been the abbot of New Minster in Winchester.

The Benedictional gives prominence to two saints especially revered at New Minster. At all events it is an established fact that the Benedictional belongs to the Winchester school of calligraphy and illumination and that liturgically it belongs to the Dunstan revival.

[123] Tassin argued that a list of books drawn up in the pontificate of Geoffry would never have referred to a volume as belonging simply to "Archbishop Robert" unless the Robert in the episcopal succession of Rouen had been intended. The issue between Saas and his assailant grew acrimonious because of the erasure on the title page where, according to Tassin, the Canon had added to *Benedictionarius Roberti Archiepiscopi* the key word *Cantuariensis*. Saas retorted that he had simply written into an erasure made long before him, the adjective that seemed appropriate in view of the datum given on a sheet of the binding: *Robertus Cantuaritarum archiepiscopus anno Christi 1050*. Although this sheet was lost in the rebinding, John Gage, writing in Archaelogia in 1832, said that the leaf could be seen in his day.

[124] V. Leroquais, op. cit., II, 300.

[125] Ordination Anointings in the Western Church before 1000 A.D., Monographs of the Mediaeval Academy of America, VIII (Cambridge, 1933), ch. vii.

of the 11th century." [126] An Ordo provincialis concilii celebrandi
(foll. 176 v. ff.) appears to this editor "to have been written in the
latter part of the 12th century." [127] Wilson rejects [128] Mabillon's
view [129] that this *ordo* dates from the pontificate of William Bona
Anima (1079–1110), but the present writer is inclined to agree
with Mabillon on an earlier date. Recent studies also tend to give
a fairly early date to the supplementary ducal *ordo* and to its
insertion in the Codex of Robert's Benedictional.[130]

Since the examination of the transmission of Robert's Benedictional, upon which the Anonymous seems clearly to depend,
has pretty well established the presence of the MS in Rouen cathedral at least by the opening of the twelfth century, it would seem
no longer legitimate to speak of the author of our Tractates as the
Anonymous of "York." Not only the older Tractates in the Codex
but also its *chef d'oeuvre*, "De consecratione," seem clearly associated with Rouen (although the problems dealt with in some of
the Tractates bear, to be sure, on English affairs).

There are still other reasons besides the dependence upon the
Robert Benedictional which constrain us to localize the "De
consecratione" in Normandy rather than York. To these we turn.

[126] Op. cit., p. 162, n. 1.
[127] Ibid., p. 153, n. 2.
[128] Ibid., p. 195.
[129] Vetera Analecta (Paris, 1676), II, 457 ff.; nov. ed. (1723), 226 ff. Mabillon
pointed out (1) that the conciliar *ordo* refers to Archbishop Maurilius (d. 1067) as
venerabilis memoriae (ed. Wilson, p. 155, l. 16), (2) that in reaffirming the condemnation of Berengarius (loc. cit.), the *ordo* seems to assume that bishops present
at the time of its composition (and insertion in the Benedictional) were also present
at the condemnation of Berengarius, and (3) that the *ordo* contains what would
appear to be a reference to the Duke, his conquests, and his council called at Lillebonne in 1080. Now Wilson has rightly shown that the third inference is unsound
as it stands, for, as he points out, the whole section (beginning "Divinae trinitatis,"
pp. 156 f.) in which these allusions are found, is taken bodily with only the
slightest changes from chapter 13 of the Eighth Council of Toledo. Mansi, X, 1221.
Nevertheless, these phrases from Toledo are quite apt for the situation in Normandy
and, in any event, could have been absorbed into the *ordo* earlier as well as later.
Moreover, Wilson's palaeographic dating has elsewhere proved too late (cf. the ducal
ordo), and such may well be the case here. Mabillon's two other arguments for the
pontificate of William still stand and to them may be added the observation that
the *ordo* assumes the presence of only one archdeacon (loc. cit., p. 153) and a single
archidiaconate is not probable after 1072. Cf. below, Chart and n. 197 on the later
multiplication of archidiaconates.
[130] Wilson had thought that the supplementary *Officium ad ducem constituendum*
(foll. 181–3), modeled on the royal *ordo* of Edgar was "written in a hand of about
1275–1300," but the Director of the Bibliothèque de la Ville has recently given the

4. The Use of the Normal Pseudo-Isidorian Collection and the Hibernensis as Evidence of a Norman Origin of the "York" Tractates

Z. N. Brooke, in his study of English canon law in the eleventh and twelfth centuries, cautiously accepts the Norman period of Böhmer's reconstructed biography of the Anonymous of "York," but cannot agree with Böhmer that, because the Anonymous "supports York against Canterbury, therefore he must have gone to England and become a canon of York." [131] Nevertheless, Brooke speaks of the Tractates as forming "the only English contribution to the mass of pamphlet literature which was evoked by the contest of *sacerdotium* and *imperium*." Brooke conjectures that the Anonymous was quite possibly at Henry's coronation because "he is able to detail the coronation rite of the English kings in his most important tract 'On the Consecration of bishops and kings' . . ." Now we have been able to show that the proficiency of the Anonymous in detailing the coronation rite was not due to his presence in Westminster on August 5, 1100, but to the availability in Rouen cathedral of the Robert Benedictional with its Edgar Ordo, copied out by the Anonymous. But Brooke's correct historical intuition that the Tractates are really from an *Anonymus Rothomagensis* rather than *Eboracensis* comes out in a most important attestation, based upon an examination of the MS itself. Brooke asserts that the Anonymous quotes from the Pseudo-Isidorian Decretals not only in his defense of Rouen, but also in the allegedly Yorkish "De consecratione." Here the Council of Chalcedon is quoted at length, and from this it is clear that the Anonymous uses "a *normal* pseudo-Isidorian collection, and not the collection introduced by Lanfranc, *which was apparently the only one current in England at this time*." [132] Elsewhere in his

---

expert opinion that "cette date est certainement beaucoup trop basse." Marc Bloch, Les rois thaumaturges: étude sur le caractère surnaturel attribué à la puissance royale particulièrement en France et en Angleterre, Publications de la Faculté des Lettres de l'Université de Strasbourg, 19 (Strasbourg, 1924), pp. 496 f. Cf. also L. Valin, Le Duc de Normandie et sa cour (902–1204), étude d'histoire juridique, thèse pour le doctorat, Faculté de Droit de l'Université de Paris (Paris, 1909), p. 43.

[131] Op. cit., p. 159.

[132] Ibid., p. 159, italics mine.

Moreover, in his quotation from the Chalcedonian Preface, the Anonymous is

study Brooke provides the evidence that makes the foregoing "apparently" an unnecessary qualification, for he shows that the Lanfranc abridgment of Pseudo-Isidore was the form in which these Decretals were first introduced to England (undoubtedly at Lanfranc's primatial Council of London in 1075) and that this Lanfranc collection continued in use until about 1150, at least until 1139 when Theobald, that other great canonist abbot, became archbishop of Canterbury.[133] Brooke's careful research into the legal MSS of our period in England and their transmission, thus indirectly but satisfactorily, adds to the cumulative evidence that the *chef d'oeuvre* of the "York" Tractates, composed most certainly within a few years of 1100, is not the creation of an ecclesiastic on English soil.

The evidence of the Hibernensis quoted in the Appendix to "De consecratione" leads to the same conclusion. No one has thus far observed that the material at the end of the Tractate, apart from the episcopal and royal *ordines* taken from the Robert Benedictional, is a miscellany of nine Greek Proverbs [134] intermingled with all but five of the nineteen chapters of liber xxv, "De regno," of the Irish Collection of Canons (A-Text).[135] These quotations, constituting about eleven pages in the Codex, are a quite unexpected addendum to the Tractate. The author had clearly introduced the lengthy episcopal and royal *ordines* with "Nunc inseramus," but we are unprepared for the Proverbs and the "De regno" from the Hibernensis. It is possible that these did not belong to the Tractate in its original form and were added later by the author on blank leaves of the original *libellus* as additional

---

quoting the *pure* Hispana, not the later Hispana Gallica or the still later Hispana Augustodunensis (the ninth century version incorporated in the False Decretals). This is demonstrated by the preservation of a certain reading (*ad coelum* instead of *ad zelum*, on which see below, n. 640). Thus, far from using the Lanfranc abridgment which Böhmer's thesis of an English origin of "De consecratione," would seem to require, the Anonymous appears at this point to know how to go back of the normal Continental Pseudo-Isidore to the original Hispana.

[133] Ibid., pp. 82, 85, 88.

[134] Given by S. Hellmann, op. cit., without regard to palaeographic peculiarities, pp. 129 ff.

[135] Hermann Wasserschleben, Die irische Kanonensammlung (2 ed.; Leipzig, 1885). This second edition is superior to that of 1874 in that it makes references to a Karlsruhe (Reichenau) and a Bodleian MS not hitherto used and takes into consideration some of the findings of H. Bradshaw.

pièces justificatives and subsequently absorbed into the present Codex by the copying scribe.[136] They are, however, by no means irrelevant to the argument of "De consecratione." Indeed certain phrases and concepts of the Tractate may derive from the "De regno" [137] while the marked biblicism of the "De consecratione" may also have been inspired by the Hibernensis, characteristic of which was its ranging of Old and New Testament texts alongside sentences from the Fathers, canons of councils, and decrees of Popes as sources for ecclesiastical law. The sense of the cosmic rôle of the king, which informs the nine Greek Proverbs, has been manifestly communicated to the Anonymous in his extreme sacramental royalism. Since the Greek Proverbs have been mediated to the West by the Celtic Church and since the Hibernensis itself bespeaks its Irish origin, one would be at first inclined to cite the Anonymous' use of these two sources as evidence for Böhmer's hypothesis of a Yorkish background for "De consecratione." But just as we have seen that the devotion of the Anonymous to the formulas of an Anglo-Saxon coronation *ordo* is no indication of his being a spokesman of the Anglo-Saxons overwhelmed by Norman conquerors, so, on examining the history of the transmission of the Hibernensis, we may conclude that Normandy was a much more likely place for a writer of the early twelfth century to make use of surviving Irish materials than England, even York.

In the first place it must be said that we cannot be quite sure whether the Anonymous was in possession of a complete Hibernensis or of only a collection in which the title "De regno" was to be found. In general, the absorption of "De regno" into composite canonical collections was not common, other titles of the Hibernensis appearing much more frequently.[138] There is some

---

[136] The nine Proverbs and the chapters from "De regno" are set off from the preceding *Ordo* as also from the second version of "De consecratione" which follows by a special sign (.;.).

[137] For example, the regent idea of "De consecratione" that consecration changes a king or priest into *another man* may well have been suggested by cap. 1 (= Item III, 23, below p. 232) which in the Anonymous' copy was more extensive than Wasserschleben's.

[138] Paul Fournier, "De l'influence de la collection irlandaise sur la formation des collections canoniques," Nouvelle revue historique de droit français et étranger, XXIII (1899), 36 ff.

reason to believe that certain quotations and concepts from titles other than liber xxv are reflected in "De consecratione." [139] All in all, it is not unlikely that the Anonymous had a complete Hibernensis before him from which he chose to copy only the relevant *titulus*. The sequence of chapters within the *titulus* as given by the Anonymous does not correspond to the order nor to the exact wording of any of the extant MSS of the Hibernensis which have been described.[140] Indeed in many of the chapters that roughly correspond to Wasserschleben's text variant readings and entirely different subsections and interpolations are very numerous.[141] Moreover, since the Anonymous intermingles nine Greek Proverbs and a quotation from Isidore's Etymologiae with the excerpts from the normal liber xxv, one might at first infer that the Anonymous did not intend to copy out liber xxv as such but merely to extract its most relevant chapters to place alongside quotations from other sources. But the fact that he copies all but five of the nineteen chapters of the *titulus* as edited by Wasserschleben gives the impression that what he transcribed was a whole *liber* as it appeared in the version of the Hibernensis before him. Moreover, two MSS of the Hibernensis give Greek Proverbs [142] and the quotation from Isidore "De nomine regni." These MSS are numbered in Wasserschleben's listing as No. 6 (Codex Vallicellanus A. 18) and No. 9 (Karlsruhe MS, XVIII). Although Wasserschleben has not collated it, No. 8 (Hatton 42

---

[139] The Anonymous, for instance, elaborates lib. i, c. 15: "Christus imaginem Dei habet, sicut episcopus imaginem Christi"; he discusses the grades of ordination through which Christ passed, summed up in lib. viii, c. 1; he could have derived several biblical quotations on obedience to the higher powers from lib. xxiv. It is, of course, possible that the Anonymous derived his Irish material not from the Hibernensis directly, but from an earlier Irish collection on which both the Hibernensis and Sedulius Scottus (in the De rectoribus and the Collectaneum) drew. S. Hellmann, op. cit., 96, 136–144, including n. 1. Could the filiation of the Irish material be worked out clearly, we should be greatly aided in identifying the ultimate source of the royalist ideas of the Anonymous.

[140] The only edition of the Hibernensis is that of H. Wasserschleben, op. cit. A new critical edition based upon all the surviving texts remains a great *desideratum*. For want of it nothing conclusive concerning filiation and localization can be inferred from the textual variants in the Anonymous.

[141] The main variants are indicated on pp. 230 ff. below.

[142] S. Hellmann supplies the one Greek Proverb in Karlsruhe MS XVIII. Op. cit., p. 132.

in the Bodleian Library) [143] apparently has the same readings, since it is described as very close to the original from which No. 6 was copied, differing from the latter primarily in the preservation of the original "Patricius" and "Gildas" (which in No. 6 have [144] been changed to "Paterius" and "Gelasius"). The three MSS mentioned belong to the B-Text, the larger and possibly the earlier version of the Hibernensis.[145] No. 6, of unknown provenance, is now in Santa Maria in Vallicella, Rome. No. 9 came originally from Spain by way of a Columbanist cloister (where the Irish Canons were added) to Reichenau.[146] No. 8 came originally from Brittany as evidenced by ninth and tenth century Breton glosses, passing to its present home in Oxford by way of Glastonbury whither it had come some time in the tenth century. Among the A-Texts, the numerous and important variant readings of the Anonymous correspond most frequently to those of Codex Sangermaniensis [147] which is likewise connected with Brittany. Brittany was, according to Henry Bradshaw, the route by which Irish influence penetrated the Continent and the center from

[143] Described by Falconer Madan, A Summary Catalogue of Western Manuscripts in the Bodleian Library at Oxford. . . . Vol. II, Part II (Oxford, 1937), item 4117, pp. 848 f.

[144] Henry Bradshaw, The Early Collection of Canons Known as the Hibernensis: Two Unfinished Papers (Cambridge, 1893), pp. 11, 16. On pp. 62 ff. are to be found the 68 tituli of Hatton 42.

[145] S. Hellmann argues against Bradshaw rather convincingly that B is actually older than A. Op. cit., pp. 142 f. H. Bradshaw argued for the priority of A. The A-Text has sixty-five tituli, the B-Text sixty-seven. The chapters of the B-Text are in most cases more numerous than those under the corresponding tituli of the A-Text. Both versions are early and Celtic in origin and, since this is the case, the dependence of the Anonymous on one recension rather than the other does not greatly help in the problem of localization in the eleventh century.

A more positive indication of remoteness from direct Celtic influence is to be noted in connection with the Anonymous' treatment of the "orders of Christ," in which he is much closer to the French than the original Insular formulations. See below, n. 277.

[146] Karl Künstle, Eine Bibliothek der Symbole und theologischer Tractate zur Bekämpfung des Priscillianismus und westgotischen Arianismus aus dem VI. Jahrhundert, Forschungen zur christlichen Litteratur- und Dogmengeschichte, I, 4 (Mainz, 1900), pp. vii, 5. Unfortunately Alfred Halder added nothing thereto in his Die Reichenauer Handschriften, I (Leipzig, 1906).

[147] Paris, B. N., lat. 12021(formerly 121). Formerly in St. Germain-des-Prés with Breton glosses. Selections from this MS are published by d'Achéry, Spicilegium, 2 ed., I, p. 496.

which numerous Celtic MSS were later dispersed in consequence of the decay of the Celtic monasteries in Brittany.[148]

In any event, the penitential and canonical literature of the Irish came to flourish in France rather than in the Island where it originated. In France and later in Italy and Germany, this literature was widely reworked and adapted, influencing the formation of Continental collections. The Anonymous clearly used a later, enlarged, adapted, and undoubtedly Continental version. For in England, according to Z. N. Brooke, "there is no evidence at all that this general collection [the Hibernensis] or the particular legislation of the Anglo-Saxon Church were used and studied, or even known, after the Conquest." [149] While our evidence is not conclusive, the quotation by the Anonymous from an expanded B-Text of the Hibernensis may be put down in favor of the Continental side of the Channel as the place of origin of the "De consecratione" no less than of the manifestly Norman Tractates of our Codex.

Perhaps the final evidence is found as we confront the older text of the Hibernensis with that of the Anonymous:

Hibernensis: "De sermone regis protegente inimicum aut vinctum, sed tunc misericordia" (lib. xxv, cap. 18).
Anonymous: "De sermone regis *aut ducis* protegente inimicum aut vin[c]tum, sed tantum misericordię gratia" (Codex, p. 203 f.).

Wasserschleben does not note this interpolated reference to a duke in any of his MSS of the Hibernensis.[150]

5. *The Concern of the Anonymous for Ducal no Less than
for Royal Authority a Further Clue of a
Norman Origin of "De Consecratione"*

With the interpolated allusion to a duke in the Appendix of "De consecratione" should be connected several instances in the body of the Tractate in which the Anonymous displays concern

---

[148] Early Collection, p. 35. Fournier was not prepared to side with or against Bradshaw in 1899. "Sur la formation," p. 29. In his great collaborative study with Gabriel le Bras, Histoire des collections canoniques en Occident (2 vols., Paris, 1931) I find no further statement concerning the Bradshaw hypothesis.

[149] Op. cit., p. 49.

[150] To be sure, the "aut ducis" is suggested by the reference to Moses in the chapter.

for the applicability, to the duke no less than to the king, of his theory of princely supremacy over the *sacerdotium*. Surely it would not have occurred to a canon of York, writing in defense of the national monarchy, to insist gratuitously upon the superiority of a duke to a bishop, by implication, say, the earl of Richmond to the archbishop of York. Yet this is the clear implication of the recurrent references of the Anonymous to dukes and princes. Shifts in the argument to secure for the duke the same rights in the Church as for the king are all the more certain an indication of the Norman provenance of the Tractate for the reason that the Anonymous is obliged to suspend his main principle — the sacerdotal character of kingship conferred by consecration — when he turns to defend the ducal authority over the *sacerdotium*. Despite the many other parallels between the royal and ducal *ordines*, the duke of Normandy was never anointed.[151] It was therefore quite pertinent for the Anonymous to remark:

Sed de Moyse quid dicemus, qui non fuit rex unctione sacratus, non fuit sacerdos, sed *dux* tantum populi fuit? [152]

The Anonymous hereupon points to the authority of Moses over Aaron and concludes with satisfaction:

Quare iustum et equum fuit, ut etiam *dux* super hęc omnia et potestatem haberet et imperium. . . . Nam secundum scripturę sacrę testimonium, sicut fuit Dominus cum Moyse, ita fuit cum Iosue et cęteris *ducibus*, quoniam et ipsi in spiritu et virtute Christi venerunt et personam eius gesserunt et vices tenuerunt, et sacramentum.[153]

The argument here becomes simply biblical. The sacramental theory, characteristic of the Tractate as a whole, is here allowed to lapse. Such a digression appears utterly extraneous in a document of allegedly English origin. It is inconceivable that a loyal cleric of the chapter of York would have enhanced the power of

---

[151] The want of consecration in the ducal *ordo* in Normandy would have been all the more keenly sensed in that the ceremony was modeled on that of the king (the Edgar Ordo) contained in the Robert Benedictional. Cf. Bloch, op. cit., p. 194, especially n. 1.

[152] J24/L4:666, 24 ff.

[153] Ibid., 29 ff.

the lords temporal at the expense of the lords spiritual, including his own alleged superior, the archbishop of York.[154]

Moreover, we should not expect to find the word *dux*, in the sense intended by the Tractate, in an English document of our period. The first *dux* in England was the Black Prince whom Edward raised to that rank in 1337, converting thereby the County of Cornwall into a duchy. In pre-Conquest times *dux* was the ordinary translation of *ealdorman*, but after the Conquest *ealdorman* or *earl* was rendered by *comes*, while up to 1337 *dux* was known only as a foreign title.[155]

To make clear that the reference to Moses as *dux* was not a chance inclusion, it remains to mention other instances of a concern for the ducal authority in ecclesiastical matters. After quoting from Romans 13:1–7, the Anonymous concludes:

Ita quippe, ut videmus, ordinata est potestas regum sive *principum*, ut etiam sacerdotibus dominetur. [156]

The word *princeps* is, to be sure, provided by Romans, but *rex* does not appear in the passage quoted. Thus the Anonymous seems to be insisting on two classes of rulers, to both of which the *sancti pontifices* must submit. Since he twice in the same paragraph distinguishes between *rex* and *princeps*, we may rightly inquire: To what *principes*, in addition to the *rex*, should such a *pontifex* as the archbishop of York or indeed any English lord spiritual be subordinate? But that Norman bishops and even the archbishop of Rouen should be *subditi* to the duke was a position traditionally defensible even among the members of the chapter of the metropolitan see.[157]

Further on in the Tractate, after quoting I Peter 2:9, 13 f., the Anonymous sums up:

[154] In Normandy, in contrast, the subordination of the archbishop of Rouen to the duke had long been normal. The investiture of Norman bishops seems first to have been seriously contested by Paschal II some time after the return of Duke Robert from the Crusade in 1100. See below, p. 117; on dux, also nn –, –.

[155] Oxford Dictionary, III, 707; William Stubbs, The Constitutional History of England, 5th ed. III (Oxford, 1903), p. 448.

[156] J24/L4:670, 24 f.; also l. 30: "regibus et principibus."

[157] Cf. the prominence of the duke in the Ordo provincialis concilii celebrandi in the Robert Benedictional (op. cit., p. 153) and in the early Norman councils (Bessin, op. cit.).

Voluntas quippe Dei est, ut rex precellat et *duces* mittantur, ut vindicent malefacta et laudent bona, et propter hoc subiectum sit ei regale sacerdotium et maxime propter Deum.[158]

Here, again, the crucial word is suggested by the Petrine text, but the foregoing three instances [159] of specifying the ducal authority, taken along with the aforementioned *aut ducis* introduced into the chapter heading copied from the Hibernensis constitute substantial evidence for a Norman rather than an English origin of the Tractate.

6. *Quotations from Ivo of Chartres, Parallels with Hugh of Fleury, and Further Evidence of a French Origin of the Tractates*

Likewise in favor of a Norman rather than an English origin of the "English" Tractates of the Codex is the evidence provided by the Anonymous' quotation of a Letter of Ivo of Chartres to Hugh of Lyons. This occurs in Tractates J28/L5:683, 23 ff. and J29/B29:480. Ivo's Letter was written in 1097.[160] This Letter was much more likely to be known in the metropolitan see of Normandy than in York in the first years following its dispatch to Lyons.[161] William Bona Anima of Rouen was, for example, in

---

[158] J24/L4:671, 27 ff.

[159] Moreover, in the second Tractate bearing on the investiture question, "De Romano pontifice" (and as such supposed by Böhmer to have been composed in England), the Anonymous quotes the same Petrine text mentioned above and insists once again on the ducal aspect of the problem of the relationship of Church and State: "Hoc quippe regis est sive *ducum*, non sacerdotis officium." J28/L5:685, 14 f. In so succinct a summary of his thought, the Anonymous would not have had to specify dukes unless he was especially concerned to extend to the duke of Normandy the theory that he had worked out for the (English) king.

[160] Edited in Libelli de lite II, pp. 640 ff. The portion quoted by J28/L5 extends from p. 642, 30 to 643, 25. J29/B29 quotes only the passage deriving from Zosimus, but refers to Gregory, Leo, and Gelasius in the same order in which they are presented by Ivo in his Letter to Hugh.

[161] Hugh the Chanter, to be sure, refers to the Epistle in discussing the investiture controversy in the time of Gerard. Historians of the Church of York (Rolls Series, LXXI), I, pp. 110 f. The reference to Ivo here is an appropriate comment of Hugh himself, writing at a time when Ivo's Letter had become well known and is not by itself evidence that it was known in York during Gerard's pontificate.

Sigebert of Gembloux, pro-imperial contemporary of Ivo, lists the Letter as a separate work, indicating thereby that it must have been widely copied and circulated. De scriptoribus ecclesiasticis, in which it appears very near the end as cap. clxvii, was finished in 1111, a year before Sigebert's death. For other instances of the early diffusion of the Letter, see Ernst Bernheim, Zur Geschichte des

correspondence with the Bishop of Chartres. They were alike vexed by the excessive claims of Hugh of Lyons (Die), who was tempted to mingle his primatial and legatine authorities, encroaching upon the ancient rights of the metropolitan sees of Rouen and Sens.[162]

In "De consecratione" the Anonymous quotes from Augustine's Sixth Sermon on John. This same selection, somewhat abbreviated, appears in the Decretum of Ivo.[163] It reappears in Ivo's Letter to Hugh in still further reduced form.[164] In this case it would appear that the Anonymous consulted the original source, but the text may well have been suggested by Ivo. In any event its presence in "De consecratione" probably attests familiarity with, and some proximity to, the canonical thought going on in Chartres.

This impression is reinforced by several other bits of evidence. For example, in Tractate J9/S the Anonymous cites Pope Calixtus I in such a way as to make probable that his source was the Panormia of Ivo rather than the Pseudo-Isidorian Decretals.[165]

Wormser Concordates (Göttingen, 1878), pp. 12 f. and n. 36. Bernheim instances the employment of the Letter of Ivo in the pro-imperial De investitura episcoporum, dated c. 1109. Cf. Libelli de lite, II, 495 ff. Our "De consecratione," however, was surely written several years before De investitura and probably also before the entry in Sigebert's De scriptoribus. Despite these evidences of a fairly early influence of Ivo's Letter, we are still justified in seeing in that *very* early citation of the Ivonian Letter in "De Romano pontifice" some evidence of proximity to the Ivonian circle of correspondents.

[162] The bishop of Chartres was, by ancient custom, the one charged with the administration of the archdiocese of Sens during a vacancy. Thus Ivo, defender of Sens, no less than William of Rouen, was directly concerned with the integrity of metropolitan authority. Theodor Schieffer, Die päpstlichen Legaten in Frankreich vom Vertrage von Meersen (870) bis zum Schisma von 1130, Historische Studien, 263 (Berlin, 1935). Willi Schwarz, "Der Investiturstreit in Frankreich," Zeitschrift für Kirchengeschichte, XLII (1923), pp. 255 ff.; XLIII (1924), pp. 92 ff. Augustin Fliche, with a view to showing the incidental character of the investiture struggle in both England and France, maintains that the controversy was opened in both countries "à la conséquence d'un incident occasionel relatif à la primatie lyonnaise." "Y-a-t-il eu en France et en Angleterre une querelle des investitures?," Revue Bénédictine, XLVI (1934), 291. Cf. Fournier and Le Bras, Histoire des collections, II, 101 f.

[163] Migne, P. L., CLXI, lib. iv, cap. 194, col. 244; L. d. l., I, 668.

[164] Libelli de lite, II, 645, 7 ff.

[165] The citation appears in MS p. 71 (= Scherrinsky, op. cit., p. 140, n. 2, where it is not identified): "Er[r]ant qui putant, *usque* refugite." The rather long passage thus cited is only the final portion (xx) of the long letter as it appears in Pseudo-Isidore, beginning "Plurimorum relatu comperimus." Hinschius, op. cit.,

Fournier and Le Bras date the Panormia c. 1094.[166] Although Ivo is classified as a moderate, it is clear that the royalist Anonymous found him a much more congenial canonist than any of the unqualified Gregorians, as witness his quotation from the famous investiture Letter and quite probably other works of the Bishop of Chartres. Surely, the Anonymous, who writes as one well acquainted with canon law, is addressing himself to men comparably well versed. Only a canonically and liturgically well informed author, writing to men similarly acquainted with the literature, would have felt free to make citations in the abbreviated form with *usque* which we encounter in many of the Tractates. The Anonymous must be counted a member of the Ivonian circle,[167] however much he remained an exponent of the pre-Gregorian usages in Church and State.

There are further bits of evidence pointing to France rather than to England as the place of origin of the allegedly English parts of the Codex. A basic element in the royalist theory of "De consecratione," for instance, is that what Christ is by nature the royal *christus* is by grace.[168] It is possible that the distinction was suggested by an address of John VIII about Charles the Bald in 877 in which the Pope maintained that what Christ has *per naturam*, the king may have *per gratiam*.[169] The fact that the Gre-

---

p. 737; Migne, P. L., CXXX, col. 131. In the Decretum of Ivo, the same general section appears but the excerpt begins several sentences before "Errant qui putant" and closes several lines before the "refugite." Ibid., CLXI, coll. 454 f. It is also found in Bonizo of Sutri's Liber de vita christiana, v, 46. Ernst Perels (Berlin, 1930) I, p. 190. But here again the selection does not begin or end as in the Anonymous. In contrast, Ivo's Panormia presents the excerpt in just the length cited by the Anonymous, except that "refugite" is rounded off with a closing phrase. Ibid., col. 1164.

The foregoing demonstration would be more important if the quotation had appeared in one of the supposedly English Tractates.

[166] Histoire des collections, II, 97.

[167] On the other aspects of the wide acquaintance of the Anonymous with canon law, see above pp. 47 ff. and below pp. 83 f.

[168] J24/L4: 665, 21–666, 23. For other instances of the Anonymous' use of the distinction between *natura* and *gratia*, cf. J12/B12:462; J22(26)/L2:653, 34; J28/L5:685, 44.

[169] Mansi, XVII, Appendix col. 172:

. . . & secundum priscam consuetudinem solemniter ad imperij Romani sceptra proveximus, & augustali nomine decoravimus, unguentes eum oleo extrinsecus, ut interioris quoque Spiritus sancti unctionis(-em) monstraremus [virtutem, qua unxit eum Dominus Deus suus prae consortibus suis, Christum hunc oleo laetitiae delibutum extrinsecus faciens, & principem populi sui]

gorian canonist Deusdedit quotes this passage in his Collectio [170] shows that John's address was still known in the eleventh century. In any event this address of John or the important excerpt therefrom is more likely to have been known in France than in England. To be sure, it is quite possible that the source of the distinction was Jerome's Tractatus in librum Psalmorum,[171] which would, of course, have no value in localizing "De consecratione." But there are so many other clearly Continental echoes in the two allegedly English religio-political Tractates that their cumulative effect is to buttress the Rouen hypothesis. We shall have occasion in Part IV to mention in other connections these specific instances of dependence upon, or affinity with, Merovingian and Carolingian documents. Here we but refer to them collectively,[172] anticipating their general support of our thesis.

Sources to one side, there is, finally, the striking parallelism of the "De consecratione" and of the contemporaneous Tractatus de

---

constituens(-entes), ad imitationem scilicet veri Regis Christi [filij sui] Domini (dei) nostri; ita ut quod ipse possidet *per naturam*, iste consequeretur(-quatur) *per gratiam.*

The forms given in parentheses appear in the text given by Deusdedit and edited by Wolf von Glanvell; the parts enclosed in brackets are wanting in the same. Die Kanonensammlung des Kardinals Deusdedit, I (Paderborn, 1905), p. 439. The text is also found in Bouquet, Recueil, VII, 694 ff. and in the so-called Collectio Anselmo [archbishop of Milan] dedicata of the ninth century (unprinted). Cf. A. Van Hove, Prolegomena, Commentarium Lovaniense in Codicem Iuris Canonici, I, tom. 1 (Mechelin, 1945), p. 314.

For a recent analysis of the rôle of John VIII in the elevation of Charles the Bald to the imperial dignity (875–877) see Percy Schramm, Der König von Frankreich: das Wesen der Monarchie vom 9. zum 16. Jahrhundert (Weimar, 1939), I, 32–48. Pope John supported the younger rival Charles over against the older Louis the German on the death of the Emperor Louis II in 875. It is possible that the contest between the younger brother Henry I and the older Duke Robert Curthose on the death of their brother William Rufus in 1100 recalled the ninth century parallel, and that the Anonymous was led directly to the Address of John in the ancient records rather than indirectly by way of a canonical collection like that of Deusdedit.

[170] I have found no other indications of the Anonymous' use of Deusdedit. Presumably, his source antedated Deusdedit.

[171] See quotation below, n. 214.

[172] For example, below, n. 253 on the assimilation of *mundus* to *ecclesia*; n. 538, n. 478, n. 534, n. 536 on the deificatory character of baptism and coronation; n. 546 on apotheosis; n. 563 on *rex et sacerdos*; n. 566 on royal sacrifice; n. 644 on the royal participation in the *numen* and *nomen Dei*; n. 653 on the king's possession of the Petrine keys; p. 195 on the Shepherd King; and n. 662 on the king as *doctor ecclesiae.*

Cf. also n. 39, n. 363, and n. 490 on echoes of the theological language of Bec.

regia potestate et sacerdotali dignitate [173] of Hugh of Fleury in the matter of such concepts as that the king bears the image of God, the bishop that of Christ,[174] that the bishop is subject to the king as the Son to the Father, that the bishop is subject not by nature but by order — all these concepts being found in the thought of the royalist monk of Fleury. This Benedictine monastery was exempt from the episcopal jurisdiction, enjoying royal protection. A royalist tradition had long flourished there. Hugh's dedication of his Tractate to Henry I of England was nothing unusual, since all of his works were dedicated to members of the English royal house. Fleury had, indeed, long maintained close connections with England. From Fleury the cloister reform under St. Dunstan had taken its rise. Abbo of Fleury spent many years in England, while many monks of this monastery filled important posts in the English church.[175] We have, thus, in Hugh's Tractate, despite its dedication and its bearing on English affairs, an authentically French production which may be cited as a parallel to make plausible the Rouen hypothesis for "De consecratione" and "De Romano pontifice."

Moreover, as for "De Romano pontifice," there is nothing here that actually bears more on English than on the French ecclesiastical situation. Indeed the discussion of monastic exemptions, the mention of the encroachment of legates (J28/L5:684,25), and the employment of *scisma* (686,25) remind one more of the woes of Rouen and the situation arising out of the Daimbert quarrel in Sens than of York. Ivo's letter to Hugh, for example, speaks of the danger of schism in the Daimbert affair.[176]

As for "De consecratione," the only specific reference to England is in the Appendix where the royal *ordo* of the English pontifical mentions the Angles and Saxons. But since this Benedictional

---

[173] Hugh's Tractate was composed shortly after 1102, related, as Ernst Sackur has shown it to be, to Hugh of Flavigny's History. Neues Archiv, XVI (1891), 369 ff.

[174] Hugh of Fleury writes: "Verumtamen rex in regni sui corpore Patris omnipotentis optinere videtur imaginem, et episcopus Christi." Libelli de lite, II, 468, 28 ff. This is, of course, ultimately dependent on Ambrosiaster.

[175] Sackur, op. cit., p. 375.

[176] Libelli de lite, II, 647, 5. Cf. Wilhelm Lühe, Hugo von Die und Lyons, Inaugural-Dissertation (Breslau, 1898), pp. 23 ff.

This is the same letter to Hugh twice quoted by the Anonymous.

as we have elsewhere shown had for some time been adapted to the use of Rouen, the Anonymous will probably have assumed that except for such phrases the "sacrament" of sacring would be pretty much the same in any Christian kingdom.

7. Seeming Allusions in "De Consecratione" to Paschal II's Letter to Henry I

While "De consecratione" does not make any specific reference to the English situation, it must be said that at several points the Tractate does seem to pick up phrases and concepts embodied in Paschal II's Letter to Henry I, April/May, 1101.[177]

At the following points it is echoed in the Tractate:

(1) In response to Henry's inquiry of the new Pope whether he would be "indulged the privilege of investing bishops and abbots," Paschal, in this Epistle, replies:

Ait enim Dominus, "Ego sum ostium. Per me si quis introierit, salvabitur." Cum autem ecclesiae ostium reges esse arrogant, fit profecto ut qui per eos ecclesiam ingrediuntur non pastores sed fures et latrones habeantur, eodem Domine dicente, "Qui non intrat per ostium in ovile ovium sed ascendit aliunde, fur est et latro."

"De consecratione" deals with the same texts (John x),[178] although there is nothing conclusive about this, for the texts were very commonly cited.

(2) Paschal cites Ambrose as to the proper place of the prince in the Church, quoting from the famous letter to Marcellina (lib. i, 20, written on the occasion of the imperial demand to surrender one basilica for the Arians) that eloquent section (19) ending:

"Adultera est enim quae non est legitimo Christi conjugio copulata." Audis, o rex, [Paschal continues] adulteram ecclesiam nuncupari, quae non legitime nupserit. Ecclesiae siquidem sponsus unusquisque aestimatur episcopus, juxta scripturam illam qua ex fratris uxore frater non sui nominis filios suscitare praecipitur, et sponsae contemptor a futuro sponso discalciari mandatur. Vides igitur, o rex, quam ignominiosum, quam periculosum sit, per filios suos matrem adulterio pollui? Si ergo

---

[177] Jaffé-Löwenfeld, No. 5868; Migne, P.L., CLXIII, coll. 70 ff.
[178] J24/L4:675, 6 ff.

ecclesiae filius es, quod utique omnis catholicus christianus est, permitte matri tuae legitimum sortiri conjugium, ut non per hominem, sed per Deum et hominem Christum, legitimo sponso copuletur ecclesia. Per Deum enim episcopos elegi cum canonice eliguntur, testatur apostolus Paulus . . . .

Further on, Paschal says: "Ecclesia filios genuit." "De consecratione," Version B, opens with an exalted conception of the royal marriage of Christ to the Church and the assertion that "the sacrament of the royal nuptials" is most fittingly associated on earth with the royal rather than the sacerdotal power. Throughout the Tractate the conception is prominent of the king as a "Christ" by grace generating Christians, children of the Church-Kingdom, baptism being their *royal* birth.

(3) Paschal continues his argument by saying that it is monstrous to conceive of a son generating his father, or of a man creating a god. The *sacerdos* and not the *rex* is the spiritual father of Christians and as such he is called a "god" in the Bible: "Sacerdotes namque in scripturis sanctis deos vocari tanquam Dei vicarios manifestum est." The entire Tractate "De consecratione" may be said to be an examination of this assertion with the conclusion that kings and the priests are alike gods and christs but that the kings are primarily, *sacerdotes* (= episcopi) only secondarily, *Christophoroi*.

(4) Paschal's appeal to his papal predecessors including Peter, his citing Aaron, his reference to "the nod of secular powers" all seem to be responded to in one portion of the Tractate or another.[179]

Such are the main points in common between the Tractate and the Letter.[180] If "De consecratione" is some kind of response to Paschal's Letter to Henry, we shall have to explain how an ecclesiastic in Rouen was apprised of its contents or otherwise account for the seeming relatedness.

Before making conjectures concerning the authorship of the

---

[179] Cf. "Nutu supernę gratię", J24/L4:676,5.

[180] The legitimacy of secular government under God is clearly asseverated by Paschal in contrast, for example, to Gregory VII, and one has the feeling that for all his firmness, the Pope is endeavoring to be as conciliatory as possible within the limits of his convictions.

Tractate, we must consider the evidence for an English origin of one further Tractate.

8. "De obediendo Romano pontifice" as Supposed Evidence for a Yorkish Background of the Later Tractates

Except for the echoes in "De consecratione" of Paschal's Letter to Henry, we have come to see that the principal claim for an English authorship of the "later" Tractates of the Codex must rest on a third treatise, "De obediendo Romano pontifice," which deals, in part, with the controversy between York and Canterbury. Böhmer understood that this Tractate was "ein sehr locker zusammenhängender Aufsatz" and even printed it in two installments, J29(I) and J30(III) in Libelli de lite and J29(II)[181] in Kirche und Staat. Nevertheless he based his conjectures concerning the circumstances of composition on an assumed unity of the three pieces. Only Part II deals with the controversy over the demand of Canterbury to consecrate the archbishop of York and receive from him the profession of obedience. Parts I and III deal with obedience to Rome. By considering the three "Parts" a unit, Böhmer was obliged to assume that when the "Tractate" was composed, Rome must have been on the side of Canterbury.[182] The upshot of Böhmer's treatment was that "De obediendo Romano pontifice" was composed around 1103/04 during the struggle between Gerard of York and Anselm of Canterbury. By insisting on finding an appropriate phase in the long quarrel when the Pope sided with Canterbury, as "required" by I and III, Böhmer was able to place the "Tractate" in the Gerard-Anselm episode and thus maintain intact his "York" thesis. Even so, Böhmer recognized that one of the two points at issue in the Tractate, namely, consecration, was not involved in the Gerard

---

[181] Since for Böhmer, these three parts were considered one Tractate, they were numbered by him 29. M. James, in describing the contents of the Codex, recognized that the three probably did not constitute a unit and numbered the last piece, 30. To indicate the "parts" in their order in the Codex, I have assigned them the Roman numerals, while preserving James' numbering in Arabic numerals. There are three different scribal hands (IV, VII, VIII) although they do not correspond exactly to Parts I, II, and III, except that Part III = Hand VIII. Part III has the distinction of being pointed to by an index. See above, n. 76. The shift of hands would tend to corroborate the view that the scribes' original was more than a single piece.

[182] Kirche, pp. 192 ff.

controversy because Gerard had already been consecrated by Anselm on becoming bishop of Hereford.[183] But Böhmer's whole procedure was unsound. To allow I and III to control II is unwarranted by the text. There is no transition in thought from I to II or from II to III. Moreover, III begins with an initial in the MS and there is a change of hand beginning with the last sentence of II which comes at the top of p. 284 in the Codex. It is, therefore, the view of the present writer that the three "Parts" are really three separate sketches which have been grouped together possibly by the copyists, perhaps because of their small size and general subject matter, namely obedience to a higher ecclesiastical authority. If this view is correct, the case for an English origin for the "later Tractates" and more specifically the designation "Tractatus Eboracenses" is reduced to the inferences that can be drawn from two and a half printed pages of J29/B29(= II) to which we turn.

Now even Böhmer must have been struck by the Anonymous' want of fire in the defense of York, in such contrast to the zeal and resourcefulness of the same writer's defense of Rouen against Lyons and Fécamp. The Tractate exhibits a detachment and moderation which may well be a clue to the distance of the writer from the scene. It is hard to imagine the Anonymous, passionate in his convictions as he was, to write thus if he were actually a canon in York cathedral: "For God wills that each [archdiocese] be of such a grandeur and dignity as neither at present is able to be." [184] Nor would he have so readily acquiesced in the primacy of Canterbury as he does had he been a party to the tremendous effort of the York chapter to secure the ancient dignities of their church. Indeed it was not until Anselm left Rome in 1103, at the beginning of his exile (1103–1106), that he received from the Pope a solemn confirmation of the primacy of Canterbury.[185] Yet the allegedly Yorkish Anonymous accepts Canterbury's hard-won

---

[183] Böhmer interpreted "De obediendo Romano pontifice" as a York reply to Paschal's brief of December 2, 1102 demanding of Gerard an oath of obedience to Anselm. Jaffé-Löwenfeld, No. 5930.

[184] J29/B29:479.

[185] Jaffé-Löwenfeld, 5955, dated November 16, 1103. Discussed by Margarete Dueball, geb. Telle, Der Suprematstreit zwischen den Erzdiozesen Canterbury und York, 1070–1126, ein Beitrag zur Geschichte der englischen Kirche im Zeitalter des Gregorianismus, Historische Studien, Heft 184 (Berlin, 1929), p. 53.

primacy without protest, seeking only to restrain any unaccustomed demands based thereon.[186] Then as if the controversy between the chapters of York and Canterbury had not long since become acrimonious, the Anonymous says quite simply:

Sed *fortasse* iterum dicet aliquis, quia sancti doctores, qui primi fidem Christi predicaverunt in Anglia, hoc constituerunt, ut Eboracensis archiepiscopus haec facere deberet Cantuariensi archiepiscopo, qui totius Britanniae haberet primatum. Sed hoc iterum *non* esse *facile* potest probari ex epistola beati Gregorii pape . . . .[187]

No canon in Yorkminster in the early twelfth century would have discussed the claims of York and Canterbury in terms of *fortasse* and *facile*. He would have contested every inch of ground. He would surely have brought up the forged *carta* of Lanfranc.[188] Nor is it probable that one who was deeply involved on the side of York would have made the following patent error of misreading the Letter of Gregory [189] which the York canons must have known *verbatim*. The Anonymous says that the archbishop of York has the right to be consecrated by his own synod (*a sua sinodo*), a privilege instead granted by Gregory to the bishop of London.[190] One has the impression of reading an opinion on the York-Canterbury controversy by a writer not directly involved. The use of the word *metropolitanus* may be a clue to Continental origin, since in a kingdom with only two archbishops, the word is not likely to occur.[191] The Anonymous speaks both in the first

---

[186] J29/B29:479:
Nam alter est archiepiscopus tantum, alter est archiepiscopus simul et primas. Sed si Cantuariensis archiepiscopus est primas, nichil plus ab Eboracensi debet exigere, quam quod in divina lege, et in sanctorum patrum decretis constitutum est, sicut omnium aecclesiarum religiosa consuetudo est.

[187] Ibid., p. 480.

[188] Heinrich Böhmer, Die Fälschungen Erzbischof Lanfranks von Canterbury (Leipzig, 1902).

[189] M.G.H., Epp. II, p. 312.

[190] J29/B29: 479.

[191] J29/B29:280: "Et ab eodem professionem extorquere nititur, quod nullus primas ecclesiastico more a metropolitanis extorquere permittitur." Elsewhere in the Tractate *archiepiscopus* is used, and this sole appearance of *metropolitanus* may have been suggested by early canons in the mind of the writer. *Metropolitanus* is not common in English MSS, as witness the entry s.v. in J. H. Baxter and Charles Johnson, Medieval Latin Word-List from British and Irish Sources, (Oxford, 1934) attesting its usage for 1335 as a noun. On the other hand, it is in common usage

person singular and plural as though he were giving the solicited opinion of his church. This impression that we have before us a third party's view is reinforced by the fact that the writer concludes quite objectively:

Si ergo Eboracensis archiepiscopus istis [the earlier Popes] vult exibere obedientiam, non debet, nisi cogatur, de [h]is respondere archiepiscopo Cantuariensi, que potius iure debet ecclesiae Londoniensi [according to Gregory I's letter].[192]

Yes, unless forced, the archbishop of York should rather defer to the bishop of London rather than to the archbishop of Canterbury! This is not the kind of argument we should expect to hear from the fiery Anonymous if he were himself one of the York clergy. That the Anonymous is, instead, writing in France is again suggested by the already discussed quotation from the famous letter of Ivo of Chartres to Hugh of Lyons wherein the bishop of Chartres cites Zosimus, Gregory, Leo IV, and Gelasius on the inviolability of ancient canons.[193]

The only other reference to Britain in all the Tractates is in J12/B12:462 where the Anonymous asks whether if all Scots or Britains were removed to Rome and all Romans removed or destroyed, the former would constitute the Roman Church and vice versa. But there is nothing about this rather fanciful question that constrains us to assign the final section of the Tractate in which it appears to England, as Böhmer suggests.[194]

9. Clues Concerning the Clerical Status of the Anonymous

In this section we shall not reëxamine all the points already made by Böhmer [195] but shall confine ourselves for the most part to a few fresh clues which indicate that our author was either archdeacon or archbishop.

---

at Rouen in our period. Cf. the Ordo provincialis concilii celebrandi in Robert's Benedictional, op. cit., p. 153; the De ordinatione episcopi, ibid., p. 162; and the Anonymous himself in other Tractates: J24/B2: 444, viii; J24/L4: 679, 21. See also Émile Lesne, La hiérarchie épiscopale en Gaule et Germanie 742–882 (Lille, 1905).

[192] J29/B29: 481.

[193] Above, pp. 55 ff. For a clue favoring Normandy rather than York as the place of origin of the related J30/L6(=III), see below n. 269.

[194] Kirche, p. 461, n. o.

[195] "Mutmassungen über Person und Lebensgang des Autors," ibid., 259 ff.

a. Was the Anonymous an Archdeacon?

In three Tractates (J4, 12, and 11, the first two with particularly marked conceptual and stylistic connections with the major Tractates printed in Libelli de lite) the allusions to "Archdeacon Stephen," protomartyr, are strangely frequent. Böhmer conjectured that the frequency of the allusion could be explained by a special devotion to the Protomartyr by reason of the author's having in his youth been a monk in some cloister dedicated to St. Stephen, probably that at Caen.[196] Archbishop William Bona Anima (1079–1110) during whose pontificate most if not all of the Tractates were written, was once abbot of Caen, and Böhmer surmised that the defender of the Archbishop in Tractate J4/L3 was a cleric whom William had brought with him from St. Stephen's on accession to the metropolitan see of Rouen.

Another explanation for the prominence of the Protomartyr, particularly in Tractate J4/L3, is that Stephen, as the patron of deacons and archdeacons, was being appealed to by one whose clerical status qualified him for the special support of the *protodiaconus*. It was during our period that the archidiaconate was rapidly reaching the summit of its significance in the cathedrals of the Continent.[197] Because of the mounting authority connected with this office, it often happened that archdeacons resisted taking priestly orders, lest they incur a loss of dignity.[198] Now in the "Apologia" the author refers frequently to the Church in Jerusalem and to what he supposes to have been the order in the Primitive Church. From these references we are able to reconstruct his

[196] Ibid., pp. 259 f.

[197] The originally single archidiaconate had in France begun to be divided in the ninth century (in Strassburg already in the eighth). But two supplements to the Robert Benedictional provide possible evidence that there was a single archidiaconate in Rouen in the middle of the eleventh century. Op. cit., pp. 153 ff., 162. On the date of these supplements see above n. 129. From certain canons of the Norman provincial councils of 1072 and thereafter we have evidence of a plurality of archdeacons in Norman cathedrals and therefore *a fortiori*, no doubt, in the metropolitan see. See below p. 96. In England the archidiaconate was not permanently established until after the Conquest. Cf. Wilhelm Levison, England and the Continent in the Eighth Century, Ford Lectures of 1943 (Oxford, 1946), p. 107. This latter fact would be of special interest had the references to archdeacon appeared in any of the Tractates supposed by Böhmer to have been composed in England.

[198] A. Amanieu, "Archidiacre," Dictionnaire de droit canonique, I (1935), 947 ff.

view of the relative importance of the various orders within the cathedral of Rouen. Reduced to a scheme, the thought of the Anonymous exhibits the following parallels: the (arch)bishop corresponds to Christ, who discharged the rôle of both priest and bishop (659, 40 f.). As such he may not be judged by another bishop (658, 2 ff.). Indeed, all bishops are *dii* [199] (658, 6 f.), taking the place of God (cf. J2/B2:445; J24/L4 passim); and since they have accepted the same faith whereby Simon became Peter, they are also *Petri* and collectively *Petrus* (657, 30 ff.). The *sacerdotes* correspond to the Apostles who are the columns of the Church, our author writes in one place (660,1). He says *sacerdotes* instead of *presbyteri* because the former include by implication the *episcopi*. He thus glosses over an obvious difficulty. He distinguishes between the Apostles and the seventy-two disciples, but since it was hard for him to think of there being more than one bishop in the Primitive Church, he refrains throughout this Tractate from deriving episcopal authority and the pattern therefor from the Twelve. He prefers to derive episcopal power directly from Christ or from the faith in Christ like unto that of the *one* Apostle, Peter. The archdeacon, though he comes third in the several passages bearing on our theme, is clearly felt to have a special authority, superior in all but name to that of the more numerous priests. This sense of the preëminence of the archidiaconate, which is evident in the author's neglect to mention by name the Apostles except for Peter while concentrating on Stephen, comes out most clearly in the following implied ratio: The archbishop is to Christ as the archdeacon is to the protomartyr and *primus archidiaconus* Stephen (659, 22; 660, 1 f., 11, 15) [200] whose dying words "Domine, ne statuas illis hoc peccatum" are felt to parallel those of Christ (J11/B11:454).

This esteem for the first archdeacon may well be self-esteem

---

[199] On bishops as *dii*, see below n. 214 and Pseudo-Isidore, ed. Hinschius, pp. 76, 228, 248.

[200] Comparable references to Stephen are found in J12/B12:458, 27; 459, 5, 34. Here, however, Stephen is mentioned along with Peter and Paul, Mary and John the Baptist, and James. Jerusalem and not Rouen is being here defended against Rome.

and, as such, could be an important clue to the clerical status of our author.[201]

We may thus have before us in J4/L3 "Quod Rothomagensis ecclesia non est subiecta Romanae" or as Böhmer styles it, "Apologia archiepiscopi Rotomagensis," the impassioned defense of William by an archdeacon of Rouen, speaking with the authority of the entire chapter. The "Apologia" could, indeed, be an address delivered before the canons on the Feast of St. Stephen, December 26, by the *magnus archidiaconus*, seizing the occasion of an annual allocution to attack the Pope for his presumptions in encroaching upon that earthly Jerusalem which was the Church of Rouen.[202]

Because of the four fires that swept Rouen in the twelfth century, destroying most of the cathedral records of the period under consideration, we are not well informed concerning the organization of the cathedral at the turn of the century. The functionaries taking part in the supposedly eleventh century *Ordinatio episcopi*

[201] Cf. the *tendenz* of Tractate J19/B19. In its arrangement of the sequence of clerical degrees through which Christ passed in such a way as to make his last grade the least distinguished (*hostiarius*), and by then connecting Christ's *first* ministerial act in the Synoptic sequence (Matt. 4:17) with the diaconate the Tractate could be further evidence of our author's concern to enhance his clerical status as archdeacon, which, though distinguished, was of a traditionally inferior clerical degree. See below, n. 277, s.v. *diaconus*, and n. 278.

By insisting on this Dominical (i.e., "historical") sequence, the Anonymous contrives also to place the (arch)deacon next the bishop. Cf. Edmund Bishop, Liturgica Historica (Oxford, 1918), p. 161. Our author's concern for the prestige of the diaconate may be connected with the fact that at Rome up to Gregory VII the Pope-elect might pass directly from the diaconate to the episcopate, whereas with Gregory's elevation and thereafter, the presbyterate was regarded as an indispensable grade. M. Andrieu, "La carrière ecclésiastique des papes," Revue des sciences religieuses, XXI (1947), p. 107.

[202] Rouen was extremely proud of its large number of relics of Apostles, martyrs, and John the Baptist. Cf. the Liber de laude sanctorum of Archbishop Vitricius of Rouen, Migne, P.L., XX, 443 ff.

Repeated reference to Stephen may also have been due to an anonymous archdeacon's desire, in his bold denunciation of the papal temple, to appeal to the authority, and to implore the aid, of the first (arch)deacon put to death because of his sermon against the Temple of Jerusalem. The popularity of Stephen in Rouen is attested by the chapel in the later Gothic cathedral in his honor and by the presence in the meagre cathedral library during the pontificate of the successor of William Bona Anima of a hagiography of the Protomartyr. H. Ormont, ed., Catalogue général des manuscrits, I, p. x. Moreover, the Benedictional of Archbishop Robert, in use in Rouen in the time of the Anonymous, features the stoning of Stephen in one of its illuminations, marking the Christ-like words of the dying martyr.

of the Robert Benedictional [203] are as follows: *metropolitanus*; *decanus*; *archidiaconus*; [204] *cantor*; *cancellarius*; 12 *presbiteri*; 7 *diaconi cum sanctis reliquiis*; 2 *subdiaconi cum crucibus*, 7 *cum evangeliorum libris*; 1 *acolitus* . . . *cum vasculo aureo*, 2 *cum turibulis*, 7 *cum candelabris et cereis*. Occasionally in the period of enhanced archidiaconal power, the offices of dean and archdeacon were in Rouen discharged by the same person, as for example, Fulbert.[205] Before following up this clue we shall want to have before us all other data which might bear on the clerical status of our author.

b. Was the Anonymous an Archbishop?

There are several indications that the Anonymous was of episcopal rank and hence, being of Rouen, archbishop. Now the "Apologia" in which "Archdeacon" Stephen bulks large is very closely related stylistically and conceptually to two other Tractates in which the possibly tell-tale allusions to Stephen do not feature.

In J2/B2, "De una ecclesia," the defense of the metropolitan dignity of Rouen is undertaken at points in the first person singular and plural and although the archbishop is referred to throughout in the third person, the Tractate could be the archbishop's own self-defense carried on in what might be called the third person of presumed objectivity. This impression is reinforced by an occasional phrase like "magisterium ecclesiae *nostrae*" [206] and by the sense of personal involvement displayed in the emotionally charged refutation of the primatial (and legatine) claims of

---

[203] Op. cit, p. 162.

[204] Jacques Lafond, in a recent study of the chapter of Rouen which does not try to trace the history before the devastating fire of 1200, distinguishes between the offices of *haut doyen* and *magnus archidiaconus* (the chief of the later six archdeacons) and says that the former was elected by the chapter and approved by the archbishop. "Histoire du chapitre de Rouen du XIVe au XVIe siècle," Positions des Thèses soutenues par les élèves de la promotion de 1930 pour obtenir le diplome d'archiviste paléographe (Paris: École nationale des Chartes, 1930), p. 74.

[205] Gallia christiana, XI, s.v. "Decani Rotomagenses," pp. 114 f; Ordericus, Historia ecclesiastica, ed. A. Le Prévost, viii, 25.

[206] J2/B2:447, ii:
   Interrogandus est Lucdunensis archiepiscopus si legem Christi sequi velit . . . . Iste tamen repetere satagit magisterium ecclesiae nostrae . . . .

Lyons supported by Rome and based upon an allegedly ancient
letter which our author insists is spurious:

Non tamen Romanos pontifices dampnare volu*mus*, set Christum et
apostolis ipsis praeferi*mus* et ordinis unitatem dividere et dignitatem
episcopalem in aliquo minuere nolu*mus*. . . . Set dicit se Lugdunensis
ecclesia habere privilegium, per quod hoc facit. Fortasse illud est, quod
in Arvernensi concilio lectum fuit. Set illud epistola quaedam fuit,
quasi ad Rotomagensem et Turonensem et Senonensem facta archiepiscopum. Ideo "quasi" dix*i*, quia ad nullum revera facta fuit. Quod
si [quis] dixerit, ad aliquem factam esse, dicat ad quem, insinuet personam, proferat eius nomen. Producat et epistolae portitorem. Quod si
facere non potest, bene dix*i* "quasi," quia revera ad nullum et per nullum missa est. Jure ergo ab omnibus falsitatis potest argui. Set in-
stantius perscruptari vol*o*. Si ad Rotomagensem archiepiscopum missa
est, quis remisit eam Lugdunensi? an forte Lucdunensis exemplar sibi
retinuit? Set eam, quae ad hoc exemplar scripta est, quis unquam vidit,
quis legit, quis etiam audivit? Nusquam revera invenitur, nisi forte in
cubiculo Lucgdunensis archiepiscopi.[260a]

The other Tractate that can be compared with the "Apologia"
is J9/S. This long polemic, directed apparently against Lyons
or Rome, falls into two parts, clearly indicated in the MS but
without seemingly sufficient break in the sense to warrant a
separate numbering as two distinct Tractates. It will be recalled,
however, that the term "Tractate" is altogether too formal a
designation for all but a few of the pieces in the Codex, while the
distinction between these Tractates, so-called, and their parts is
not always easily drawn. It will be convenient to refer to the
second part of Tractate J9 as J9 II.[207] Both parts defend Rouen
from the invasion of new laws and practices promoted by a Pope
or other prelate (legate or primate) utterly wanting in Apostolic
humility and charity. The vehemence of the accusations of Part
I is not readily explained by contemporaneous facts.[208] For the
present purpose we can leave it to one side and concentrate on

---

[260a] Ibid., pp. 445 f.

[207] It begins at the top of p. 72 in the MS with an initital: "Pro temporum
necessitatibus de usurpatione plurimum," which may be an old heading absorbed
into the text by the copyist. It is set off from J9 I by an emphatic termination
(*ameN.;.*).

[208] But see below n. 413 on *terroribus*.

Part II, which has a number of points in common with J4/L3, the "Apologia." In this Part the Anonymous charges his foe with usurping the office of God. He then goes on to write *as one bishop to another*, upon whom alike Christ has bestowed powers:

Prius [209] enim quam tu [210] fieres et patres tui formarentur a seculo et usque in seculum omnium Dominus est. Et omnia quę patres tui habuerunt ideo nunc habes, ipse sua gratia vobis contulit hoc tamen divinę glorię privilegium nequaquam tribuit sed nobis commisit, ut videlicet de animabus iudicemus, ut peccata populi remittamus et retineamus, ut celum claudamus et aperiamus, ut spiritum sanctum conferamus et auferamus ut etiam de angelis iudicemus. Quin immo ipse in nobis hęc omnia facit Deus, qui etiam hanc nobis contulit gratiam et potestatem ut ipsi nos [211] viri et dicamur et simus dii et angeli et ianitores paradisii, et tanta est virtus nostra, ut portę inferi non prevaleant adversus eam, sed potius ipsa prevaleat spoliare inferos et calcare super omnem virtutem inimici et foras eicere mundi principem. Vobis igitur quibus hanc potestatem minime contulit sed gratię nostre summisit, nolite extollere in altum cornu vestrum, nolite loqui adversus Deum iniquitatem, ut dicatis nobis in curiam vestram non inveniemus propter consuetudinem, quia curia nostra curia Dei est et in ea Deus vel dampnat impios vel absolvit pios.[212]

The Anonymous seems to be comparing *his* (archi-)episcopal court with that of Rome. He is writing as one of episcopal dignity (*nos dii*). The impression is reinforced by the "bene, frater" near the close of the document.[213] For clearly, the Anonymous is addressing someone of at least episcopal rank as the tone and the argumentation of the whole piece testify. If after all the vehemence of the "Tractate," the Anonymous can speak of his adver-

---

[209] *Primus* in MS. Böhmer (Scherrinsky) reads *scimus*.

[210] The Anonymous addresses his opponent sometimes in the singular, at other times in the plural. Sometimes he writes as an individual, other times (thinking of himself as representative of the chapter?) in the first person plural.

[211] The *s* is malformed. Böhmer (Scherrinsky) reads *nos vestri dicamus*.

[212] J9/S:147; MS p. 83. Cf. also the thrice quoted "Qui vos spernit . . . . recipit" (Matt. 10:40 + Lk. 10:16) which in J2/B2:442; J4/L3:658, 2 f.; J28/L5:682, 38 f. the Anonymous uses to support episcopal authority. This recurrent combination of Matthew and Luke in defense of episcopal authority is quoted from Pseudo-Isidore's letter ascribed to Pope Clement, actually, of course, from the Pseudo-Clementine Recognitiones. Hinschius, pp. 41, 53; 76, 227 f., etc. The Anonymous is advancing what purports to be a papal and canonical and not simply biblical argument in defense of episcopal inviolability.

[213] J9/S: 148, 14.

sary as a brother, this must be in the official ecclesiastical sense of one of comparable dignity and office. Moreover, his assertion about "nos . . . . dii et angeli et ianitores paradisii" should be compared with a similar statement in the "Apologia": "Omnes etenim episcopi dii sunt, et dii nisi a solo Deo iudicandi." [214] Previously, in the "Apologia" the writer had argued that there is one Christ and one Peter represented alike in the "Romanus pontifex et Rothomagensis." [215] This same manner of thought lies behind the "hanc nobis contulit gratiam" of J9 II and thus greatly strengthens the thesis that the Anonymous is to be numbered among bishops.

It should be noted further that throughout his Tractates, even in the most royalist, our author guards zealously the power and authority of the local bishop or archbishop. In J13/B13a, "De electione pontificis," the Anonymous grounds the authority of the bishop in divine election (combining thus predestination and vocation = profession) and justifies the settling of a bishop over an unwilling chapter (and diocese — populus) so long as his credentials are divine and not human. In the preëminently royalist "De consecratione," the Anonymous insists again and again that the sacerdotes (=episcopi) as sancti are qualified to rule their subditi just as are kings. That the Anonymous was already priest and possibly pontiff when composing Tractate J18/B18 is indicated by the nobis in the discussion of the validity of the rite of episcopal consecration.[216]

[214] J4/L3:658, 6 f.; cf. J24/L4:665, 17; also J31/W. I am assuming that the anti-Gregorian Anonymous is here accepting, for polemical purposes, the clericalized restriction of dii in Ps. 81:6 to sacerdotes. The Didascalia and then Constantine (Rufinus, H. E., P. L. XXI, col. 468) had indeed applied the term to bishops alone, but an equally long tradition had applied it to all Christians as co-rulers with Christ: Clement of Alexandria (n. 548, below); Jerome ("Quod dii sumus, non sumus natura, sed gratia," Tractatus in librum Psalmorum, ed. by Germain Morin, Anecdota Maredsolana, III:2, p. 77), Augustine (P. L., XXXVII, col. 1050), Walafrid (P. L., CXIII, col. 982); the Venerable Bede ascribes christship to both kings and bishops (n. 548, below). Ordinarily the Anonymous finds Bede or the broadly deificatory tradition more congenial, but in Tractates J4/L3 and J9/S he evidently prefers to make the most of the express "deity" of all diocesan sacerdotes against the Roman sacerdos.

For the references in Pseudo-Isidore see above, n. 199.

[215] J4/L3: 657, 29 ff.

[216] P. 472: "Si enim Christus non cooperatur nobis, immo, si non operatur in nobis, quoniam omne sacramentum solius divine virtutis est operatio et sine precepto et auctoritate Dei nulla eius potest fieri institutio. . . ." Here the sentence breaks

In Tractate J3/W the Anonymous refers to the competence of the *bishop* [217] in a context where it would be quite natural to say instead, priest. The Tractate is not polemical. It is a tortuous exegetical study addressed to a single person and referring to others who hold a contrary view on the forgiveness of sexual sins. The author has Rome in mind in a general way, perhaps, when he remarks that the Celestial Jerusalem cannot be identified with any earthly city.[218] The fact that the work is exegetical and moral rather than polemical makes the casual reference to the episcopate a likely indication that the author is himself a bishop.[219] This reference is all the more important for our purpose in that the Tractate probably belongs among the earliest in the Codex and could indicate that the Anonymous was a bishop as early as 1080.

There are other points about our author that we may bring together here. In Tractate J11/B11 we have specific reference to the author's acquaintance with rites and usages of other churches, which might indicate wide travel, study, or both. He mentions Rome, Milan, Vienne, Rheims, and Spain. He is obviously very familiar with canon law no less than with the liturgy. He is exceedingly well schooled in the Scriptures, from which he marshals arguments with skill and cunning. He seems to know large sections of the Bible by heart, many of his smaller quotations displaying those slight displacements or substitutions and conflations that indicate citation from memory rather than direct quotation from the text. His long quotations show markedly less variation.

---

off. With this may be compared the *nos* of J11/B11: 457: "Sic fecit Christus et sic apostolus instituit mandatum eis donans exemplum hos per omnia immitari *nos* oportet." Böhmer thought he could connect the former passage with the translation of Gerard from Hereford to York against the will of the York chapter. Kirche, p. 197.

That the Anonymous may have considered himself a *sanctus* in the sense of a monk is indicated by the phrasing of J24A/W:228, *Ex quibus — **.

[217] See below, p. 218, *Apud — **.

[218] The whole Tractate is discussed briefly below, n. 516.

[219] For other allusions, see J24A/W:228, *Ex — ** and J24d/W.

If, as I conjecture, J3/W is primarily concerned with the sins of priests rather than laymen, it is quite natural that our writer should refer to the competence of the bishop to administer penitential discipline.

He quotes many of the Fathers and, as Dempf remarks, knows the Augustinian corpus at first hand. His copying out in Tractate J21/SW of four chapters from the Enchiridion on the essence of God and the good is among the several indications that our ecclesiastic had some interest in pure theology. And on the basis of the technical terms relating to free will and grace employed in "An liceat sacerdotibus inire matrimonium," Fliche has definitely connected the author of our Codex with the school of Anselm at Bec, despite the Anonymous' anti-Gregorian conclusions on clerical marriage.[220]

Finally, our writer is one who can expect his readers to be familiar with his writings ("Sed de his alibi satis diximus").[221] The present anonymity of his literary remains is probably due not to intentional concealment but to the accidents of transmission. Our author was undoubtedly well known in his own day. He writes with the power and confidence of one in authority. He is clearly a high-placed ecclesiastic who not only has at hand a good collection of canon law but also, which is more important for identification, has access to the cathedral pontifical. Moreover, from it he quotes the royal and episcopal *ordines* almost as though he knew them by heart.[222] And this indicates an ecclesiastic who was high enough in the cathedral to participate responsibly at consecrations.

We shall now turn to the significance of one or two quotations from the liturgy which not only throw some further light on the clerical status and competence of the author but also provide a possible clue to the occasion of his writing the *chef d'oeuvre* of the Codex.

10. *Some Liturgical References in "De consecratione"*

"De consecratione regum et pontificum" is for the most part a fine polemical piece. The author has in mind allies [223] and foes,[224]

---

[220] See above, pp. 18, 26.

[221] J12/B12: 461, iii.

[222] The quotations from the *ordines* in the body of the Tractate show more variations from the Robert Benedictional than the complete copies given in the Appendix, where the writer or his scribe undoubtedly had the Benedictional open before him.

[223] Notice, for example, the third person plurals in 667, 24 and 30.

[224] For example, 667, 27; 679, 24.

near and far. That the Tractate went through the heat of real controversy is evidenced by the differences in the two versions.[225] The distinctive opening section of the Tractate seems to stand apart in its solemn tone and style.[226] It will be recalled that only Version B of "De consecratione" has this section which Böhmer calls an "Exordium." [227] Although this Exordium is an integral part of the present Tractate, it may once have formed a separate compositon. For the moment it can be considered apart. It opens with a sermon allegedly of St. Augustine [228] beginning, the Anonymous says, "Recte festa ęcclesię colunt." [229] It is in the Homiliarium [230] assembled by Paul the Deacon at the request of Charlemagne that the sermon is ascribed to Augustine. Outside of the Homiliarium it is included among the works of St. Maximus of Turin [231] and in an altered version (lacking also the distinctive *initium*) among the writings of the Galican Eusebius.[232] It is therefore reasonable to assume that the Anonymous was quoting from the Homiliarium.[233] Here it appears in the "Commune sanctorum" among four other sermons all relating to the dedication of churches and altars.[234]

This brings us to a possible coincidence of liturgical and historical dates that deserves mention. The "Astitit regina" (Ps. 44:10)

---

[225] See above, pp. 30 f.

[226] Possible outcroppings of this festive stratum are recognizable in the remainder of the Tractate.

[227] See above, n. 79.

[228] J24/L4: 662, 30.

[229] Unidentified by Böhmer. Migne, P. L., XXXIV, col. 2171.

[230] Ibid., XCV, col. 1457, homilia cxcix; Friedrich Wiegand, das Homiliarium Karls des Grossen, Studien zur Geschichte der Theologie und Kirche, Bd. I, Heft 2 (1897), No. 128, p. 64.

[231] Migne, P. L., LVII, col. 883.

[232] Maxima bibliotheca veterum patrum (Lyons, 1577), VI, p. 675, homilia i, "In natalem Ecclesiae."

[233] The offhand allusion, "et beatus Augustinus in sermone, cuius initium est . . . ," takes for granted a general familiarity, on the part of the reader (or hearer) with the Homiliarium, and as such it is a clue to the clerical status of the Anonymous. The Homiliarium was originally intended for the use of clerics at the *officium nocturnale*. Wiegand, op. cit., p. 84.

[234] Two of these sermons are ascribed to Augustine, three to Bede. The first of the suppositious sermons of Augustine is now assigned by P. Lejay to Caesarius of Arles. Dictionnaire de Théologie catholique, III, 2, 2170. It is found in the present Roman Breviary in the "Commune dedicationis Ecclesiae," lectio iv. It may be noted here that Robert's Benedictional contains a dedication sermon (op. cit., pp. 69 ff.) of which there may be echoes in our Tractates.

which is cited in the Exordium (662,29) was most certainly suggested by the supposititious Augustinian sermon in which it likewise appears prominently. Now this Psalm, which to be sure
recurs frequently throughout the liturgical year, is chanted at the
Feast of the Dedication of Santa Maria Maggiore, one of the
Roman churches, the anniversary of whose consecration is observed throughout Latin Christendom.[235] The anniversary falls
on August 5. This is also the date of the coronation of Henry I in
Westminster, 1100.[236] Since there are several reasons to connect
the argument of "De consecratione" with the new situation in England on the accession of Henry I, it is possible that the opening
reference to a sermon in the Homiliarium (which the clerics in
attendance at the coronation will have read early in the morning as
appropriate to the concurrent feast of dedication) is an additional
clue to the date and occasion of the composition of at least the
Exordium of Version B of "De consecratione."

From the ecclesio-political implications of a sermon in *dedica-
tione ecclesiae*, the Anonymous moves on to another event of the
liturgical year, Epiphany, and to the inferences that can be drawn
therefrom for the rôle of the king in the Church. Having just
quoted Zachariah 9:9 ("Ecce rex tuus venit tibi, iustus et salvator") and Jeremiah 23:5 f. ("Ecce dies veniunt . . . et suscitabo
David") — passages especially appropriate to the accession of a
new king — the Anonymous proceeds at once to relate the king
to the Church. The key to the relationship he finds in the "nuptials of the Church." Böhmer thought that these "nuptiae sanctae
ecclesiae" [237] referred to the act of episcopal investiture including
the royal presentation of the ring and staff to the bishop,[238] but the
much more likely meaning is the royal consecration during which
the king is joined to his Church-Kingdom by the sacrament of
royal unction.[239] This interpretation of the text is suggested by

---

[235] Other feasts of dedication observed in the present Roman Calendar are the
Lateran on November 9, St. Peter's, and St. Paul's on November 18.

[236] Flores hist., "Rolls Series," II, 34.

On the possible connection between the dedicatory elements in "De consecratione" and the dedication of St. Stephen's in Caen, 1077, see below, p. 104.

[237] J24/L4: 662, 36; also called "sacramentum harum nuptiarum" (663, 4).

[238] Kirche, p. 226.

[239] Cf. Peter Damiani's *inunctio regis*, Migne, P. L., CXLIV, col. 899 (*"sermo"*
lxix). Eduard Eichmann says that this letter is falsely ascribed to Peter Damiani

two facts in addition to the foregoing observations which have disposed us to this view: 1) throughout the Tractate the Anonymous argues that the Church and the realm are one and 2) he derives the prerogatives of the king in the Church chiefly from the rights and attributes accorded the king in the coronation *ordo*. Nowhere in the Tractate does the Anonymous appeal to the former privileges claimed by the king or duke at the consecration and investiture of a bishop. Since these very rights have been challenged in the Hildebrandine Reform, it would serve no purpose to cite the papally deprecated usages connected with investiture. Instead, the chosen tactic of the Anonymous is to argue from biblical precedent, pre-Gregorian canon law, and especially from the implications of the "sacrament" of royal unction, conceived as the royal nuptials of the Church. To be sure, the consecration of a bishop is also a marriage to the (diocesan) Church. Therefore the Anonymous is at pains to show that the *principal* "nuptiae sanctae ecclesiae" are royal rather than sacerdotal. In the liturgical joining of a king to his Church-Kingdom, the eternal marriage of the Bridegroom is reënacted, the king becoming in the moment of his consecration the *christus* of the national Church, as the Anonymous proceeds to argue in the body of the Tractate. But he must first prove that the nuptials of the Church are royal, that it is a king or rather a *rex et sacerdos* in his royal capacity who is wedded to the Church. For proof, the Anonymous introduces an antiphon from the office of Epiphany:

Hodie coelesti sponso iuncta est ecclesia
[quoniam in Iordane lavit Christus eius crimina:
current cum muneribus] ad regales nuptias:
[et ex aqua facto vino laetantur conviviae].[240]

and, following Josef Braun, S.J., holds that it was probably written by Nicholas, notary of St. Bernard. "Königs- und Bischofsweihe," S.B., Bayrische Akademie der Wissenschaften, phil.-hist. Kl., 1928, No. 6, p. 13, n. 2. But even if the letter is withdrawn from Damiani, the sentiment is authentically his. Despite his Gregorian sympathies, Damiani was quite prepared to acknowledge that "reges et imperatores propter sacram unctionem *christi* nuncupantur." Liber gratissimus, Migne, P. L., CXLV, col. 113B; pointed out by Oppenheim, op. cit., p. 47.

[240] J24/L4: 663, 2 f. Cf. Liber responsalis, Migne, P.L., LXXVIII, col. 743. The bracketed portions do not appear in "De consecratione," being indicated only by the *usque*. Cf. Magistretti, Manuale Ambrosianum, II, p. 91 where marriage and baptism are emphasized in the corresponding antiphon in Epiphany, quoted below, n. 628; also F. C. Conybeare, Rituale Armenorum (Oxford, 1905), pp. 426, 428.

A second glance at this antiphon will make clear why the Anonymous is confident in calling the coronation the royal nuptials of the Church. The ancient feast of Epiphany combines a number of liturgical motifs, in part, pre-Christian in origin.[241] In the foregoing antiphon four elements in the celebration are referred to: 1) the baptism of Christ at Jordan, which is 2) his consecration (coronation) as the Son of God, the Messiah, 3) the appearance of Christ to the Gentiles (the Magi), and 4) the marriage at Cana. This extraordinary conflation of religious motifs in a single formulary permits the Anonymous to call the coronation (=baptism-consecration)[242] the royal nuptials (*regales nuptiae*), in which the Church-Kingdom (*ecclesia*)[243] is joined to her spouse (*sponsus*) who is in heaven (*coelestus*) Christ [244] but on earth the royal *christus* during the sacring. But the Anonymous has first to dispose of the prevailing notion of the bishop's being espoused to his church, for unless this conception can be limited, it will be prejudicial to the Anonymous' confident assertion:

Unde et sacramentum harum nuptiarum *magis convenit regię dignitati, quam sacerdotali*, et ideo reges qui Christi regis imaginem preferunt, his nuptiis [mentioned in the antiphon of Epiphany] magis apti sunt, quarum sacramentum magis preferunt.[245]

But why is the royal sacrament of marriage superior to the episcopal? Surely not simply because the king is joined to the national

[241] Karl Holl, "Der Ursprung des Epiphanienfestes," S.B., Berliner Akademie der Wissenschaften, I, II (1917), pp. 402 ff.; Hermann Usener, "Heilige Handlung, I: Wasserweihe," Kleine Schriften, IV (Leipzig, 1914); Anselm Strittmatter, "Christmas and Epiphany, Origins and Antecedents," Thought, XVII (1942), pp. 800 ff. For a discussion of Epiphany as an adaptation of the Jewish Feast of Tabernacles and the redemptive significance of the waters of Siloam, see E. C. Selwyn, "The Feast of Tabernacles, Epiphany and Baptism," Journal of Theological Studies, XIII (1912), p. 225.

[242] The baptismal character of the royal consecration, as illuminated by Wilhelm Berges, will be discussed presently.

[243] Elsewhere the Anonymous defines the *ecclesia* as *mundus* (J24/L4: 663, 27), *genus electum, regale sacerdotium*, etc. See below, p. 179. At the moment of liturgical coronation, it would be particularly natural to refer to the Christian realm simply as *ecclesia*. The fact that the Anonymous himself never hyphenates the terms is not prejudicial to the thesis here presented in view of his frequent definition in the above sense.

[244] Interestingly, in another Tractate (J4/L3) where the Anonymous clearly distinguishes between *Deus, Christus*, and *Spiritus sanctus* (658, 23 f.), he speaks of the Church as the *Patris sponsa* (659, 38). Cf. n. 524 below.

[245] J24/L4: 663, 4 ff.

Church, while the bishop is joined solely to a part thereof, the diocese. The answer is suggested by Wilhelm Berges in his documentation of the corporate and the baptismal character of the medieval coronation.[246] The coronation, with its religious significance centering in the anointing of the king's head was apparently felt to be a collective act whereby the whole people (the church-realm) were vicariously and corporately cleansed and anointed anew after the hazardous interregnum, reduced to a minimum, in the interests of public peace.[247] We have already noted that Jesus' baptism in Jordan was at once his Epiphany as the Son of God and his consecration as the Messiah. The relation between baptism and royal consecration was more readily sensed by the medieval attendant at a coronation, for the reason that the medieval rite of baptism retained the ancient practice of anointing the child's head after the immersion.[248]

[246] Op. cit., discussed above, pp. 21.

[247] Recall how Henry I hastened from Winchester to Westminster to legitimize his rule by the royal unction on Sunday August 5 at the hand of Bishop Maurice of London (in the absence of Anselm). William Rufus had been killed by a stray arrow on the afternoon of August 2.

[248] A *pannus lineus*, a cap customarily used at baptism to protect the sacred oil was, beginning with the twelfth century, employed in the royal consecration. Its ritual removal a few days later was called *dealbatio*. Schramm, English Coronation, p. 138.

The royal and marital imagery of baptism abounded. Medieval baptismal practices and language made the rebirth particularly vivid. The font was called an "immaculate womb." The waters of the font were addressed as those flowing from Paradise in four rivers. The baptismal recovery of Paradisiac purity was thus vividly shown forth.

In the Benediction of the Font in the Gelasian Sacramentary (ed. H. Wilson, p. 85), the priest's dividing of the waters with his right hand in the form of a cross is followed with words alluding to the Holy Spirit:

Qui hanc aquam regenerandis hominibus praeparatam arcana sui luminis admixtione foecundet: ut sanctificatione concepta, ab immaculato divini fontis *utero* in novam renata creaturam progenies coelestis emergat.

The many Scriptural rôles of water are then mentioned.

We may note here also the baptismal practice of placing a lighted candle in the hand of the baptized infant as a symbol of his preparedness to attend the heavenly marriage of Christ and his Church. Having asked the name of the child, the priest says:

Accipe lampadem ardentem et irreprehensibilem: custodi baptismum tuum, serva mandata, ut cum venerit dominus *ad nuptias*, possis ei occurrere una cum sanctis in aula coelesti: ut habeas vitam aeternam et vivas in saecula saeculorum.

William Maskell, Monumenta Ritualia Ecclesiae Anglicanae (Oxford, 1882), I, 27.

On the royal imagery in baptism see further below, n. 478, and on the nuptial imagery, pp. 146 ff.

To complete his argument, the Anonymous must now show that Christ himself is joined to the Church, his spouse, primarily as a king and only secondarily as a priest. This he does by recalling that in Hebrews 7:17 Christ is Priest after the order of Melchizedek,[249] that is, as *rex iustitiae*, as the Anonymous points out, alluding to the Etymologiae of Isidore. Christ is wedded to the Church as King, his *sacerdotium* derives from his *regnum*,[250] his primary relationship to the Church is that of lordship over her. Earthly *christi* co-rule (*conregnant*)[251] with Christ this Church-Kingdom, the Anonymous contends, in alluding to an unidentified passage in Gregory Nazianzus.[252] That the Church and kingdom which the king co-rules with Christ are one realm, the Anonymous maintains, by assimilating *mundus* to *ecclesia* in the Gelasian formula which he quotes with a royalist intention, seemingly innocent of the original sense:

Mundum hic [Gelasius] appellat sanctam ęcclesiam, quę in hoc mundo peregrinatur. In hoc igitur mundo [= ecclesia] habent principatum *sacri* regiminis sacerdotalis auctoritas et regalis potestas.[253]

The government of the *mundus-ecclesia* has become sanctified in a Christian sense and the anointed king is the ruler thereof. It is not Christian to separate the spirituality from the temporality, for, quoting Luke 11:17, "Omne regnum in se ipsum divisum

---

[249] J24/L4: 663, 18 ff. His insistence here that Christ was made priest "non secundum ordinem leviticum, sed secundum ordinem regis iusticię" may echo Jerome's "non secundum ordinem Aaron, sed Melchisedech." Tractatus in librum Psalmorum, ed. G. Morin, III: 2, p. 46, 7.

[250] J24/L4: 663, 10 f.

[251] Ibid., l. 22. On *conregnum* see further below, p. 187.

[252] Gregory is not mentioned here but in a parallel passage in J28/L5: 685, 16 ff.

[253] J24/L4: 663, 26; cf. J28/L5: 684, 45 f. This assimilation of *mundus* to *ecclesia* has a long Frankish history. Cf., for example, the letter (c. 845) of Guenilo, archbishop of Sens, to the Archbishop of Lyons saying that Christ "potestatem suam ad eandem gubernandam ecclesiam in sacerdotes divisit et reges ut, quod sancti docerent pontifices, et ipsi implerent et impleri facerent devotissimi reges." M.G.H., Epp. VI, 73.

The Anonymous, needless to say, recognizes the existence of the universal *ecclesia* no less than that of the diocesan, the monastic, the provincial, and the national *ecclesia*, but the universal tends to be purely spiritual, based as it is upon election — which the Anonymous repeatedly presses — and confirmed by baptism. It is set over against the equally universal *ecclesia Sathanae* which the Anonymous, however, tends to localize in Rome. A typical utterance on the universal Church is that in Tractate J24D/W: 235, ** Sed — **.

desolabitur." [254] The anointed king rules both bodies and souls, and is aided in this by the bishop who is likewise consecrated, "ut et ipse *regat* sanctam ecclesiam [=his diocese] *secundum formam doctrinę* a Deo sibi traditam," [255] under the king.[256]

In a few swift lines the Anonymous has 1) restricted the claim of the bishop to be the spouse of the Church in such a way as to make the king the bridegroom of the national Church and 2) completely reversed the Gelasian formula in favor of the *regalis potestas*. Details of the theoretical relationship of the royal and the episcopal *christi* are worked out in the body of the Tractate. The Exordium peculiar to Version B ends with the establishment of the two foregoing points.

We have already suggested that the occasion of the Exordium was the "royal nuptials" of the *regnum-ecclesia*, namely, some royal consecration. Because of the coincidence of the *Dedicatio sanctae Mariae ad nives* [257] (August 5) and the coronation of Henry I — supported by other clues — it is even possible that this Exordium was originally composed as an allocution or a portion thereof on that memorable occasion. On this view the Exordium will have been subsequently enlarged and amply documented to appear as our present Version B. Version A would then be an enlargement of B (less the Exordium analyzed above) with the addition of an Appendix of *pièces justificatives*. The absence of the Exordium from Version A could be explained on the ground that as the memory of the coronation ceremony which (may have) originally induced the author to write receded, the arguments based upon this royal marriage-baptism-coronation were dropped in favor of more sober biblical, canonistic, and liturgical arguments without reference to any immediate situation. That the Exordium is the nucleus or original portion of the Tractate and as such a possible clue to the date and occasion of the composition is indicated by the fact that Version A, in its opening

[254] J24/L4: 663, 43 f.

[255] Ibid., ll. 24 f.

[256] The relationship between king and bishop will be dealt with systematically in Part IV below.

[257] It is pertinent to remark that the chrismation of a church at its dedication or consecration is a parallel to baptismal christening. The imagery and rites are drawn from baptism. P. de Puniet, "Dedicaces des Églises," D. A. C. L., IV: 1, 374 ff.

sentence betrays a clear familiarity with the Exordium in its use of four key words which appear at the end of the suppressed Exordium, two of them in a quotation.[258]

11. *Remaining Clues*

We turn to a few remaining bits of evidence concerning the date and locale of our Codex.

Intriguing without really yielding any clues, is the Anonymous' interest in Greek etymologies. A saint (*hagios*), he says, is one *extra terram*, a mediator; the king and the priest are preeminently saints since they stand between heaven and earth.[259] The pejorative sense of *laicus* (which he derives from the Greek *lai* [sic] = *publicani*) is discussed in J24c/W, *apotheosis* in J24/-L4:665, 30 f, *cacia*(=*kakia*) is used in J31/B30, but here in a quotation from Jerome. He has, of course, no first hand acquaintance with Greek but he does not seem to be confined to Isidore.[259a]

We have already discussed some evidence that the Anonymous may have traveled widely.[260] A reference to the relationship of Peter to Paul in a Roman painting of Christ in Glory might yield a clue. In J23a/B23a the Anonymous writes:

Sed et cum maiestas Christi Romae pingitur, Paulus pociori parte, id est dextera, Petrus vero in minus digna, id est sinistra, quasi divino iure compingitur, in quo et precellens esse monstratur.[261]

It is with this thought that the Anonymous triumphantly closes this Tractate against Petrine authority. Yet the representation

[258] For the textual problem here, see above, n. 79. That J28/L5, which quotes and paraphrases "De consecratione," is dependent upon Version B instead of A is evident from parallels between the Exordium of B (J24/L4: 663, 25–664, 13) and J28/L5: 684, 45–685, 22. The latter is then followed by a direct quotation from the former: J24/L4: 670, 41–671, 22 = J28/L5: 685, 23–31. (There are two other long quotations in J28/L5 from J24/L4 noted in the edited text.) J28/L5 deals with the prerogatives of the king primarily in respect to episcopal investiture, whereas J24/L4 deals with the prerogatives of the king in terms of the *royal* investiture, namely, coronation.

[259] In the "magna digressio" in J24/L4 omitted by Böhmer; see Appendix. For discussion thereof, see below p. 160.

[259a] On *apostolus* = *missus* (J28/L5 and J29/L6 quoted in nn. 456 f.) cf. Etym. vii, 9, 1 and on *laicus* = *popularis* (Isidore) and *publicanus* (Anon.) cf. ibid., 14, 10.

[260] See above, p. 73.

[261] J23a/B23a:477.

of Peter at the left of Christ is the customary one. In the eleventh century the question of the theological implications of Roman iconography had become so widespread that Peter Damiani devoted an opuscule to it.[262] It is just as possible that the reference of the Anonymous is based upon Damiani's writing as upon direct observation in Rome.

Elsewhere the Anonymous writes of the reading of the *privilegium* granted to Lyons at the Council of Clermont in a way, suggesting that he might be recalling the actual scene as he wrote: "Fortasse illud est, quod in Arvernensi [263] concilio lectum fuit." [264] In reading Tractates J4/L3 and J12/B12 one has the impression that the prominence of Jerusalem, *civitas ipsa Jerusalem*, could be due to the indelible impression made by the ancient scenes and relics upon the author during a pilgrimage to the Holy Land.

Of the Tractates first to be published by Scherrinsky, J9/S yields the most clues, but these too are inconclusive. We have already mentioned several. The Tractate appears to have been written about the time of J4/L3, the "Apologia Archiepiscopi Rotomagensis," dated by Böhmer between March and December, 1096.[265] Much more acrimonious than this, it makes obscure but impassioned references to the cruelty of the prelate against whom it is directed.[266] It makes a distinction between conciliar canons and decretals that are universally, provincially, and locally valid

---

[262] Migne, P. L., CXLV, 529, De picturis principum apostolorum. That Christian iconography preserved the ancient Roman feeling for the left as the place of honor was unknown to Damiani who had to resort to other explanations for the embarrassing fact. A. L. Frothingham, "Ancient Orientation Unveiled, III: The Left as the Place of Honor in Roman and Christian Art," American Journal of Archaeology, 2nd series, XXI (1917), pp. 313 ff.

[263] In passing it should be mentioned that Funk, op. cit., criticized Böhmer for correcting the textual *arumnensi* to *Arvernensi* (=Clermont, 1096), but the Council of Clermont is often so designated in contemporary accounts, and therefore Böhmer's is the obvious emendation. Cf. Bessin, op. cit.

[264] J2/B2: 446, ix. In J11/B11, as we have observed above, p. 73, the Anonymous speaks familiarly of Rome and Milan, Rheims and Lyons. But cf. J2/B2: 440: "Nam et Rothomagensis ecclesia, cui se Lugdunensis prefere contendit, in celebriori et prestantiori loco sita est, ut aiunt, qui utriusque loci habent notionem." The final phrase implies that the author himself had not seen Lyons, at least.

[265] Kirche, 187 ff. Böhmer knew this Tractate only in excerpts at the time of his publication. Because of the citation of what must have been a chapter in Ivo's Panormia, this Tractate must be dated in any event after c. 1094. See above, pp. 56 f.

[266] Particularly J9/S: 133 f. (MS, pp. 60–62).

(*universalia, particularia, singularia*). The council at Rouen is considered an instance of *singularia* (for a whole people or province).[267] Yet the Anonymous contrasts *transmarinum* and *citramarinum*,[268] speaking also of *terra nostra*,[269] as though he might be writing from the British Isles. But apart from these words, the Tractate very much resembles in locale, intensity, and subject matter the J4/L3, the "Apologia." [270] The humility of the Christ is eloquently contrasted with the pride of the offending prelate.[271] The fact that Augustine was once a heretic and then became a revered bishop is cited in favor of the threatened archbishop.[272]

A short Tractate, J6/S "De temperandis legibus," concludes: "Propter necessitatem quoque et utilitatem, licet episcopos de suis aecclesiis ad alias transmigrare, quod sine necessitate fieri in sacris canonibus omnino prohibitum." [273] This flexibility in regard to canon law is quite characteristic of the Anonymous, but does not help much in localizing the Tractate. In general the Anonymous seems to have been a master of canon law, but he employed his learning to refute it (in the name of Christ and the king or the Holy Spirit and the episcopate, depending on the Tractate), to proclaim anew the Pauline contrast between law and grace and to insist upon the liberty of the Christian over against the newer curial law.

[267] Ibid., p. 140 (MS, p. 73).

[268] Ibid., p. 141 (MS, p. 73).

[269] Ibid., p. 146 (MS, p. 82): "Nunc autem adversus laicos agendum est, qui ministris Dei audent dicere. Vos inquam nullam iusticiam vel potestatem habetis in *terra nostra*, necque antecessores vestri umquam habuerunt, nec patiemus ut novas consuetudines super nos inducatis." The reference to the laity in the foregoing is not clear from the context. With this reference to *terra nostra* in J9 we may connect an allusion in J29/L6, where the Anonymous argues that the Pope has no need of exercizing his allegedly emissary functions in the land where the Anonymous lives in order to teach the latter's countrymen Scriptures, "quia nos scripturas propheticas et evangelicas et apostolicas [habemus] in quibus omnia mandata Dei continentur et horum *scientia* plenius est *apud nos* quam apud illum [the Pope], et perfectior habetur et celebrius colitur" (687, 13 ff.). The Tractate in which this proud sentence occurs is one for which Böhmer, it will be recalled, claimed a Yorkish origin. But the "scientia . . . celebrius colitur" would be a much more appropriate claim for the province containing Bec and Caen than for the province of York.

[270] See above, pp. 84 ff.

[271] J9/S: 133 (MS, p. 60).

[272] Ibid., p. 136 (MS, p. 66).

[273] Ibid., p. 131 (MS, p. 55). The Tractate quotes from Paul and several papal decretals including Pope John's "Necessitas non habet legem." Ibid., p. 130. Cf. Felix IV, Pseudo-Isidore, ed. Hinschius, p. 700.

Nor are the clues provided by the Anonymous' references to the degrees of clerical order in several of the published Tractates of much aid in identifying the author and the scene of his labors. A great many of the Tractates of Codex 415 deal with the question, directly or indirectly, while three [274] of them make specific reference to a peculiar, early medieval notion that Christ himself went through all the grades or degrees of ordination. Of these there were usually held to be seven. André Wilmart has assembled various medieval lists of "the orders of Christ" and demonstrated their ultimate dependence upon an Egyptian ascetic of the fourth or fifth century.[275] The full sequence in order of rank in the Anonymous is as follows: doorkeeper, reader, exorcist, acolyte, subdeacon, deacon, priest (*presbiter* once, *sacerdos* twice), and bishop. Wilmart observes that the Iro-Scots were particularly fond of pondering over the ecclesiastical offices of Christ and finding appropriate texts for each of the orders. Lists, however, that stem from Irish sources lack the order of the acolyte. The list of Ivo of Chartres leaves out the bishop who is placed in a category apart from the usual degrees. This is done to preserve the number seven (including the well established order of acolyte) and the corresponding sevenfold grace of the Holy Spirit. A composite list made of the Anonymous' several references to the orders of Christ never entirely agrees with any of the ten variant lists distinguished by Wilmart,[276] but he is closest to Ivo of Chartres.[277]

---

[274] J2/B2: 441; J11/B11: 457; J19/B19: 473 f.

[275] "Les ordres du Christ," Revue des sciences religieuses, III (1923), pp. 305 ff.

[276] Wilmart prints the following variant lists (A–J) represented by one or more MSS:
  A. Missal of Bobbio, Paris, B.N. 13246, seventh century.
  B. Cologne, Chap. 15, et al., ninth century.
  C. St. Gall 40, et al., ninth century.
  D. Hibernensis, seventh century.
  E. Chronicle of "Malalianus," eighth century.
  F. Monte Cassino 217, eleventh century.
  G. Florence, Ashburnham 32, ninth century.
  H. Dunstan and Egbert Pontificals, tenth century.
  I. Honorius of Autun (c. 1125–1130), De sacramentis.
  J. Ivo of Chartres (d. 1115), De excellentia ecclesiasticorum ordinum.

[277] As to the *hostiarius*, the Anonymous in J19/B19: 473 f. agrees with G and J in understanding Christ as having discharged this office in driving the money-changers from the Temple. He also agrees with A, B, C, D, and H in construing the opening of the gates of Hell as a final instance of Christ's having been *hostiarius*. He does not go with E and H in appealing to the opening and shutting of the

The original intention of the compilers of hierarchical lists was to ground the authority of every order in the life of Christ. But the intention of the Anonymous is to open to question the stringency of canonical law regarding orders. For example, while purporting to be tremendously concerned about the orders of Christ, he discovers that Christ went through the degrees in a different sequence from that obtaining in canon law.[278] In Tractates J11/-B11 and J13b/B13b he raises embarrassing questions about the

doors of the Ark, nor with I and J in appealing to the words of John, "I am the door." The earlier lists place the office of *hostiarius* between that of presbyter and that of bishop.

All lists including the Anonymous', agree in conceiving of Christ as discharging the office of *lector* when he read from Isaiah in the synagogue.

The Anonymous agrees with the lists except E in beholding Christ as *exorcista* in driving out the demons. But unlike them he does not specify the scene in which Christ uses saliva (J) nor the episode concerning Mary Magdalene's seven devils. E does not list the exorcist, but revives in his place to make the seven, the ancient *fossarius*.

Only the Anonymous, F, J, and I list the *acolytus*. Significantly these are not the Anglo-Saxon pontificals, but Monte Cassino, Honorius, and Ivo of Chartres. The last two would be the only ones to consider in connection with the sources and the environment of the Anonymous. An *acolytus* tallies with the Anonymous' already mentioned allusions to, and dependencies on, Ivo in several Tractates. As for Honorius, while he does mention eight instead of seven grades as does the Anonymous in one list (J2/B2: 441), he places the lector after the exorcist, contrary to the Anonymous, and, of course, his later date (a quarter of a century after the Anonymous flourished) is against him and even his milieu as a source for the Anonymous.

Only with J (Ivo) again does the Anonymous agree in beholding Christ as *subdiaconus* in the washing of the feet of the disciples. E mentions the laving along with the changing of the water into wine at the marriage at Cana. All the others mention only the latter.

Only with H and J does the Anonymous agree in connecting the *diaconus* with the Dominical act of breaking the bread, but H specifies the breaking of the loaves for the five and the four thousand. J and the Anonymous are alone in connecting the diaconate with the breaking of bread in Holy Week. Even these two diverge, however, in that J adds Christ's praying at Gethsemane, while the Anonymous in J19/B19: 474 confines Christ's diaconate to preaching penitence in Matthew 4:17, a text *unique* in its application among all the surviving references.

All the lists pretty much agree on the priestly rôle of Christ at the Last Supper, although different phases may be singled out for emphasis. G and J alone see Christ's priestly rôle consummated on the Cross. *Sacerdos* instead of *presbyter* is used by C, D, F, G. This usage is likewise observed by the Anonymous twice.

[278] In J19/B19, 473 f. he contends with what may be mock earnestness that Christ was first *diaconus*, then he discharged the other offices in the following sequence: lector, exorcista, acolitus, hostiarius, and then simultaneously, *subdiaconus* and *sacerdos*.

We have already suggested a possible connection between the Anonymous' challenge to the traditional sequence of clerical orders and the preëminence of the archdeacon in the cathedrals. Cf. above, n. 201.

sequence of clerical ordination and deals with the case of a cleric who, wittingly or unwittingly, inaccurately apprised the consecrator of his real clerical status.[279]

In Tractate J2/B2 the Anonymous names eight orders including the bishop. In the two remaining Tractates he does not include the bishop, but this conformity with the pattern of Ivo is inconclusive because J11 is confined to the three main orders and J19 ends in the middle of a sentence, although the impression given by both these Tractates is that it was not the author's intention to include the bishop. The importance of this observation may well be that the Anonymous intended to spare the episcopate from his none too subtle depreciation of the lower orders and the doubt he diffuses concerning the historicity of initiatory rites.

In other Tractates, the Anonymous reveals still further his skepticism about orders because of the diversity of rites East and West. We cannot be at all sure that we are in possession of those Dominically enjoined.[280] In fact, the rites clearly cannot stem from the Apostles. Yet surely it cannot be said that no valid consecration has taken place since the passing of the Apostles.[281] He goes on to argue that either the original rites were abandoned, in which case the present practices would be manifestly inferior, or the Apostolic practices themselves were inferior and in need of improvement, a deficiency impossible to ascribe to the first companions of Christ.[282] Can it be, he queries with perhaps mock seriousness, that the Apostles performed the Eucharistic service without proper ordination?

Ipsi [the Apostles] enim aut his ordinibus fuerunt ordinati aut sine his ordinibus corpus Christi conficiebant et sanguinem. Sed hoc non est

---

[279] There may be a relationship between these Tractates and Epistle 185 of Ivo addressed to Archbishop Bona Anima. See below, p. 122.

[280] J18/B18: 472, iii: "Quae res [the diversity of rites] nobis inditio est aut nos aut illos aut forsitan utrosque divinam auctoritatem non sequi nec nostris vel illorum orationibus inesse vim vel potentiam consecrandi."

[281] J13b/B13b: 463.

[282] Ibid., 464: "Quod si quis dicat hoc [these rites and their elaboration] esse factum ad au[g]mentum et perfectionem christianae religionis, sequitur, ut dicat, quod in apostolis et primis patribus non fuit perfecta christiana religio. . . . Quod contra si eorum religio et institutio sufficiens et perfecta fuit, constat, quod haec non sunt inventa ad au[g]mentum et perfectionem, sed ad eorum correctionem et suggilationem."

credendum. Fuerunt igitur ordinati. Sed quo tempore, ut immitemur
eos? [283]

It is at this point that the Anonymous gives his unusual views
about the Dominical sequence of discharging the seven offices.

With these last rather inconsequential bits of evidence we
bring to a close our search for clues relating to the locale of composition of the "later" Tractates and to the clerical status of their
author. We turn now to the interpretation of the assembled data
and shall consider, in the order of increasing probability, three
possible candidates for authorship.

PART III

CONJECTURES CONCERNING THE AUTHORSHIP
OF THE CODEX

Our examination of all the clues grudgingly yielded by the several Tractates tends to localize the Codex in its entirety in Rouen,
although two of them seem to deal with the investiture controversy in the reign of Henry and one with the struggle between
York and Canterbury. There is no reason to doubt but that all the
Tractates, except J10/W, came from the hand of the same writer
who was a learned, traveled, high-placed ecclesiastic well versed
in Scriptures and the liturgy, especially well read in Augustine,
and quite competent to marshal arguments from canon law. In
the major Tractates he gives the impression of one writing with
considerable authority and, as he frequently uses the first person
plural, we may infer that he speaks not for himself alone but for
his chapter or for whatever other body he belonged to. Although
some scholars have thought that he remained deliberately anonymous, the much more likely explanation of the anonymity is that
we have here in the Codex the first drafts or transcripts of publicist writings which remained with the author after the scribally
prepared documents had been severally dispatched to the Pope, the
archbishop of Lyons, and the others to whom the Tractates proper
were most certainly directed. With these first drafts have been

[283] J11/B11: 457, vii.

assembled, possibly by the writer himself, abstract school discussions, sketches and notes that may constitute his youthful writings.

Of the clerics of Rouen cathedral in our period, there are four about whom enough is known to warrant their consideration as possible authors of the Codex: Archbishop Gerard of York, Bishop William Giffard of Winchester, Archdeacon and Dean Fulbert of Rouen, and Archbishop William Bona Anima of Rouen.

Ideally, we should hypothesize as author a canon of the cathedral in Rouen who eventually went to England whither he took his collected papers, adding a bit thereto during his English sojourn. On such a hypothesis we should be able to embrace all the facts, including the transmission of the MS to an English library. While we are not required by the assembled evidence to find the Anonymous ending up in England, the transmission of a primarily Norman Codex to England and the survival there of this markedly anti-papal and anti-monastic collection could be best explained by its having been carried across the Channel by the author himself, who in his new position would be sufficiently important to secure for these papers a permanent place, possibly in a cathedral library, whence they could later find their way into the Parker Collection.

There are only two known canons of Rouen in the period under consideration who were called to English posts: Gerard, former precentor who became archbishop of York in 1101, and William Giffard, dean of Rouen who was elected bishop of Winchester in the previous year. As we have noted, Böhmer on good grounds [284] was obliged to withdraw his original advocacy of Gerard and satisfied himself with postulating a cleric from Rouen in the entourage of Gerard. But as we have seen, there is no real evidence for localizing any of the Tractates in York. Moreover, since the Anonymous was himself well-informed and on occasion wrote with a sense of authority and corporate responsibility, we should hardly expect to find him obscurely trailing the former precentor of Rouen from Hereford [285] to York.

[284] Gerard was more or less continuously in England from 1090 on. He was present as royal chaplain at Bath, on January 27 of that year. Monasticon Anglicanum, W. Dugdale and J. Caley, eds. (London, 1817 ff.), II, 266. In the Chronica de archiepiscopis Eboracensibus, Gerard is mentioned as chancellor under both William I and William II. "Roll Series," LXXI, II, 521.

[285] Gerard was bishop of Hereford from 1095 to 1100.

1. *Bishop William Giffard of Winchester*

There remains William Giffard. Dean of the Rouen chapter,[286] Giffard was a royal chaplain under William the Conqueror,[287] and chancellor [288] from 1094 under William Rufus, into the first year of Henry I. One of the first acts of the new king, after seizing the royal treasury, was to nominate William bishop of Winchester, August 5, 1100, to signalize a reversal of his brother's policy of despoiling vacant sees. Against the Gregorian regulations, however, he invested Giffard with ring and staff.[289]

Because of ensuing controversy, Giffard was not to be consecrated until August 11, 1107.[290] He was at the center of what was in effect the English analogue of the investiture controversy; he went with Anselm into exile in Normandy in April, 1103.[291] Although commonly considered on the side of Anselm, he was not a Gregorian [292] and in his Norman exile apparently fell out with

---

[286] In 1080, according to Pommeraye, Histoire de la cathédrale, p. 302.

[287] As early as 1091. H. W. C. Davis, Regesta Anglo-Normannorum 1066–1154, Vol. I: Regesta Willelmi Conquestoris et Willelmi Rufi 1066–1100 (Oxford, 1913), No. 315.

[288] Ibid., No. 349.

[289] Matthew Paris, in his Historia Anglorum, "Rolls Series," XXXXIV, Vol. II, p. 181, writes: "Rex itaque Henricus in regem, ut dictum est, coronatus, dedit episcopatum Wintoniensem Willelmo Giffard, et continuo de possessionibus cunctis ad episcopatum pertinentibus illum, contra novi statuta concilii, de quo superius mentionem fecimus tam *fratrissans* quam *patrissans* investivit, *remuneratus.*" The final word, suggesting Giffard's involvement in simony, is added to the MS. The reference to the imitation of William Rufus and William the Conqueror does not appear in the corresponding place in the Chronica majora, ed. by Luard. "Rolls Series," LVII, ii, p. 118.

Henry of Huntington in his Historia Anglorum, "Rolls Series," LXXIV, p. 233, writes of the same event: "Sepultus autem est [William Rufus] in crastino perditionis suae apud Wincestre, et Henricus, ibidem in regem electus, dedit episcopatum Wincestriae Willelmo Giffard, pergensque Londoniam sacratus est ibi a Mauricio Londonensi episcopo. . . ."

[290] Giffard at length received, first priestly ordination, then episcopal consecration at the hands of Anselm. Migne, P.L., CLIX, lib. iii, ep. 7.

[291] Matthew Paris, Historia Anglorum, "Rolls Series," XLIV, II, 192.

[292] Cf. Böhmer: "Auch Wilhelm von Winchester und Reinhelm von Hereford waren keineswegs Gregorianer, sondern wollten sich nur nicht von Gerhard von York weihen lassen." Kirche, p. 159, n. 3.

A co-exile of Anselm need not be *ipso facto* eliminated from consideration as the author of our royalist Tractates. A defender, such as was the Anonymous, of metropolitan authority and a profound believer in the efficacy of a properly administered consecration, might conceivably resist the king on this one issue, even though in other respects utterly royalist. Moreover, the outspoken royalist, Gerard, is to be found among the signatories of a letter to Anselm, appealing to him to

Anselm because of his machinations with a view to recovering his see.[293] Evidence for this are two letters written from Lyons which indicate the extent to which Giffard had broken away from Anselm in spirit. The precise nature of Giffard's temptation, concerning which Anselm gives earnest counsel, is not made clear in Epistle 105,[294] although its political character is obvious. In Epistle 98 [295] the involvements of William Giffard are stated. He was apparently tempted to turn over to Henry a castle which he held from Duke Robert.[296] Giffard gives as his justification the alleged wrongs of Duke Robert against him. Anselm in his firm and solemn communication to Giffard, associating himself in this

---

return like Mattathias to Zion. Migne, P.L., CLIV, lib. iii, ep. 121. Cf. also ep. 91. Of the five other signatories of the former epistle, three are the excommunicated *royalist* bishops, Gerard, Herbert of Thetford-Norwich, and Robert of Chester. Giffard apparently found royalist company congenial.

[293] At what time Giffard parted company with Anselm is not certain. Anselm's three extant letters of recommendation of William Giffard addressed to leading men of Normandy may fall at the end of the Roman trip. Migne, P.L., CLIX, lib. iv, ep. 24, to Duke Robert, 25, to Archbishop Bona Anima, 26, to his "friend" Roger, probably of Bec.

[294] Ibid., lib. iii, coll. 142 f.: Omnes qui contra sinceritatem honestatis et justitiae suggerunt, venosi serpentes sunt, filii serpentis antiqui. Rogo igitur vos, ut dilectum amicum, et consulo, ut filio charissimo, ut si quis hujusmodi vobis aliquid contra consilium Dei consulere voluerit, nunquam tantum insibilet auribus vestris promittendo, minando, blandiendo, rogando, ut mentem vestram invenenet persuadendo. Vos scitis quia Dominus reprobat consilia principum, consilium autem Domini manet in aeternum.

[295] Ibid., coll. 137 f.

[296] William Giffard was a "vir alti sanguinis" "de semine Karoli-magni" according to Rudborne in Anglia Sacra, I, p. 279 f. He was related to the Giffards of Longueville. Pommeraye (Histoire de la cathédrale, p. 238) says that he was the son of Walter Giffard III, Count of Longueville and Earl of Buckingham. But this must be a mistaken identification. There were three Walter Giffards of Longueville and Buckingham: Walter I died in 1084, having received his earldom as a reward for his services to the Conqueror. Walter II supported William Rufus in Normandy (Ordericus, op. cit., viii, 9), but he later joined the league for placing Robert Curthose on the throne of England (ibid., x, 17), dying July 15, 1102. Interestingly, William Giffard was in charge of the Tower of London when Ralph Flambard made good his escape to Normandy, rousing Robert to contest the crown. Walter III was a minor on the death of his father, and his mother Agnes (who was enamored of Duke Robert and promised to give him her lands if he would marry her on the death of Duchess Sibylla) managed his hereditary domains for him for many years (ibid., xi, 4); he died without issue. William Giffard was manifestly not his son; he was more probably the son of Walter I and hence nephew of Walter II on whose death, during the minority of the heir and the governance of Agnes, the exiled Bishop-elect quite conceivably tried to regain the favor of Henry and make amends for his uncle's (?) disloyalty by turning over to the King a portion of the strategic holdings around Dieppe, which might otherwise have fallen directly into the hands of Henry's brother and foe.

message with the Primate of France with whom he is sojourning, discerns the true motive of the Bishop-elect namely, his willingness to compromise his principles in order to regain his position in England:

Cujus consilii, in quantum intelleximus, haec est summa, videlicet, utrum de castello quod de comite Roberto tenetis, possitis fratri ejus regi Henrico contra eumdem comitem deservire, propter injustitias quas idem comes vobis facit, sicut mandastis. Quod nequaquam coram Deo et coram justis hominibus licite fieri posse intelligimus. Nam, etiamsi vos de hoc absolvit, quod illi deleatis per hominium, aut per fidem promissam, sive per aliquam communem conventionem, non vos potuit absolvere de hoc quod Deo et proximo propter Deum debetis per christianam religionem. Quapropter intelligimus quia non debetis praefatum comitem de hoc quod de illo habetis exhaeredare et haereditatam ejus inimico suo tradere. In hoc quoque vos multum oportet intendere quod nondum vestra dilectio suscepit episcopi consecrationem, et si hoc faceretis quod a vobis rex exigit, nullus posset exstinguere exsecrabilem famam, quia hoc factum esset propter episcopatum, quem perdere timeretis, redemptionem.[297]

From these letters of Anselm it is clear that William Giffard was anxious about the temporary loss of his see (and the ear of the King) [298] and very much concerned about consecration. He stood, in exile, between Anselm, who had gone to Rome to learn at first hand the wishes of the Pope concerning investiture in the Island Kingdom, and the King, who, for all his insistence upon the right of investiture, was a veritable messianic ruler in contrast to the tyrant whom he had succeeded. "De consecratione" could have

---

[297] Migne, P.L., CLIX, lib. iii, ep. 98, coll. 137 f.

[298] The Appendix of Version A of "De consecratione" ends with cap. 18, of lib. xxv of the Hibernensis: "De sermone regis aut ducis, . . . ," closing thus: "Utinam sermo regis disolvisset me et, ut solvit Ioseph et ut liberaret me Danielem liberavit de lacu leonum et ut Mardocheum de angustia sua." Like these three ancients, Giffard had risen to prominence in a land not his own, a Norman, statesman and churchman in England. It is just possible that the conclusion of "De consecratione" with this excerpt from the Hibernensis is an allusion to the current plight of the Anonymous, and on the Giffard hypothesis, a reference to his desire to return to England and the King's favor. In connection with the Anselm correspondence on the matter of Giffard's giving up a castle to Henry against Robert, the interpolated "aut ducis" would have very special significance. On the interpolation, see above, p. 52. But there is so much else quoted in a miscellaneous way in the Appendix that I should scarcely wish to press the connection.

received, on this view, its first formulation in connection with Giffard's participation in the precipitate coronation of August 5, 1100 and with the attendant elevation of our chancellor to the episcopate, a coincidence which could explain the liturgical allusions detected in the festive and distinctive (indeed detachable) Exordium, while the full-blown Tractate will have been composed in Rouen cathedral during the Bishop-elect's exile. On this hypothesis we should be able to explain the author's seeming familiarity with the contents of Paschal's letter of April/May 1101 [299] and at the same time his use of the Robert Benedictional. "De consecratione" could be his reconsidered statement of the proper relationship between king and bishop, thought out in terms of the sacramental power of royal and episcopal anointment. Giffard in exile was undoubtedly preoccupied with the question of consecration, since without it he was obliged to satisfy himself with the title of bishop-elect. The Giffard hypothesis accounts for more of the assembled facts than the Gerard theory, but like the latter, it suffers from the canon's early departure from Rouen. Yet he apparently remained a canon of Rouen for some time after becoming chancellor in 1094 and is indeed still referred to as canon and dean of Rouen after 1100 in a letter of Anselm to Arch-

[299] Since on this hypothesis "De consecratione" could be a response of some kind to Paschal's Epistle (cf. above, pp. 60 ff.), it is important to ascertain whether William was still heading the royal chancery at the time the Epistle was received in England. Giffard witnesses as chancellor in a royal grant to Rochester, March 12, 1101. Monasticon Anglicanum, I, 164, No. xiv. Giffard's successor as chancellor, Roger (royal chaplain and afterwards bishop of Salisbury), is first recorded under the date of September 3. It is not impossible, therefore, that Giffard served as chancellor for several months after March and could have been next to the King when Paschal's letter arrived. This is the assumption of J. Armitage Robinson without reference, to be sure, to our particular problem. He supposes that Giffard was chancellor until September. Gilbert Crispin, Abbot of Westminster (Cambridge, 1911), p. 142, No. 20. H. W. C. Davis, however, says that Giffard will probably have laid down the chancellorship at least before Easter (April 21), when, at the crown-wearing at Winchester, Anselm approved of Giffard as bishop of Winchester. E.H.R., XXVI (1911), p. 86. The Easter reference on which this conjecture is based is in Annales monastici, ed. H. Luard, "Rolls Series," XXXVI, II, 4. In any event, Giffard is the only one of the three men we are considering who is recorded as having witnessed the momentous coronation of Henry at Westminster on August 5, 1100. F. Liebermann, Die Gesetze der Angelsachsen, I, 521 ff. He attests Henry's charter of liberties granted at the time of the coronation.

bishop William Bona Anima,[300] and in any event spent the greater part of the years 1096–1100 in Normandy [301] as well as part of his exile beginning in April 1103. He is also recorded with the King and Archbishop William in Rouen in 1106.[302] Nevertheless, it is hard to think of him as continuing to be so involved in the affairs of the cathedral that he would have composed those Tractates of the Codex which most certainly fall in the year of the Council of Clermont and shortly thereafter. Until some new evidence comes forward, Giffard's authorship of the Tractates can be only an hypothesis.[303]

[300] Migne, P.L., CLIX, lib. iv, ep. 25. Actually, Giffard could not have been dean after 1093, in which year John I witnesses to a document as dean of Rouen. Gallia christiana, XI, p. 115. Cf. Chart, p. 96 below.

[301] Charles H. Haskins, Norman Institutions, Harvard Historical Studies, XXIV (Cambridge, 1948), pp. 79 and 82. An undated testimony of William Giffard around 1100 indicates by implication the power which he still exerted in the cathedral after he became royal chaplain and then chancellor:

> Notum sit omnibus quod ego Willelmus Wintoniensis episcopus, secundi Willelmi Regis cancellarius, primi autem Willelmi capellanus, testimonium Rothomagensi ecclesie perhibeo, quod tempore primi Willelmi regis vel secundi nullus cancellarius vel capellanus habuit potestatem in ecclesia Rothomagi aliquid in choro disponendi, vel cantandi xpristus vincit, vel aliquid aliud faciendi.

This deposition may have been extracted from William by fellow-canons during the exiled Bishop-elect's sojourn in his old haunts, but since he refers to himself as bishop rather than as bishop-elect, the document could belong to the period after his consecration in 1107. It is found in the Chartulary of the Cathedral, MS Y44 (Bibliothèque de la Ville, MS 1193), printed in Valin, op. cit., p. 258. Discussed by Ernst H. Kantorowicz, Laudes Regiae: A Study in Liturgical Acclamations and Medieval Ruler Worship (Berkeley and Los Angeles, 1946), pp. 169 f. Thus every festive entry of William Rufus into the cathedral of Rouen would have found William Giffard singing the laudes regiae though he had no right thereto as he afterwards confesses. There is obviously some connection between the Christus vincit (royal lauds) and the christological ideas of "De consecratione."

From contemporary records it appears that the singing of the Christus vincit was a privilege accorded to only a few, usually the royal chaplains, sometimes the king's men-at-arms. With the privilege went the so-called presbyterium. Cf. Kantorowicz, ibid., pp. 175 f. and notes.

[302] See below, p. 118.

[303] It should be added, however, that the Tractate on the York-Canterbury controversy could be very well explained on the Giffard hypothesis. William was prebendary of London, which could account for the positive attitude taken toward London in "De obediendo." John Le Neve and Thomas Hardy, Fasti Anglicani (Oxford, 1854), II, 379. In the Thurstan-Ralph controversy, Giffard was personally involved. Chronica Pontificum ecclesiae Eboracensis, Historians of the Church of York, "Rolls Series," LXXI, II, 373; Annales ecclesiae Wintoniensis, Annales Monastici, "Rolls Series," XXXVI, I, pp. 297 f. He was present at Westminster in 1109 when the consecration of Archbishop Thomas was debated during the Whitsuntide court. W. Farrer, op. cit., No. 227.

We are therefore thrown back upon the two cathedral digni-
taries of Rouen, Archbishop William Bona Anima and Archdeacon and Dean Fulbert.[304]

2. Archdeacon and Dean Fulbert of Rouen

There are three Fulberts in Rouen in our period: Fulbert (I)
the Sophist,[305] archdeacon of Rouen and hagiographer, Fulbert
(II), archdeacon and dean of Rouen who at the end of his life
became a monk of St. Ouen,[306] and Fulbert (III), hagiographer
and monk of St. Ouen. It is little wonder that these three near contemporaries have been confused by even the most discerning of
historians! Our attention is directed toward Fulbert II whom we
must be at pains to distinguish from Fulbert I. We may leave
Fulbert III to one side, since he never featured in the life of the
cathedral chapter.[307] That Fulbert I and Fulbert II are not the
same person comes out clearly when we consider the lapse of time

Another fact of interest is that Giffard represented Archbishop Ralph at the
nuptial Mass for Henry I and Adelaide of Louvain. The Archbishop was himself
incapacitated and insisted on designating Giffard against the bishop of Salisbury
who claimed the privilege as a "parochial" right. Eadmer, Historia novorum, "Rolls
Series," LXXXI, pp. 292 f. The marriage took place a few days before the Feast of
the Purification of Mary. The King's intention to marry Adelaide had first been
made known on Epiphany. William Farrer, An Outline Itinerary of Henry I (Oxford, 1919), pp. 90 f. It is remotely possible that the nuptial and epiphanal imagery
of the Exordium of "De consecratione" could be connected with Giffard's prominent
part in the royal marriage.

Mention might also be made of the fact that Giffard was present at the Council
of London in 1102 which condemned sodomy (Canon 28). Mansi, XX, Col. 1153.
Tractate J3/W, in which this problem is frequently mentioned, might be connected
with Giffard on this score.

We may add further that a poem composed on the death of Giffard in 1129
styles him "os . . . plebis . . . Regis secretior auris." He is credited by the same
eulogist with having understood well the proper claims of Caesar and God:

Ecclesiae curam, Regi reddebat honorem;
Debita distinguens Caesaris atque Dei.

It is not clear whether the poet intends to have his words understood as a Gregorian
or a Henrician compliment. Anglia Sacra, I, 280 f. Other bits of evidence favoring
the Giffard hypothesis may be found in my "The Bearing of Christology . . . ,"
pp. 111–31.

[304] Böhmer was certain that Fulbert could not be the author, but this was because
he was sure that the Anonymous had to be found in York. Kirche, p. 264.

[305] So-called in a positive sense by Ordericus, op. cit., iii, 3.

[306] Ibid., viii, 25.

[307] He is discussed in Histoire littéraire de France, VIII, 379 and by Ceillier, op.
cit., 2nd ed., XIII, 469. He wrote on the miracles of St. Ouen and a Life of St.
Achart. He died c. 1092.

CHART

The Deans, Archdeacons, and Chancellors of Rouen Cathedral

(1045–1130)

Arch-bishop	Decanus	Archdiaconus *	Cancellarius
1044	c. '45 Osbern, Gx, ins 12A	c. '45 Hugh, ibid.	c. '45 FULBERT, ibid.
1046			
1048			
1050			
1052		'52 Hugh,§ Gx, ins 13A	
1054		'55 FULBERT, Gx, ins 13C	
1056		'56 FULBERT, Or, iii, 3	
1058			
1060			
1062			
1064		'64 William BA,¶ Or, iv, 6	
1066			
1068		'67 FULBERT, R, 88	
1070			
1072			
1074	c. '75 Robert I, Pm 302	'74 FULBERT, Gx, ins 17C	
1076			
1078		c. '80 Bernard, R, 1212	
1080	'80 Wm. Giffard, Pm 302	'80 Benedict, R, 919	
1082		'82 [Benedict] Dv, xvi	
1084			
1086		'88 [2] FULBERT [1] Benedict, HE	[3] Urso
1088		'91/5 FULBERT, HE	
1090		'91/2 FULBERT, #Pr 323, 19	[Richard] [Urso]
1092	'93 John I, Gx 115	'92–1110 FULBERT Benedict, Ca, 21	
1094		'94–9 FULBERT, Dv, No. 423	
1096		'96 FULBERT, Or, ix, 3	
		'96 FULBERT Benedict	Richard,
1098			Gx, ins 20A
1100			
1102			
1104			
1106		'06 [2] FULBERT [1] Benedict	[3] Richard Gx, ins 128A **
		'07 FULBERT Benedict	Richard Ursell
			Fr, No. 167A; HF
		'07–22, FULBERT "& chapter of Rouen," Fr, No. 185	
1108			
1110			
1112			
1114			
1116			
1118		'19	Rich. Osmund Gx, ins 20A
1120			
1122			
1124	'24 Geoffrey I, Pm 302		
1126			
1128	'28 FULBERT, Or, viii, 25	'28 FULBERT	
1130	'30 [6] Nicholas, Gx, ins 22D	[5] Fulbert §§	[1] Rich. [2] Osmund [3,4]

Archbishops (left column, spanning rows): MAUGER · MAURILIUS · JOHN · WILLIAM BONA ANIMA · GEOFFREY · HUGH

KEYS, NOTES, AND ABBREVIATIONS IN CHART

Ca = Cartulaire de l'Abbaye de Saint-Étienne de Caen, edited by Étienne Deville, "Notices sur quelques manuscrits normands conservés à la Bibliothèque Sainte-Geneviève," IV, Revue catholique de Normandie, XV (1905), 15 ff.

Gx = Gallia christiana, XI.

H = C. Haskins, Norman Institutions: Ap E, No. 6; E, No. 7 not clearly identified with Rouen; F, No. 1.

ins = Instrumenta in Gx.

Or = Ordericus Vitalis, op. cit.

Pm = Pommeraye, Histoire de la cathédrale.

Pr = P r o u, Recueil des Actes de Philippe Ier roi de France (1059–1108), (Paris, 1908).

R = J. H. Round, ed., Calendar of Documents Preserved in France, I (London, 1899).

Dv = Davis, Regesta, I.

Fr = Farrar, op. cit.

* There was a plurality of archdeacons after 1096 and probably from 1072 or earlier, since the canons of two Norman councils under John and the Council of Lillebonne in 1080 deal with archidiaconates in the plural. Cf. Bessin, op. cit. (1072), p. 55, c. 2, p. 56, c. 14; (1074), p. 64, c. 1 (here the office is spoken of in the singular); (1080), p. 68, cc. 6, 7.

§ Hugh signs as one "unworthy of being archdeacon."

¶ William Bona Anima must have given up his archidiaconate when he left for Jerusalem c. 1064.

Witness of a grant signed by Philip I. Richard, presumably the later archdeacon, signs as *capellanus*, while Urso, presumably the later archdeacon Ursell, signs as *canonicus*.

** The three are indicated as "archdeacons of Rouen"; Benedict precedes Fulbert, but since on either side of this date we have a record of Fulbert signing first, we may assume that the exceptional change in the order of precedence does not betoken a new Fulbert.

§§ This is clearly Fulbert IV as is indicated by his rank, the fifth to sign. Richard, first noted 1001/2 as *capellanus* and in 1096 as third archdeacon, is now first archdeacon. Valeran and Robert are named third and fourth archdeacons before the new dean who comes sixth.

between the first mention of a Fulbert (as chancellor) at Rouen (c. 1045) [308] and our last (c. 1128) as archdeacon and dean.[309] The difference between these dates is eighty-three years — and an infant could not begin as a chancellor. We must therefore try to divide these eighty-three years between the two Fulberts and since almost our only sources apart from Ordericus are the quite impersonal charters and conciliar canons to which the name of "Fulbert" is affixed, we must proceed schematically. The accompaning Chart gives all the references we have to the dean, archdeacon(s), and chancellor of the cathedral from c. 1045 to c. 1128.

From the foregoing chronological arrangement of the scattered notices of deans and archdeacons in Rouen it would appear that there is but one obvious grouping: c. 1045–c. 1074 for Fulbert I and c. 1088–c. 1128 for Fulbert II.[310] Fulbert I would thus be the counsellor and archdeacon under Archbishop Maurilius (1055–1067), which is the way Ordericus associated him, and Fulbert II would be the archdeacon and finally the dean under William Bona Anima (1079–1110). To be sure, the signature of 1074 is difficult to assign, but since it is, by seven years, nearer the cluster of entries for Fulbert I than for the first entry of Fulbert II, I am disposed to ascribe it to the earlier Fulbert. It is probable that the archidiaconate of Rouen became especially powerful during the years of the infirmity and deposition of John of Avranches (1069–1079).[311] In any event it is clear from the clustering of notices between 1088 and 1107 that an Archdeacon Fulbert has become a very important personage. During this period Fulbert II appears to be contesting the rank of first archdeacon [312] with a certain Benedict.

The archidiaconate appears to be expanding considerably during the pontificate of William Bona Anima. With this diplo-

---

[308] Gallia christiana, Instrumenta, 12A.

[309] Ordericus, op. cit., viii, 25. Böhmer, by mistake, says December 21, 1121. Kirche, p. 264. There seems to be a Fulbert IV in 1130. See Chart.

[310] To be sure, L'histoire littéraire de France conjectures that Fulbert I died c. 1092, but this is the date of Fulbert III's death, which can be ascertained within a few years. The writer has presumably confused the two Fulberts at this point, although he elsewhere carefully distinguishes them.

[311] Acta Rhotomagensium archiepiscoporum, Migne, P. L., CXLVII, 273 ff.

[312] He usually signs first and may have become what was later called the "Grand Archdeacon," the first of six. See above, n. 204.

matic evidence concerning the cathedral chapter that has chanced to survive may be connected the words of Ordericus concerning the expansion of William's diocesan organization: " . . . magnamque partem oneris sui decanis [313] et archipresbyteris sine invidia distribuebat, bonisque nihilominus ad participationem honoris avide asciscebat." [314] By 1107 there are at least four archdeacons and Fulbert is their head. As of 1128 Fulbert II is called *archidiaconus et decanus, gloria metropolis, cleri decus et diadema, illa profunda fontis inexhausti sapientia.*[315] And when did he become dean? In 1093 John I is dean and in 1107/22 Fulbert is still styled archdeacon only. Sometime after 1107/22, therefore, he will have assumed the decanal dignity while remaining first archdeacon. (It is regrettable that the document here cannot be dated more accurately.) Geoffrey may have replaced him in 1124, which is possibly the year Fulbert left the cathedral to become a monk in St. Ouen (instead of 1128 as is commonly supposed on the basis of Ordericus' account). Tentatively, then, we may think of Fulbert II, first as archdeacon and then as dean, presiding powerfully over the chapter of Rouen from about 1088 to about 1128, a plausible span of forty years of active canonical life.

It will be recalled that in the search of clues in the Tractates of our Codex, we were impressed by the prominence of Stephen and, by implication, of the archidiaconate in the thought of our author, particularly in J4/L3, dated by Böhmer between March and September 1096.[316] For 1096 Fulbert II is attested twice and

---

[313] Reference here is undoubtedly to rural deans. See Pierre Andrieu, "Pour servir à l'histoire des doyens ruraux des origines au XIIIᵉ siècle," Revue catholique de Normandie, XLI (1932), pp. 113–143.

[314] Op. cit., v, 4.

[315] Ibid., viii, 25.

[316] Böhmer, Kirche, p. 189. It is even possible that the "Apologia" was an address by the archdeacon before the synod in February in anticipation of the papal suspension. The archdeacon, being next in precedence after the metropolitan at a provincial synod, will undoubtedly have delivered, in the absence of Archbishop William, the allocution normally expected at this time. Cf. the Ordo concilii celebrandi, loc. cit., p. 153. Indeed, it would be in just such unusual circumstances as here hypothesized, that a naturally proud archdeacon would have made the supernumerary allusions to Archdeacon Stephen which we have noted in the "Tractate." This synodical address, moreover, before the provincial episcopate will have been delivered in the cathedral. Thus we could explain the gesture-like allusions to Archbishop William's numerous improvements in the cathedral fabric. J4/L3: 661, 12–25.

possibly thrice as archdeacon or first archdeacon. He took a very prominent place in February at the provincial synod called at Rouen where he appears to have represented Archbishop William. It is thus possible that it was this Archdeacon Fulbert II who was the author of the "Apologia archiepiscopi Rotomagensis" after the threatened papal suspension became effective in March — and hence of all the Tractates of our Codex which we have shown to come from one hand.

An outstanding archdeacon like Fulbert will have been well instructed in canon law,[317] concerned with ecclesiastical holdings and the rights of temporal sovereigns, and as archdeacon and dean well versed in the liturgy,[318] and a good preacher. He is

[317] Cf. the duties of the archdeacon in the Ordo concilii celebrandi, loc. cit., pp. 154 f.

[318] In view of the fact that Archdeacon Fulbert eventually became dean, Pommeraye's description of the seventeenth century powers, prerogatives, and liturgical functions of the dean of Rouen are especially interesting and the more so for the reason that as chief functionary in the twelfth century the archdeacon, even without annexing the decanal office, doubtless discharged many of the functions here assigned to a chief functionary of the seventeenth century:

> Il occupe aux Festes solomnelles la premiere Chaire dans l'Eglise, même un Evesque assistant au Choeur il ne luy doit pas ceder sa place, mais l'Evesque prend seance au côté gauche en l'absence de l'Archevêque; il officie aux principales Festes de l'année, et en toutes les occasions que appartiennent aux droits honorifiques de sa dignité. A raison de cette dignité, il doit faire au Chapitre, ou quelqu'autre à sa place, deux oraisons ou exhortations Latines, l'une la veille de Pasques, et l'autre la veille de l'Assomption. Il preside dans les Chapitres generaux, et en fait l'ouverture, c'est luy qui fait la ceremonie et la Harangue, lorsque les Rois, Reynes, Princes, et personnes de marque sont receus dans la Cathedrale. . . . Il avoit seance aux Eschequiers de Normandie et dans celuy du Bailliage de Roüen après l'Abbé de Jumieges. . . . Enfin le Chapitre luy fait l'honneur après sa mort de faire ses obseques dans le Choeur de la Cathedrale et une Chappelle ardante, ce qui ne se faisoit autrefois que pour les Roys les Princes ou pour les Archevesques.

Histoire de l'Eglise cathédrale de Rouen (Rouen, 1686), pp. 297 and 289. If the eleventh century dean or archdeacon of Rouen delivered orations on the eves of Easter and the Assumption and on all occasions when royalty was present at the cathedral, this would be a valuable clue for the purpose of ascertaining the authorship of "De consecratione." First as to the oration on the eve of Easter. This responsibility was perhaps connected with the first three canons of the Council of Rouen of 1072 under John, Archbishop of Rouen, 1069–1079. Bessin, op. cit., pp. 54 f. John had formerly been bishop of Avranches and while administering the affairs of this see composed De officiis, in which among other matters he laid emphasis upon the use of oils and chrisms. Migne, P. L., CXXXVII, col. 270.

As it was the custom to prepare the oils and chrisms for the year at Eastertime, it is quite possible to think of some of the material of "De consecratione" as having once constituted a portion of an Eastertide allocution in Rouen cathedral. In De officiis John has a passage on the Olive Branch brought by the Dove, the Holy Spirit, after the Flood. Ibid., col. 49; cf. H. A. Wilson, ed., The Gelasian

recorded as witness to a charter signed by Philip I bearing on the feudal relations between the archbishop of Rouen and the king of France.[319] Apart from these notices, however, we have nothing to go on to connect Fulbert II with the radical royalism [320] of the two investiture Tractates. The several "Tractates" on the orders of Christ could be the half-serious musings of an archdeacon troubled by the fact that despite the vast authority of the archidiaconate, technically his status was below that of a simple priest.[321] All in all, the epitaph of Fulbert given by Ordericus [322] could be applied without any hesitation to the author of our Tractates. Unfortunately we have no identified writing from the pen of Archdeacon Fulbert II with which to compare our anonymous documents.[323]

Sacramentary under Charles the Great, Henry Bradshaw Society, XLIX (London, 1915), p. 71. The olive is of course the oil of the New Covenant, a type of the Holy Spirit brought into the world in the New Dispensation of Christ. This conception of dispensational history connected with the Holy Spirit and the oil is the very stuff of "De consecratione." "De consecratione" may well contain material drawn from a once successful decanal-archidiaconal exhortation during Holy Week.

[319] Cf. the Charter of Philip I signed by Fulbert and the discussion of the temporal authority over villas and lands in J24/L4 and J28/15. Prou, op. cit., 321 ff. See following note.

[320] Actually, the Anonymous is not so radical in the specific matter of investiture as one might think from the over-all impression his Tractates leave. See J28/L5: 685, 40 ff. quoted below, n. 639. A very similar statement is made in "De consecratione," 667, 40 ff. Such a view would be quite compatible with the thought of a *responsible* canon of the metropolitan cathedral, such as Archdeacon Fulbert obviously was.

It is in the defense of *episcopal* rights against the Pope more than in the defense of *royal* rights in the investiture Tractates that the Anonymous shows himself to be most radical or, rather, conservative and even "reactionary," since he wished to preserve intact the pre-Gregorian dignities of the episcopate.

[321] See above, pp. 66 ff.

[322] Quoted in part, p. 99, above.

[323] There are four writings that have been ascribed with varying degrees of uncertainty to "Fulbert": 1) The Life of St. Romanus of Rouen, 2) the Life of St. Remigius of Rouen, 3) the Ordo concilii celebrandi in Robert's Benedictional, and 4) the Acta Rhotomagensium archiepiscoporum. If any of these could be reassigned to Fulbert II, we should be in possession of an invaluable stylistic proof or disproof of our Fulbert hypothesis, but we are apparently not so fortunate.

Ad 1. There are four ancient Lives of Romanus. The one in question is printed by Nicolas Rigault (Paris, 1609), where it lacks its Preface later supplied by E. Martène and U. Durand, Thesaurus novus anecdotorum (Paris, 1717), I, 181 ff. Without knowledge of the Preface, Mabillon (Vet. an.) had supposed the Life to be of very early date. With the publication of the Preface, however, it was clear that the author was Fulbert I, addressing himself to "Dominis et confratribus suis." It was almost certainly composed before 1079, because the author of the Acta, which closes with the accession of Bona Anima, says that St. Ouen possessed a copy thereof. The Life is discussed in Histoire littéraire de France, VIII, 373 ff. Martène

3. Archbishop William Bona Anima of Rouen

Were it not for the fact that the "Apologia archiepiscopi Roto-magensis" describes William Bona Anima [324] in the third person,[325] one would have immediately thought of the Archbishop himself as a possible author of the Tractates.

William was the son of Radbod of Flers, a widower who entered the priesthood and became bishop of Séez.[326] With this paternity Böhmer connected the discussions in our Codex of the legitimacy

confused Fulbert I and II. Op. cit., III, 1651 f. But Ceillier makes clear that the Life was written by Fulbert I the Sophist. Op. cit., 2nd ed., XIII, 468. The editors of the Acta Sanctorum agree in assigning, without hesitation, the Life of Romanus to Fulbert I. Op. cit., LVIII, Oct. X (Paris & Rome, 1869), pp. 75 f. Since the florid style of the Preface with its self-conscious references to vocabulary and grammar is what one might expect from one styled a Sophist, I have not felt it necessary to try to procure the rare Rigault volume for further confirmation of the generally held view. Stylistically, the Preface thereto is quite different from the writings of our Codex 415.

Ad 2. The Life of Remigius is printed by Martène, op. cit., III, 1665 ff.; it is discussed in Histoire littéraire de France, VIII, 376 f. and by Ceillier, op. cit., 2nd ed., XIII, 468 f. A likeness in style is noted by the writers between this and the foregoing Life. The author is less easily identified than the former by his words, but he clearly is of the cathedral chapter and has access to its archives. The less florid style of this hagiography is more like what one could expect from the author of our Tractates, but there is nothing conclusive here.

Ad 3. The Ordo concilii celebrandi, most recently edited by Wilson, op. cit., pp. 153 ff. Wilson dated this addendum to the Benedictional as late twelfth century against Mabillon who dated it in the pontificate of Bona Anima or his predecessor. Histoire littéraire de France, following the lead of Mabillon, conjectured (légers indices) that the Ordo was inserted by Fulbert I who had himself participated in the condemnation of Berengarius which features in the Ordo. Op. cit., VIII, 378 f. See above, n. 129.

Ad. 4. The Acta is printed in Migne, P. L., CXLVII, 273 ff. The possible attribution of the Acta to Fulbert I is due to Mabillon who, however, favored Theodoric of St. Ouen as a more probable candidate for authorship. Vetera analecta, n.e. (Paris, 1723), p. 226. They begin with a reference to the provincial catalogus with which the Anonymous (J2/B2: 443, vii) and Ordericus were also familiar. Böhmer, Kirche und Staat, p. 186, n. 3. Since the Acta ends with the accession of Bona Anima, it cannot antedate 1079 which comes within the period I have tentatively assigned to Fulbert II. The author is especially well acquainted with the details of the pontificate of John. The Acta does not suggest the style of the Anonymous.

[324] His biography is to be found in Gallia christiana, XI, coll. 37–41; Pommeraye, Histoire des archevesques, pp. 276–300; Histoire littéraire de France, IX, pp. 496–502; Ceillier, op. cit., 2nd ed., XIV, 56 f. The main source of all these accounts is Ordericus. I have not been able to consult Georges Dubosc, "Un archevêque de Rouen en Syrie au XIe siècle," Journal de Rouen, Dec. 28, 1919; reprinted by H. Defontaine, ed., Par ci, par là, 1st series (Rouen, 1922), pp. 169–177.

[325] J4/L3: 661, 13–25.

[326] He is attested as bishop 1025 to 1032.

of the ordination of the sons of priests.[327] William was a cousin of William I, bishop of Evreux (1046-1066), whose father was the powerful Gerard Flertel.[328] Archbishop Maurilius of Rouen (1055–1069) was attracted to William Bona Anima and made him archdeacon. William in turn was responsible for introducing the young cleric Gundulf, destined to become bishop of Rochester, to the archiepiscopal *mensa*, at which one dined holding high converse on spiritual themes.[329] In 1056 William, Gundulf, and a monk, Herbert of Montreuil, set out with the aged and harried Theodoric, abbot of Evroult, for the Holy Land.[330] If Bona Anima were the author of the Tractates, we should have in his pilgrimage a very good explanation for the prominence in our Codex of Jerusalem [331] as the mother of all churches, while the journey through distant regions would account for the references in our Tractates to various liturgies and usages including the Greek.[332] The original band made its way by the land route to Antioch. At Antioch the company, increased in Austria, resolved to separate, Theodoric, William, and Gundulf going from thence by sea. The latter were deeply moved by the dying words of their saintly companion, Theodoric, who collapsed before reaching Jerusalem, declaring that although he had set his face toward the earthly Jerusalem, he was quite prepared to turn his face to the heavenly Jerusalem instead.[333] A storm attending the return journey of the pilgrims so alarmed William and Gundulf that they resolved to take monastic vows, if they should ever be delivered safely.[334] William appears to have put off his entry into a monas-

---

[327] Particularly, J22(26)/L2. See below, pp. 147 f.

[328] Ordericus, op. cit., iv, 6. He is characterized as of high birth and great benevolence. Ibid., v, 9, 46.

[329] Vita Gundulfi Roffensis episcopi, Migne, P. L., CLIX, coll. 815 f. The most recent account of Gundulf is that of R. A. L. Smith, "The Place of Gundulf in the Anglo-Norman Church," E. H. R., LVIII (1943), p. 257.

[330] Ordericus, op. cit., iii, 4; iv, 6; Vita Gundulfi, coll. 815 f. On Theodoric of Mathonville see further L. Hommey, Histoire. . . . du Diocèse de Séez. . . . (Alençon, 1899), II, 59–61.

[331] Particularly J2/B2: 651, 28; J3/W: (MS, pp. 35 f.) ; J4/L3: 659, 27; J9/S; J12/B12: 459.

[332] J11/B11: 455 f.; J18/B18: 472, iii.

[333] Ordericus, op. cit., iii, 4.

[334] Vita Gundulfi, col. 816. Up to this point they had been "non sponte clerici."

tery, but at length chose St. Stephen's in Caen.[335] As that foundation was newly organized it seemed best to his counselors to send
him to Bec for the benefit of the teaching and discipline prevailing there.[336] From Bec he accompanied Lanfranc to Caen presumably in 1063 [337] when the latter was made abbot of St. Stephen's. William was assigned the task of instructing the novitiates,
which could conveniently explain the "school pieces" among the
Tractates.

When at length Lanfranc was raised to the throne of Canterbury, William was chosen to succeed him in St. Stephen's which
he ruled as abbot from 1070 to 1079.[338] The consecration of the
monastery, begun under Abbot Lanfranc, took place in 1077 [339]
under Bona Anima. William the Conqueror had secured a portion of the arm of St. Stephen and other relics of the royal
saint to add glory to the royal-ducal sanctuary and school, destined also to be the royal sepulchre. The presence of the Conqueror and his consort and a great concourse of barons, bishops,
and abbots with their retinues bearing gifts enhanced the splendor
of the dedicatory rites.[340] Archbishops Lanfranc, Thomas, and
John were present to represent the three ecclesiastical provinces
of the Conqueror's domains. Although it was John of Rouen who
presided during the ceremonies, it is almost certain that Abbot
William will have had some part in the extended celebration. The
"Exordium" of Version B of "De consecratione" could, indeed,
have been composed for this very occasion by Abbot William. It
will be recalled that this part of J24/L4 bears the marks of

[335] Ibid. That allusions to *sanctus* in our Codex may imply a monkish status
for our author, see above, n. 216.
[336] "Iste Willelmus cum habitum religionis Cadomi suscepisset, missus est Beccum,
ut ordinem ibi addisceret, quia novella plantatio ipsius loci nondum poterat alios
perfecte instruere." "Vita Lanfranci," cap. x, Vita abbatum Beccensium. Lanfranc,
Opera, ed. by J. A. Giles (Oxford, 1844), I, p. 291.
[337] For a review of the literature on Lanfranc's call to Bec (1063 or 1066) see
A. J. MacDonald, Lanfranc: A Study of His Life and Writings (Oxford, 1926),
p. 56, n. 2.
[338] Ordericus, op. cit., iv, 6. Cf. C. Hippeau, L'abbaye de Saint-Étienne de Caen
(Caen, 1855), pp. 25–29. This account of Abbot William is based on Ordericus.
[339] Ordericus, op. cit., v, 2, 16; Cartulaire, ed. by E. Deville, loc. cit., XIV
(1904), p. 272. Chronicon sancti Stephani Cadomensis dates the dedication in 1073.
Ed. André Duchesne, Historiae Normannorum scriptores (Paris, 1619), p. 1018.
[340] Ordericus, op. cit., v, 2. Cf. Cartulary of St. Stephen's, Gallia christiana, XI,
Inst., coll. 66 ff. William of Poitiers, Gesta, Migne, P. L., CXLIX, col. 1267.

earlier composition.[341] Festive in spirit and replete with liturgical allusions, this "allocution" on the royal nuptials of the Church would have fitted very well into the dedicatory service of the royal-ducal monastery of St. Stephen's in 1077. And this conjecture is reinforced by a passage in the Tractate wherein the Anonymous gives what may be rhetorical prominence to the fact that Solomon, too, built, constructed, dedicated, sanctified a house of God, and "solemnitatem dedicationis fecit." [341a] Significantly this passage occurs in connection with the Anonymous' assertion that Moses as *dux* had the same power over the *sacerdotes* as an anointed *rex*, that as *dux* he, too, sanctified and dedicated the sanctuary.[341b]

Two of the metropolitans present at the abbatial dedication, Lanfranc and Thomas, had recently returned from Rome where, as envoys of the Conqueror, they had secured from the Pope a confirmation of all the ancient rights which the Conqueror had demanded.[342] We cannot doubt but that the munificence of the King and Duke and his manifest espousal of the moral and cultural aspects of ecclesiastical Reform will have elicited sentiments of utter devotion in the learned Abbot of St. Stephen's, who, amid the splendor of the dedication, will have been understandably moved to proclaim the royal nature of the Church. That Bona Anima's loyalty to the Conqueror was abiding is vouched for by the record of his later solicitude for the dying ruler, wretchedly abandoned by time servers, feudal and clerical alike.[343] To conjectures in the realm of psychology and temperament we may add the evidence of textual emendation. It will be recalled that the Exordium of "De consecratione" yields clues that could connect this once possibly separate section of the present Tractate with some festive occasion like a coronation, a royal marriage, or a dedication. It quotes, for example, a sermon ascribed to Augustine which is found among the sermons appropriate for the dedication of a church or the anniversaries thereof in the Homiliarium.[344]

---

[341] See above, n. 79 and ff.
[341a] See below, n. 569.
[341b] See below, n. 665.
[342] Ordericus, op. cit., v, 2.
[343] See below, p. 111.
[344] See above, Part II, Section 10.

We have noted,[345] moreover, in the Exordium that the contrasting divine authorities are the *sacerdos* and *rex*, while in the body of the Tractate the terms are *pontifex* and *rex*.[346] The change is all the more significant for the reason that the shift is obviously intentional, occurring in the very sentence which is, as it were, the suture, in the edited text of the Tractate, between the Exordium and Version A. On the Bona Anima hypothesis, the Exordium will have been composed by the *abbas* of St. Stephen's for whom *sacerdos* would be the appropriate generic term when thinking of the relationship of the clergy to the king in the language of the Old Testament, while the remainder of the Tractate will have been a subsequent enlargement by the *pontifex* of Rouen in the interest of defending the old order in Church and State.

It remains to link William Bona Anima with the observed resemblance between the scripts of our Codex and certain manuscripts known to come from Bec.[347] It is worth noting that the very hand in our Codex which most markedly resembles that of a known Bec book is that in which the first four of the Tractates of our collection is written.[348] One of these Tractates is a typical "school piece" and one a disciplinary disquisition on a problem especially prominent in monastic life. Two of the Tractates in this Bec-like hand were composed in Rouen shortly after William left St. Stephen's to take up his new pontifical duties, accompanied undoubtedly by several brethren from Bec and Caen. Significantly, it is precisely in one of these early defenses of the metropolitanate of Rouen that Stephen the protomartyr is given such uncommon prominence.

All in all, William's pilgrimage to Jerusalem and his early

---

[345] See above, n. 79.

[346] The outcropping of *sacerdos* in the main body of the Tractate as a synonym of *episcopus* and *pontifex* may mark the passages containing this more general term as belonging to an older stratum, of which the Exordium would be the largest surviving fragment.

[347] See above, p. 32.

[348] The script of the final Tractate is written in the same or a quite similar hand, and we have already noted the similarity of its ornamentation to that of a known Bec book. See above, p. 32. The subject matter of the piece is love and obedience, which could well be the exhortation of the sometime master of the novitiates, William the Good Soul. If the Tractate filled an entire quire by itself, we should say that it had been displaced in the rebinding and thus separated from the first four seemingly and, in two cases quite certainly, early pieces of the collection.

monastic career, first as master of the novitiates and then as abbot, fit very well the clues we have hitherto assembled: the prominence of Jerusalem in several of the Tractates, the palaeographic evidence connecting the first four Tractates with Bec (and possibly the last), the linguistic evidence (to which we shall presently turn) [349] connecting certain philosophical terms with the school of Bec, the festive character of the Exordium, and lastly the frequent allusions to Stephen the protomartyr, notably in the early pontifical "Apologia." We turn to William's career as metropolitan, 1079–1110.

It was on or perhaps before [350] the death of the infirm and deposed Archbishop John that William was appointed by the Conqueror to the metropolitan see of Rouen. Ordericus, who was later ordained priest by William and always described him with reverence and esteem, says that the Archbishop was "good, cheerful, and courteous." He continues:

He furnished the mother church with ample stores of all the ornaments necessary for divine worship, and rebuilt from the foundation the cloisters of the bishop's palace and convenient offices.[351] The relics of St. Romanus the bishop were translated with great ceremony. . . .[352] Like a tender father, this bishop was kind to the clergy and monks, and all who were under his rule. He occupied himself continually with psalms, and hymns, and spiritual songs, and celebrated regularly the sacred mysteries. He was a stranger to deceit and malice, but scourged the indigent as occasion required.[353] He had naturally a fine voice, and

---

[349] On this, see below, p. 110.

[350] "Reccesit hinc [John], imo processit; nam duobus ante obitum ejus. annis inthronizatus est dominus Guillelmus. . . . cum apostolica auctoritate, tum regio munere, tum denique communi electione." Acta Rotomagensium archiepiscopum, Migne, P. L., CXVI, col. 280.

The uncertainty concerning the exact date of the accession is discussed by Pommeraye, Histoire des archevesques, p. 278. Cf. Böhmer, Kirche, p. 188, n. 3.

[351] I have not been able to consult the writings of Georges Lanfry on the results of excavations relating to the Romanesque predecessor of the present Gothic cathedral: "La cathédrale de Rouen au XIe siècle," Bulletin des Amis des monuments rouennais, 1928–1931, pp. 117–134; "La crypte et le déambulatoire," Bulletin de la Commission des antiquités, Seine-Inférieure, XVIII (1933), pp. 152–6; "La crypte romane," Bulletin monumental, XCV (1936), pp. 181–201.

[352] Cf. J4/L3: 661, 12 ff. The name of St. Nicaise of St. Clair-sur-Epte was annexed to the episcopal lists of Rouen under William. H. Leclercq, "Rouen," D. A. C. L., XV, p. 114.

[353] The combination of sternness and kindliness suggested here is especially marked in J7/W which is a small piece concerning the meting out of punishment in a

was a skilful chanter; was deeply versed in ecclesiastical law, and had a great command of clear and expressive language in preaching the word of God to the uninstructed. His patience and benevolence charmed all who enjoyed his society, and he committed without jealousy a large share of his official burdens to his deans and archpriests, admitting good men without reserve to a participation in the honours of his station.[354]

The testimony of Ordericus that William occupied himself incessantly with "psalmis et hymnis et canticis spiritualibus, sacrisque mysteriis," that he was "In usu ecclesiastico doctissime instructus," and that he was skilful in preaching to the faithful could clearly strengthen the hypothesis of William's authorship of the Tractates, wherein the liturgical and canonical bulk large and where the homiletical is not absent. The author of our Tractates is so obviously well instructed in canon law and liturgics that we could not possibly expect to find him among the lower clerics and lesser figures of his day.

At the very beginning of his pontificate William had to face what he considered a threat to the metropolitan dignity in the pronouncement of Gregory VII in favor of the primatial authority of Lyons over the provinces of Rouen, Sens, and Tours. Gregory's Epistle, extending the primacy of Lyons, was addressed to Gebuin.[355] It represented, as Böhmer observes,[356] the new policy of Gregory to withdraw Normandy from the ecclesiastical influence of William I, against whom he had decided in that very year,

---

cathedral or monastery. That this "Tractate" concerns monks or canons is suggested by the reference to the hypothetical guilty person as *frater*. Tractate J3/W, which is a full-length exploration of the biblical sources of penitence, manifests the same combination of sternness and magnanimity, thus reinforcing the plausibility of William the Good Soul's authorship. Moreover, since we have reason to suppose that the author of J3/W was at the time of composition (c. 1080; see below, n. 516) a bishop (above, p. 73), the Bona Anima hypothesis is further strengthened, since he is the only one of the three Rouen clerics we are considering who was a bishop that early. Fulbert never became bishop, and Giffard became bishop in Winchester only in 1100. On courtesy, cf. J4/L3: 661, 26.

[354] Ordericus, op cit., v, 4; translation by Thomas Forester, Bohn's Antiquarian Library (London, 1852), II, 123 f. Cf. Vita Lanfranci: ". . . vir generosis natalibus ortus, simplex, bonis moribus ornatus. . . ." Loc. cit., p. 291. Also Acta archiepiscopum Rotomagensium: ". . . vir sane et generis nobilitate elucens morum praerogativa praepollens." Migne, P. L., CXLVII, col. 780.

[355] Jaffé-Löwenfeld, Nos. 5125 f.

[356] Kirche, pp. 184 ff.

1079, to take up a stern policy.[357] At the same time, against the Archbishop of Rouen Gregory took up an equally hostile attitude, allegedly on the sole ground of the illegitimacy of Bona Anima's birth as the son of a priest.[358] Possibly Tractates J16/B16, "De depositione pontificis," and J17/B17, certainly J22(26)/L2, "Apologia pro filiis sacerdotum," and J25/L1 belong to this period of William's pontificate. The first two argue that only that which is bad in a priest or bishop may be taken from him, but not that which is good, namely, his God-given order.[359] This spirit is entirely in keeping with what we know of Bona Anima. The "Apologia pro filiis sacerdotum" is more palpably personal. It bears the marks of angry brooding over the papal stricture. It is the work of a keen, *responsible* cleric, who makes clear his hatred of license but who lays bare the papal sophistry of refusing ordination for reason of one's earthly birth when membership in the Church itself depends solely on spiritual rebirth. While this defense could have been written by one other than the Archbishop himself, the closing words suggest that this Tractate was composed by the one directly affected by the charge and by one fully prepared to accept the consequences of his daring thought.[360]

J25/L1, "An liceat sacerdotibus inire matrimonium," is really a plea not to allow canonical regulations to interfere with God's predestined recruitment of citizens of the Heavenly Jerusalem. Here the writer is obsessed with the thought that (he or) some good Christian might not have been, had this canon been observed. One whose whole thought is shot through with the Pauline-Augustinian predestinarianism (bordering at times on fatalism) cannot

---

[357] Willi Schwarz is inclined, nevertheless, to discern moderation and the spirit of compromise in Gregory's dealings with William the Conqueror even after 1079, since Gregory, of course, needed his support, or at least his neutrality, in the papal struggle with Philip I and Henry IV. "Der Investiturstreit in Frankreich," Zeitschrift für Kirchengeschichte, XLII (1923), esp. pp. 325 ff.

[358] Jaffé-Löwenfeld, No. 5135.

[359] J16/B16: 469: "Quare laborandum est, ut destruatur in eo, quod malus est, et reservatur, quod bonus est." J17/B17: 470: "Quare non potest deponere *pontificem* seu sacerdotem, qui virtutem, quam ei dat Deus, destruere vel auferre non potest."

[360] J22/L2: 655, 38 ff.:
Sed fortasse dicturus es: Lex canonum prohibit, ut tales ordinentur. Ad quod respondemus: Apostolus dicit: "Si spiritu ducimini, non estis sub lege." . . . Et hęc quidem dicta sufficiant. Quę si bene et fideliter dicta sunt, gratulamur. Sin autem, correctionem libenter accipiemus.

but justify clerical marriage. For God who rules all (J21/SW) can bring good (a saint or virgin) out of a relative evil (clerical marriage). Quite willing to accept celibacy and continence as a good for those called thereto, the Anonymous concludes that a cleric's desire to marry is God's prompting to "minister" in the birth of a predestined soul, while the desire to be continent is an equally divine prompting! We have already taken note of Fliche's identification of the technical language of this discussion as belonging to the school of Anselm at Bec.[361] He calls it a third Norman version of the Rescript of Ulrich and dates it around 1080, following Böhmer.[362] Although the author of J25/L1, "An liceat," is dependent upon Ulrich of Imola and possibly the two other Norman versions,[363] Fliche is willing to concede a certain originality to our author. All four tracts considered by Fliche are concerned to suppress, by means of clerical marriage, the evils of fornication and sodomy.[364] Outright papal approval of clerical marriage wherever desired was their program as against the strictures of Cardinal Damiani. The important point wherewith we may connect the last of these writings with William Bona Anima is the fact that prior to his elevation to the archiepiscopal throne, William had spent some time at Bec and succeeded Lanfranc in the allied center at Caen. In Bec he will have become acquainted with the Anselmian terms employed in our Tractate.[365] Thus along with other evidence pointing in the same direction, it is not hard to imagine this Tractate to have been the work of the good-hearted

[361] See above, p. 26. Anselm's work on which this claim for affinity is based is his De concordia praescientiae et praedestinationis necnon gratiae Dei cum libero arbitrio. Migne, P. L., CLVIII, coll. 507 ff.

[362] A second version he dates between 1074 and 1080. It is discussed in connection with the problem of transmission above, p. 26. The first Norman version is the Tractatus pro clericorum connubiis by an author who, according to Fliche, came from Italy to Normandy.

[363] In these the following influences may be noted: the False Decretals, Augustine, Atto, bishop of Vercelli (924–961) and grand chancellor of Lothair II of France, in addition to Ulrich and Anselm.

[364] J3/W in our Codex is concerned with another aspect of this problem, punishment for, and forgiveness of, sexual vagaries of the priesthood. Here the Anonymous deals with the incest of Lot, for instance, which is prominent in the "second version."

[365] The key terms are *praescientia, praedestinatio, praecogitatio*, as they are related to *gratia, mandatum*, and *liberum arbitrium*. Fliche says that the last is not taken into account in J25/L1 but elsewhere in the Codex it is used in a kindred context.

Archbishop, whose elevation had been opposed by Gregory VII because of an allegedly illegitimate birth as the son of a priest. In the synod and diet of Lillebonne in 1080 [366] to which William I summoned William Bona Anima and the nobles and clergy of Normandy, the King and Duke, despite the new sternness of the Pope toward him, proved to be much more vigorous in insisting upon the carrying out of certain Hildebrandine principles than was the Archbishop, who could not be expected to take a lively interest in the prosecution of married clerics. Article III of the Canons of Lillebonne deals with the problem. It is probable that Tractate J25/L1, which is open-minded about clerical marriage, is a literary deposit of the controversy occasioned by the Duke's synod. The canons of Lillebonne also manifest especial interest in the maintenance of civil order in the duchy. The truce of God is the first concern of the assembly. Article X forbids the investiture of priests by laymen. By implication, however, the investiture of the higher clerics remains unchallenged.

From 1081 onward for a period of uncertain duration, William was papally suspended from his office. [367] For the year 1082 we have a record of the controversy with the abbot of Saint-Wandrille, William having refused to bless a new *ferrum judicii* to replace the one accidentally destroyed at the Abbey. [368] We learn that it was William, loyal to the last to the beneficent patron of Caen, who arranged for the fitting burial of the Conqueror. William had died in a monastic cell on the outskirts of Rouen, wretchedly abandoned by barons and despoiled by servants. The Archbishop ordered the body to be conveyed to Caen and he himself presided at the ceremony in St. Stephen's, although it was Gilbert of Evreux who delivered the funeral oration. [369]

In 1090 William Bona Anima laid an interdict over all of Normandy because Duke Robert took away Gisors, which had belonged to the *temporalia* of the cathedral of Rouen. Gisors was a key point in the defense of Normandy. [370] The abbey of Fécamp

---

[366] Mansi, XX, 555 ff. No papal legate presided over this very important reforming council. Cf. Gregory's letter to Bona Anima concerning the latter's lack of respect toward papal legates. Jaffé-Löwenfeld, No. 5204.

[367] Böhmer, Kirche, pp. 187 f.

[368] Lemarignier, op. cit., p. 81, n. 74.   [369] Ordericus, op. cit., vii, 16.

[370] Philip I had aided Duke Robert against William Rufus. Gallia christiana,

refused to consider itself as falling under the Archbishop's jurisdiction in the imposition of the interdict and therewith began the
struggle with Fécamp reflected in our Codex.[371] When Urban II,
defending the privileges of Fécamp, intervened to deprive Bona
Anima of his pallium, Duke Robert thereupon sided with the
Archbishop. The conflict lasted from 1090 to 1094. It was the
occasion of the Archbishop's second suspension, beginning in
1093.[372]

In the same year, 1093, Anselm was made Archbishop of Canterbury and his place as abbot of Bec was filled by one of whom
Duke Robert and Anselm alike approved. As metropolitan, William Bona Anima was present at the consecration of the new
Abbot the following year, 1094, while the Duke invested him with
the *temporalia*. At this ceremony a conflict broke out between
William Bona Anima and the Duke over the control of Bec. Bona
Anima, as we have just noted, was indisposed to permit the existence of any autonomous ecclesiastical enclave within his province.
At the very opening of the ceremony of consecration, the Abbot-
elect, already mitred, was apprised of the intention of Bona Anima
not to proceed with the consecration unless the Abbot-elect made
a profession of obedience which the latter refused to do, appealing
by messenger to the Duke, who this time took the Abbot's side.
The Archbishop, very much irritated, was obliged under ducal
duress, to proceed with the ceremony.[373]

It was also in 1093 that Bona Anima is said by William of
Malmesbury to have solemnized the marriage of Philip I of France
and Bertrade de Montfort after the king abandoned Bertha.

XI, 18 f. For a discussion of the problem raised, cf. Böhmer, Kirche, p. 143. For
the importance of Gisors: Ordericus, op. cit., x, 18.

We may mention here for completeness, though it has no direct bearing on the
possible relation of our Codex to Bona Anima, that in 1091 he held a Council at
Rouen. Ordericus, op. cit., viii, 18; Mansi, XX, 739. At this time William, with the
approval of Duke Robert and the assent of the assembled suffragans appointed
Serlo, Abbot of St. Evroult, Bishop of Séez. Serlo was destined to suffer much in
his diocese, overrun by cruel and rapacious nobles, and to endure exile several times
in England and Italy. It was this appointee of William Bona Anima who later
encouraged Henry I, in a moving Easter sermon, to restore regal order to Normandy.
Ibid., xii, 11.

[371] J5/B3 and J27/S,A, in the latter by name.
[372] Discussed, with the literature, by Lemarignier, op. cit., p. 194.
[373] The occasion is described in J. Picard's notes, Migne, P. L., CLIX, col. 28.

William Bona Anima, since he was already under papal suspension, could, according to the chronicler, afford to demean himself to perform a service that was frowned upon by almost all. Recent research has, however, cleared our Archbishop of Malmesbury's charge [374] although he was undoubtedly present at the nuptial mass. That William was broadminded in matters of marriage is attested by a letter addressed to him by Hildebert, bishop of Le Mans and later archbishop of Tours.[375] Hildebert writes that he refuses to descend with William and his suffragans to do evil that good might abound, to countenance a breach of the laws on consanguinity in order that two warring baronial houses might through wedlock be brought to peace and quiet. The adaptability here ascribed to Bona Anima is quite in accord with a certain ethical relativism or, shall we say, magnanimous casuistry of several of our Tractates, including J15/S, "De nuptiis." [376]

At the Council of Clermont in November 1095, Gregorian principles were restated with great effectiveness and the suffragans of Archbishop William were greatly impressed. His entire province, however, resented the reassertion of the primatial dignity of Lyons, which seemed to William's suffragans an encroachment upon the metropolitan dignity of Rouen. It was moreover alleged by them that the claims of Lyons were based upon falsified docu-

---

[374] According to Malmesbury, William of Rouen finally presided at the nuptial mass after the king had vainly besought Ivo of Chartres to acquiesce in the adulterous union. De gestis regum Anglorum, "Rolls Series," II, p. 980. Ordericus says that it was Odo of Bayeux who consecrated the marriage. Op. cit., viii, 20. The truth is apparently to be found in Urban's letter to Reynold of Rheims in which Urison of Senlis is held responsible. Jaffé-Löwenfeld, No. 5469. The whole problem is discussed by Augustin Fliche, Le Règne de Philippe Ier, Roi de France (Paris, 1912), pp. 40 ff. It is quite probable that William was present, as also Odo, and by their presence assented to the act.

[375] Migne, P. L., CLXXI, coll. 221 f. Discussed in Histoire littéraire, XI, 292.

[376] The occasion of this Tractate on the dissolubility of marriage between Christians and Saracens or Jews may have been the outbreak of anti-semitism in Rouen in 1096. Annales Rotomagenses: "1096 Hic ivit comes Robertus Jerusalem. Eodem anno interfecti Iudaeorum apud Rotomagum." Felix Liebermann, Ungedruckte anglo-normannische Geschichtsquellen (Strassburg, 1879), p. 47. It is much more likely, however, that it was written in view of the problem of the returning Crusaders who had taken Jewish or Mohammedan wives. On this supposition, J15/S will have been composed after 1096 and most likely around 1100. It is of interest to note that the Thomas Phillipps MS 7817 which contains A. Fliche's "Norman version I" of Ulrich's Rescript on sacerdotal marriage (paralleling our J25/L1 = Fliche's "Norman version III") likewise contains a treatise on the legitimacy of marriage with a Saracen or Jewess. G. Waitz, "Handschriften. . . ." Neues Archiv, IV (1879), p. 596.

ments, otherwise the Gallican metropolitans would themselves have copies of the basic documents in their archives from ancient times. We have already noted how Ivo of Chartres defended metropolitan autonomy for the province of Sens and how his Letter of 1097 to Hugh of Lyons, twice quoted in the Tractates of Codex 415, was a contribution in this struggle. Several of the Tractates in our Corpus are clearly the corresponding defense for the metropolitanate of Rouen, notably J2/B2, J4/L3, and J12/B12; and it is plausible that it was William himself who wrote them.

The provincial synod of Rouen in February 1096 [377] ratified the decrees of the Ecumenical Council of the preceding year, but its principal concern was manifestly the recovery of order in the baron-ridden province. The first canon deals with the Truce of God. Other canons deal with asylum and similar measures for the protection of the people. Parish militias are encouraged as a means of defense against marauders. Investiture with ring and staff are tacitly retained for the bishops, only the investiture of priests and lower clergy by laymen is expressly forbidden.[378] We have already observed that William himself does not seem to have presided at this synod,[379] possibly because he had failed to comply with papal instructions concerning submission to Hugh of Lyons as Primate within the three months' period set by the Council of Clermont and was, in consequence, suspended from office.[380] How-

---

[377] Ordericus, op. cit., ix, 3; Mansi, XX, coll. 921 ff.; Bessin, op. cit., 76 ff.

[378] It will be noted that William's synod differed markedly from the Council of Clermont on the matter of lay control and investiture. The Rouen synod was silent, for example, on episcopal investiture:

Canon V: Statuit etiam sancta synodus, ut omnes ecclesiae ita sint saisiatae de rebus suis, sicut fuerunt tempore Guillelmi regis. . . .

Canon VI: Statuit etiam, ut nullus laicus det vel adimat *presbyterum* ecclesiae, sine consensu praesulis nec vendat, nec pecuniam inde accipiat. . . .

Canon VII: Nullus laicus habeat consuetudines episcopales, vel justitiam quae pertinet ad curam animarum. . . .

Canon VIII: Nullus *presbyter* efficiatur homo laici. . . . — Mansi, XX, 739 f., 921 ff.; Bessin, op. cit., 76 ff.

Compare the fully Gregorian canons 15–20 of the Council of Clermont. Mansi, XX, 817 f. The author of "De consecratione" could have accepted the foregoing canons without relinquishing any of his convictions about the anointed king and his relationship to the anointed bishop.

[379] See above on Archdeacon Fulbert, p. 100.

[380] Böhmer says that William will have been automatically suspended on March 1 (i.e., after the provincial synod). Kirche, p. 189.

ever this may be, it is possible that in this very period when Bona
Anima was under suspension and suffering from the primatial
presumptions of Hugh that he made common cause with Ivo
(Chartres-Sens) and, employing certain of the latter's arguments,[381] went to an extreme in defending Philip I [382] as anointed
king (the Daimbert affair) and himself as anointed metropolitan
(despite suspension) from primatial (and ultimately papal) inter-
ference based on new and, from his point of view, pretentious
canons. So might we explain Version A of "De consecratione
with its dual concern for king *and* bishop and its documentary
Appendix made up of excerpts from the cathedral pontifical and
ancient canons.

Or again, it is possible that we can connect Bona Anima and
the three or four publicist Tractates with the investiture controversy between Duke Robert and Pope Paschal, brought to
light by the discovery of a letter published by Wilhelm Levison.[383]
Levison does not date it any more precisely than 1101–1106, but
he takes up the possibility of its having been connected with the
controversy over Lisieux in which Bona Anima had an important
but not entirely creditable part, complying as he did with the low
aims of Duke Robert.

Duke Robert Curthose, it will be recalled, transferred in September, 1096, the administration of his duchy to his brother William
Rufus in return for financial assistance in undertaking the Crusade. Royal and ducal government [384] were thus joined until the
accidental death of William Rufus in 1100 and the concurrent
return of the Crusader. Until the battle of Tinchebrai in Septem-

---

[381] See above, pp. 55 ff.

[382] Though there seem to be echoes in "De consecratione" of Paschal's Letter to
Henry, it will be borne in mind that even Böhmer connected the Tractate with
Henry I "nur infolge eines ganz gelegentlichen Citats aus der englischen Krönungs-
formel." Kirche, p. 203. But we have now shown that the *ordo* cited was taken
from a pontifical in Rouen. Part II, Section 2. Therefore a connection with Philip I
is not out of the question.

[383] Neues Archiv, XXXV (1909), pp. 457–81. Augustin Fliche makes no mention
of this new evidence, holding that the investiture struggle in France and England
was but a passing and incidental phase of the extension of the primatial authority of
Lyons. "Y-a-t-il eu en France et en Angleterre une querelle des investitures?", Revue
Bénédictine, XLVI (1934), pp. 283 ff.

[384] William did not, however, assume the ducal style during his administration of
the Duchy. F. M. Powicke, ed., Handbook of British Chronology, Royal Historical
Society Guides and Handbooks, No. 2 (London, 1939), p. 32.

ber, 1106, when with the defeat and imprisonment of Robert
Curthose, royal and ducal government could be fully rejoined in
the same hands as in the days of William the Conqueror, Normandy suffered wretchedly under the misrule of the returned
Crusader and his favorites. It is not clear whether Bona Anima
can be counted among the early supporters of the anti-ducal party,
which looked to Henry as the salvation of stricken Normandy.[385]

It seems clear enough, however, in the first years after the return
of the Crusader, that Archbishop William was willing to oblige
the Duke and ordain Fulcher, the almost illiterate brother of the
ill-reputed Ralph Flambard,[386] as bishop of Lisieux. This was in
June 1103. Duke Robert had invested Fulcher out of consideration for the renegade Flambard, the despoiler of English churches
and the justiciar during much of the tyrannical reign of William
Rufus. Imprisoned by Henry I, he had escaped to Normandy,
establishing himself as the chief minister of the slothful Duke who
allowed himself to be incited to a futile campaign against his now
royal brother. Fulcher died a few months after consecration and
was replaced by Flambard's sons, the older aged twelve, the Duke
once again endeavoring to please his favorite. Since Flambard
was already bishop of Durham, he avoided the charge of seeming
to be in possession of two sees at once, by administering the
diocese as a "steward" rather than as himself its bishop.[387]

Ivo, viewing the decay of canonical practice in the neighboring
archdiocese, wrote two letters to the metropolitan ultimately responsible, William Bona Anima, calling the affair of Lisieux "big-
amous." [388] He complained also directly to Pope Paschal.[389]

---

[385] In 1101 the Archbishop baptized the son of the Duke and the Duchess Sibylla,
whom Robert had brought back with him from Apulia. The child was named
William after the Archbishop. He later composed Sibylla's epitaph. Ordericus, op.
cit., xi, 4.

[386] For a recent treatment, see R. W. Southern, "Ranulph Flambard," Royal Historical Society, Transactions, XVI (1933), pp. 95 ff.

[387] Ordericus, op. cit., x, 18.

[388] Migne, P. L., CLXII, ep. 153, col. 157. The other is ep. 149, coll. 154 f.
Tractate J8/B8 concerning the mercenary and *digamus* pastor, who if he is not truly
a pastor, need not be obeyed or heeded, may be connected with the Lisieux episode.

[389] Migne, P. L., CLXII, ep. 157, col. 162.

It is at this juncture, possibly, that Paschal addressed his letter to Robert:[390]

Tu autem te ipsum ostium efficisti, et per anulum et virgam investituram aeclesie, non ut sponse Christi, sed sicut ancille, hostibus tradis ejus regimen usurpantibus, deserentibus Deum qui vere ostium est, per quem qui non ingreditur fur est et latro.

Levison observes that Paschal's letter to Robert has stylistically and conceptually much in common with his letter to Henry I in 1101.[391] Thus the echoes [392] of Paschal in "De consecratione," which seemed to imply some proximity to the English *curia regis* might be explained instead by the Paschal-Robert correspondence. Bona Anima was presumably involved on the ducal side, since 1) he was himself under papal suspension and 2) had consecrated Fulcher to oblige the Duke. It will be recalled that "De consecratione" mentions the ducal authority along with the royal in its general defense of princely rights in the Church.[393]

The reason that the notorious affair of Lisieux was not cleared up before Duke Robert's imprisonment after Tinchebrai in 1106 was that there was some question about whether John of Serlo, the cleric elected to replace Flambard's sons, might be properly consecrated by Bona Anima in view of the papal suspension of the Metropolitan, which remained in force until 1105. We know, for example, that John communicated with Ivo asking whether a suffragan of the suspended Metropolitan might perform the consecration as a deputy.[394] In the meantime Flambard sold the benefice to William of Pacy. Eventually Bona Anima was constrained to condemn this William of Pacy but not until the new Duke, King Henry, had expedited the elevation of the archdeacon of Serlo to the episcopal throne of Lisieux. This belated condemnation of Pacy took place in 1106 some time after the assembly presided over by Henry I at Lisieux in the middle of October at

---

[390] Levison: "Es liegt nahe, an das Bistum Lisieux zu denken, dessen Verhältnisse in diesen Jahren dem Papst mehr als einmal nicht unberechtigen Anlass zum Einschreiten geben konnten." Op cit., p. 430.

[391] Ibid., p. 428, n. 5.

[392] Discussed above, pp. 60 ff. Two of the concepts, the Church as *sponsa Christi* and *ego sum ostium*, are contained in the letter to Robert.

[393] Part II, Section 5.

[394] Migne, P. L., CLXII, col. 162AB.

which the victor of Tinchebrai (September) enunciated his governmental and ecclesiastical principles.[395]

During these same years Bona Anima was also concerned with a third investiture quarrel ending in the deposition of Turold of Bayeux (1097–1107).[395a] Thus there were at least three major Gallic ecclesio-political episodes (Sens, Liesieux, Bayeux) with which Bona Anima was more or less connected. His involvement in any one might have issued in just such publicist Tractates as our Codex contains. Nor does this possibility in any way impair the theory advanced above connecting the Exordium and earlier strata of "De consecratione" with the dedication of St. Stephen's.

In November a drawn out conflict between Fécamp and a small monastery was brought to a close in the royal and ducal presence in the chamber of Archbishop William.[396] It is worth noting that both William Bona Anima and William Giffard were present on this occasion on the side of Fécamp. Already by the spring of 1106 Bona Anima had recovered his jurisdiction. Anselm, despite recent strained relations betwen the two prelates,[397] had been moved to intervene in behalf of the suspended Metropolitan of Rouen. Shortly after his appeal to the Pope, we have a record

[395] Ordericus, op. cit., xi, 21. Flambard made his peace with Henry, probably having deserted Robert's cause at Tinchebrai. At all events he was restored to his see at Durham, while most of Henry's other foes were treated severely.

[395a] Paschal sternly informs William of his impatience with Turold, ep. 179, March 30, 1106; Migne, P. L., col. 188. The reconstruction of the ecclesio-political issue at Bayeux has been made possible by the publication of a hitherto unedited letter of Paschal, addressed to the Gregorian chapter of Bayeux, Oct. 8, 1104. G. Morin, "Lettre inédite de Pascal II," R. H. E., V (1904), p. 284. The most recent reconstruction of the episode is that of Sarell Gleason, An Ecclesiastical Barony of the Middle Ages, Harvard Historical Monographs X (Cambridge, 1936), pp. 17–23. With Turold's appointment "per secularem potestatem," with his hasty assumption of the diaconate out of canonical sequence, with his deposition by Pope and chapter several Tractates of our Codex could be connected, esp. J13a, 13b, 16, and 19.

[396] Gallia christiana, XI, Instrumenta, col. 127: "Natum sit igitur, tam futuris quam presentibus, quod anno. . . . 1106, indictione 15, vii idus Novembris, lis quaedam seu calumpnia ante regem Anglorum jamque ducem Normannorum, Rotomagi in camera archiepiscopi Willelmi ipso praesente fuit finita. . . .

[397] In ep. 67 (lib. iii) Anselm had reproached Bona Anima for his failure to recall a certain intrusive monastic under his control, saying: "Videte ne nobis necesse sit, ut familiariter reverendo meo Patri loquar, clamare ad Deum de vobis, ad quem pertinet hoc corrigere, si contemnitis."

of two letters of Paschal II which betoken the new relationship between Rouen and the Holy See.[398] Paschal suggests that bad counselors had perhaps been the cause of William's many *pravitates*. Significantly, the "Apologia" opens with the refutation of the papal-legatine charge of *infidelitas* (656, 25–9) before taking up the charges of *inobedientia* (29ff.) and *contemptum ordinis* (661, 12ff.).

Ludovico Frati, on the basis of a Bologna MS, holds that a possible reason for William's recurrent difficulties [399] with the Papacy may have been an interest in alchemy.[400] Now Böhmer, in discussing Gerard of York as a possible author of the Tractates, had taken note of the interest of that archbishop in astrology, and had suggested a connection between his interest in the occult and the fatalistic determinism of several of the Tractates.[401] By the same token, the manifest fascination experienced

[398] Migne, P. L., CLXIII, epp. 178, 179, the latter already cited above in connection with Turold.

[399] William was suspended altogether three times: 1081–, 1093–, 1100–1105. Böhmer, Kirche, p. 187.

[400] "Guglielmo arcivesco di Rouen ed Arnaldo da Villanova," Archivum Romanicum, V (1921), pp. 260–63.

Frati discovered in the University Library of Bologna in MS 457 an old French version of the Perfectum magisterium commonly attributed to Arnold of Villeneuve (1235–1313). On the otherwise blank *verso* of the second leaf is written: "Livre de Mr Guillaume de Rouen imprimé en latin sous le nom d'Arnault: Perfecti magisterii." On comparing the Latin with the French, Frati discovered, indeed, a marked correspondence. The "Pere reverend" of what Frati considers the older text becomes however, "charissime fili" in the Latin which is dedicated to the king of Aragon. Frati holds that the alchemical treatise was originally addressed to the reverend father, William Bona Anima, and later reworked by Arnold. The conjecture is supported by the following *explicit*: "Ceste science fut accompli a Rouen, ville pres de Paris, le vendredi et de l'oeuvre mil ij^e seize et communiquée par le Mr Guille de Rouan." Since the second William of Rouen began his pontificate in 1274, Frati feels confident in dismissing the date 1216 as an anachronism not at all detracting from his theory of the interest taken by Bona Anima in alchemical seances as a supplementary reason for his bad relations with the Holy See.

[401] Kirche, pp. 262 f.; 207, n. 3.

It is of some interest in this connection that in J9/S Augustine is cited as a bishop who once held Manichaean views and who nevertheless had become a sainted bishop (p. 136). The allusion to Augustine is quite natural for so devoted an Augustinian as our Norman divine, but it suggests the possibility that he who is manifestly very well versed in the Augustinian corpus may have been for a while affected by the thought of the very Manichaeans whom Augustine was opposing in his anti-Manichaean writings. In any event our writer, who we have reason to believe was himself a bishop, is quite willing to admit that he has done something amiss but insists that that which God has given him (his clerical rank) cannot be

by the author of "De consecratione," as he considered the well-nigh magical potency of oils and chrisms in changing a king or bishop into an *alius vir*, might be connected with the newly discovered evidence, supposedly demonstrating Bona Anima's interest in alchemy.[402] Significantly, Alois Dempf has drawn our attention to the characteristic fusion of the natural and the supernatural in the thought of the Anonymous, particularly in the discussion of marriage, virginity, and predestination [403] in Tractates J25/L1 and J22/L2 and of the mystery of liturgical kingship in J24/L4.[404] This sense of the interpenetration of the natural and the divine is quite consonant with what we should expect from a cleric interested in occult science. If Frati's conjecture were sound in connecting his Bologna MS with Archbishop William, it would strengthen our hypothesis of William's authorship of our Tractates. Unfortunately, Frati's suggestion, however attractive and welcome as an enrichment of a meagre bibliography, does not hold up on close inspection.[405] But Paschal's reproof of Bona

---

taken from him. Cf. Hugh Williamson, The Arrow and the Sword (London, 1947), pp. 108 ff. on the possible Neo-Manichaeism and Margaret Murray, The God of the Witches (London, 1933), pp. 160 ff. on the witchery in the court of William Rufus.

[402] Oils and the guidance of the alchemist by the Holy Spirit are two matters which touch upon elements in our Tractates. See particularly Arnold's own (reworked?) Preface (lacking in Mangetus), Histoire littéraire, XXVIII (1881), pp. 82 ff. It is of some interest that J10/W: 224, *Quod si —** makes use of an alchemical image when comparing a king upon whom sacerdotal power has been conferred with livid lead turned into shining gold. I have elsewhere indicated, however, that this Tractate is almost certainly not from the hand of the author of the other Tractates of our Codex. See above, pp. 35 ff.

[403] See below, n. 499.

[404] The sense of the mystery and the magic of nature and the royal will and their interdependence manifest in the Greek Proverb, appended to "De consecratione," might be a point of contact between our Codex and Bona Anima's interest in alchemy.

[405] In the first place, an interest in alchemy in Rouen as early as the end of the eleventh century would in itself be quite extraordinary. Secondly, the French alchemical text which Frati holds to be prior to Arnold's Latin adaptation is not in its present form of the eleventh century. Thirdly, it is not credible that the vernacular would have been used for so learned a subject. Fourthly, when one compares Frati's French version with Latin alchemical compendia containing the same sequence of materials, it becomes clear that Frati has been misled. In Lehigh University alchemical compendium MS 1, the Latin *explicit* which corresponds to the French of Frati's MS 457 quoted above, n. 400, is the following: "Ars hec fuit completa et perfecta apud *Romum* prope Parisio die parasceue sancte anno domini 1216 et communicata per magistrum Guillermum reverendo archiepiscopo Remensi." Described in Osiris, VI (1939), American alchemical MS 57, especially

Anima's many *pravitates* may well indicate something more than perverse insubordination, namely, heresy. So construed Paschal's letter could account for the uniqueness of our Codex.[406]

In the same year 1106 we have a record [407] of the Archbishop's approval of a certain monastery's becoming a cell of Fécamp. And the following year we have a record of his ordination and benediction of the new abbot of Fécamp, Roger of Bayeux, and his participation in the dedication of the new building.[408] Apparently the Metropolitan and the monastery of Fécamp were at long last on good terms.

In the same year, 1107, Bona Anima ordained Ordericus priest. It is doubtless to some extent because of Ordericus' personal relationship with the Archbishop that we have the rather numerous details from the pontificate of William Bona Anima which we have been able to recount. On the occasion of Ordericus' ordination "great numbers of the clergy assembled at Rouen, and the household of Christ received happily an accession of nearly seven hundred clerks in orders of different degree." [409] The mass ordination took place on the Feast of St. Thomas the Apostle, a hundred and twenty priests and two hundred and forty-four deacons receiving orders. Pommeraye conjectures [410] that the mass ordination of 1107 may have been the occasion of William Bona

---

pp. 475, 503. *Apud Romum* is not *apud Rothomagum*, whatever it may be. Moreover, it is clear that William is *magister* and is distinguished from the archbishop. And the date tallies with that in the French. While Frati probably did not know of the Lehigh MS, he had himself described elsewhere a similar Latin MS containing the same material, which should have cautioned him against making so facile a conjecture. Ludovico Frati, "Indici dei codici latini conservati nella R. Biblioteca Universitaria di Bologna," Studi italiani di filologia classica, XVI (1908), MS 169, 12 and 13, p. 174.

[406] Heresy would 1) make plausible the strange combination in MS 415 of freethought, "spirituality," and *ex opere* sacramentalism, 2) help explain the later suspensions of Bona Anima and clarify the condition of the third papal restitution ("ut malos consiliarios, quorum instinctu multas pravitates incurristi, a tua familiaritate repellas," Paschal, ep. 178), 3) help account for the anonymity and uniqueness of the Codex since the writings of a thrice suspended prelate would not have been widely copied and preserved, and thus 4) account for the want of any identified literary remains surviving from the hand of one who was after all a learned, important, and beloved abbot and metropolitan in a flourishing and strategically important province.

[407] Gallia christiana, XI, Instrumenta, col. 127.

[408] Ordericus, op. cit., xi, 30.

[409] Ordericus, op. cit., xi, 30.

[410] Histoire de la cathédrale, p. 299.

Anima's letter to Ivo of Chartres, to which reference is made in the reply of the latter, Epistle 185.[411] It is just possible that Tractate J11/B11 reflects the controversy that appears to have raged when, by oversight or misrepresentation, a cleric was ordained to a higher degree before having passed through the usually required preliminary ones. The fact that Bona Anima himself wrote to Ivo of Chartres seeking canonical advice, shows that the problem had exercised the chapter of Rouen.[412]

Finally, there is the suggestive coincidence of the renowned magnanimity and kindliness of William (evidenced by the sobriquet *Bona Anima* and by Ordericus' description of him)[412a] and the recurrent emphasis in our Codex upon the Christ in all believers, upon love (notably in J31/B30, "De charitate"), upon forgiveness and Apostolic humility. Especially significant is the fact that the Matt. 25:41f. which is given prominence in William's writ for his foundation for the poor, the sick, and for pilgrims at Caen[413] appears with comparable prominence and intention in one of our Tractates.[413a]

---

[411] Migne, P. L., CLXII, col. 186.

[412] It is possible also that the several Tractates in the Codex which make light of the traditional sequence of ordination and the strict adherence to traditional formulas of ordination reflect the controversy of 1107. But the problem of faulty sequence in ordination had occupied several Norman synods before. Bessin, op. cit., p. 55, c. 9; p. 65, c. 11.

[412a] See above, n. 353.

[413] We have only three letters from the hand of William, none of them long enough nor of enough consequence to make a stylistic comparison with our Tractates possible. Migne, P. L., CLXII, epp. 7 and 98, coll. 650, 683 (to Lambert of Arras); Eadmer, Historia novorum, "Rolls Series," LXXXI, p. 38 (to Anselm). The message of only one of these might be brought into connection with our Codex. The brief ep. 7, after commending to Lambert a certain Richard ordained to the priesthood by William, continues: "Eum sub tui custodia nullis precor sinas subjacere vel lacerari terroribus." The terrors obscurely alluded to here suggest a possible connection with those mentioned in J9/S: 133 f.

A goodly number of charters are attested by William, some of which reveal something of his personal manner and temperament behind the diplomatic style. For instance, there is the capitulary act of St. Stephen's beginning, "Ego Willelmus, Cadomensis caenobii peccator abbas," which witnesses to William's concern to serve Christ (Matth. 25: 41 f.) by succoring the poor, the sick, and also pilgrims. Cartulary of St. Stephen's, ed. by Étienne Deville, "Notices," IV, Revue Catholique de Normandie, XV (1905), pp. 19 f. Cf. ibid., XIV (1904), p. 269. Cf. J24/A/W: 227, *Volo —** and J4/L3: 661, 23 f.

The parchment which records Archbishop William's turning over a certain church to St. Stephen's in Caen scarcely helps us in making stylistic comparisons. Lemarignier, op. cit., Pièce justificative III, p. 298. We do have, however, in

Such is the evidence in favor of William's authorship of the Codex. The fact that many events in the early life, the rule, and the pontificate of William Bona Anima are reflected in the Codex and the coordinate fact that no appreciable body of known writings [413] has survived from this moderately important preceptor, abbot, canonist, liturgist and archbishop tempt one to suggest that the diverse Tractates of our Codex, demonstrably the work of one writer, could be his.

As we have already noted, there have been two main deterrents to suggesting William as the author, despite the clear connection of many of the Tractates with the personal and administrative problems of his career: 1) that two of the Tractates allegedly deal with the English investiture question and one concerns the struggle between York and Canterbury, and 2) that one or two of the Tractates seem to be written in the Archbishop's defense rather than by the Archbishop himself.

Now the first objection can be easily removed both by the fact that the investiture Tractates use French, indeed Rouen, sources (the Robert Benedictional, for example) and the fact that Frenchmen less directly concerned with the English investiture controversy than a Norman wrote on the subject, namely, Ivo of Chartres and Hugh of Fleury. But more important than this, there is absolutely nothing in either Tractate to connect them with specifically English affairs. And as for the Tractate on the York-Canterbury dispute, we have already taken note of the impression it gives of remoteness from the scene. [414] It is not hard to imagine that the stout defender of the metropolitan dignity of Rouen against Lyons would, given the occasion, have taken the side of the metropolitan of York against Canterbury. The opportunity might have been afforded by the messengers of Thomas II sent to Normandy to make inquiries of friends, probably in Bay-

---

William's charter of exemption from episcopal jurisdiction granted to Bec, something more personal and more extended than most documents of this type. Migne, P. L., CL, coll. 552 f. The language and the concerns of this document are compatible with those of our Tractate, even if they do not positively support the Bona Anima hypothesis. But for the positive witness of this grant on another count, see below, p. 124.

[413a] J3/W: n. 734.

[414] See above, pp. 63.

eux, and of the King then in Normandy.[415] Or, if the Tractate was occasioned by the previous York-Canterbury controversy, that between Gerard and Anselm, it is possible that William Bona Anima would have taken an interest in the struggle of a former canon of Rouen. However this may be, the fact that one of the Tractates deals with an English matter can no longer be held prejudicial to a Rouen authorship for the entire Codex.

The second objection which has hitherto removed Archbishop William from consideration as a possible author of the Tractates is that he is described in the third person in the "Apologia archiepiscopi Rotomagensis" and elsewhere. But in Part II, Section 9, we showed that the third person might be explained by the desire to give an air of objectivity to the discussion.

Since on other grounds also we have already become reasonably certain that the author of our Codex could have been of episcopal rank it is a temptation to conclude that the *Pontifex Rothomagensis* of J2, J4, and J9 is William Bona Anima writing about himself. On this hypothesis, these *apologiae* have been made impersonal for greater effectiveness. It is most instructive to compare in this connection William's charter of episcopal exemption to Bec [416] with the "Apologia." Here also the writer moves from the first person singular, through the third person singular, to the first person plural and back again. Admittedly, this document from the hand of Archbishop William is in the official style of charters, but the quick shifts in grammatical person make more plausible, at least, the suggestion that the "Apologia" could be from the hand of Archbishop William, even though he is referred to in the third person. There can be no doubt that the "Apologia," written with great feeling, represents the corporate views of the

---

[415] Eadmer, Historia novorum, p. 204.

[416] Migne, P. L., CL, col. 553:

. . . *ego* . . . Willelmus, Dei gratia Rothomagensium archiepiscopus . . . decrev*i* . . . et propter salutem animae *m*eae, antecessorumque *m*eorum, necnon et successorum, conced*o* ut Ecclesia [Beccensis] . . . perpetuo sit libera ab omni episcopali exactione. . . . Si autem in eadem parochia talis causa orta fuerit . . . *archiepiscopus* ferrum judicii ad locum illum per ministros *suos* destinabit, judiciumque ibi coram *archiepiscopi* ministris portabitur. . . . In caeteris autem parochiis . . . hoc solum concessi*mus*, ut manu pastos suos laicos quietos habeat. . . . Haec autem ex consulto clericorum *nostorum* fecimus. Cf. another charter for Bec by William, 1106/7, C. Haskins, Norman Institutions, p. 293.

cathedral chapter, which would explain the predominantly collective "pro ipso apologeticum faciamus responsum."[417] But the ideas, the arguments, and even the style could very well be that of the learned canonist himself.

4. Conclusion as to Authorship

The reasonably assured results of the foregoing exploration are that the Tractates of Codex 415, with the exception of J10/W are the writings of one author (this, against Philipp Funk), that in consequence any generalizations based upon a supposed homogeneity of the Codex stand uncontested on this score (this, in favor of Alois Dempf, particularly), that the author thereof should henceforth be known as the *Anonymus Rothomagensis* (this, against Heinrich Böhmer), and that as an apparently responsible and highly placed ecclesiastic, the Anonymous is probably more representative of his generation (at least of his fellow clerics of the cathedral) than has been hitherto supposed (this, against Z. N. Brooke). Finally, we may say that the Anonymous is rightly considered in some ways a proto-Protestant of the Cranmer-Henrician type (this in favor of Gavin and Lapparent). On this we shall have more to say presently.

The Bona Anima hypothesis is strengthened by, or takes account of, every one of the eleven major clues established under Part Two: Behind Anonymity, including three which might seem to favor rival claimants to the honor. Clue 10, for example, concerning the festive Exordium of "De consecratione" which could be used to favor William Giffard since he was in attendance at the coronation of Henry I in 1100, may, with perhaps greater cogency, be construed in support of William Bona Anima's authorship for the reason, as we have seen, that it fits extraordinarily well into the ducal dedication in 1077 of St. Stephen's at Caen when Bona Anima was abbot. Similarly, clue 7 concerning the echoes of Paschal's letter on investiture, which points to William Giffard, retiring royal chancellor, can very well be made to support William Bona Anima's authorship of all our Tractates on investi-

---

[417] J4/L3: 656, 24 f. That after all, however, one person is primarily involved is betrayed obliquely in the query which is placed on the lips of the opponent (659, 15) and by the first person used in 680, 39.

ture in view of the three purely Norman investiture episodes brought to light with which our Archbishop was more or less connected and notably with the Paschal-Robert dispute. Finally, clue 9a concerning the peculiar prominence of Stephen in the "Apologia" which is the principal evidence pointing to Archdeacon Fulbert, can also be connected with our Archbishop's devotion to the saint over whose royal abbey at Caen he formerly ruled as abbot. Moreover, for neither Giffard nor Fulbert is there such external evidence as we have for Bona Anima with which to account for the topical diversity of a corpus demonstrably homogeneous in style and tendency. And as for chronology, Giffard appears to have left Rouen a little too soon and Fulbert to have arrived on the scene a little too late for either to account for the full range of the Tractates. Yet every piece of the Codex can be connected with the kindly priest's son William Bona Anima: archdeacon and pilgrim, teacher and abbot, liturgist and canonist, builder and preacher; beloved metropolitan thrice suspended by Gregory VII, Urban II, and Paschal II; ally or foe of Lanfranc, Anselm, Ivo, and Hugh of Lyons; friend and supporter of William I, Robert, and Philip I. Unfortunately, there is no unequivocal internal or external evidence which could make certain our ascription of the Tractates to him.

If Archbishop William Bona Anima is the most likely author of the Codex, his archdeacon, Fulbert, is the next most probable. Several of the points used in favor of the Archbishop could be used, indeed, with almost equal cogency in favor of his chief Archdeacon, for many of the matters we have just taken up would have concerned the entire chapter, of which Fulbert was for a number of crucial years the able spokesman. Some of the Tractates may indeed have been collaborative. Surely an author who had access to the cathedral archives and took such a commanding place in the affairs of his time and who was, withal so well informed in canon law and so well versed in liturgy, is to be found among those in the cathedral of whom we have some notices in the contemporaneous records. And if one is constrained to attach especial importance to the reflection in "De consecratione" of Paschal's epistle to Henry I and remains unimpressed by the extent of the purely Norman-French investiture episodes, then clearly, William Giffard is a much more likely author than a hypothetical former canon of Rouen in the entourage of the Bishop of Hereford, later Archbishop of York.

Provisionally, then, we may say that to the two French clerics who contributed to the literature of the English investiture controversy, Ivo of Chartres and Hugh of Fleury, we may add a third Frenchman, the Anonymous of Rouen. The three were neighbors and there is some evidence that each knew of, and came to terms with, the thought of the other. However this may be, it is clear that the fact that the Anonymous may have dealt with the English investiture question does not alone qualify him to rank as an English publicist. His home was Normandy. His sources were Continental. It is even possible that "De consecratione" and "De Romano pontifice" bear as much on the French and the Norman investiture problems under Philip and Robert, occasioned by the disputes over Daimbert of Sens, Flambard in Lisieux and Turold of Bayeux, as upon the English controversy under Henry. And at least an indirect interest in the imperial-papal struggle is indicated.[418]

To the bearing of the whole theology of the Anonymous of Rouen on his conception of the relationship of Church and State and to a fresh evaluation thereof we may now turn.

PART IV

REGNUM AND *SACERDOTIUM* IN THE THOUGHT OF THE ANONYMOUS OF ROUEN

Even apart from the specifically ecclesio-political Tractates, the thought of the Anonymous of Rouen is markedly "royalist." The prevailing imagery is royal rather than sacerdotal. Christ as

---

[418] It will be remembered that though dedicated to Henry, Hugh of Fleury's Tractate may well have been intended to answer the problems posed in the Empire. Sackur, op. cit., p. 375. The Anonymous expressly mentions the emperor at one point in connection with coronation, J28/L5: 685, 33 f.: "Et hęc quidem sublimis et gloriosa investitura est, qua Deus *imperatorem* sive regem investit, ut habeat potestatem celitus datam super omnes hominis. . . ." Throughout "De consecratione," the references to the Roman emperors may be in part explained by the writer's interest in the Empire of his own day.

rex et sacerdos is divinely King and only humanly a Priest. Upon this distinction between *Christus Rex* and *christus sacerdos* the political theology of our Norman divine can be made to rest as we assemble it from the diverse homiletical musings, publicist polemics, and theological *parerga* of Codex 415. We shall begin with his Christology.

1. *Christology*: *Christus per naturam, Christus per gratiam*

Jesus of Nazareth was, according to the Anonymous, Christ by grace in respect to his human nature and Christ by nature in respect to the Incarnating Presence. There were thus in Jesus of Nazareth not simply two Natures but also two "Christs," the *christus per gratiam*, his anointed humanity and the *Christus per naturam*, his Divine Nature.[419] Herein lay his claim to uniqueness as King of kings. Although the sacerdotal function of *Christus-christus* is made by the Anonymous to correspond to his humanity, nevertheless even in this priestly rôle he was Priest according to the order of Melchizedek, the King of righteousness: [420]

Melchisedech enim interpretatur rex iusticię. Non enim secundum ordinem leviticum, sed secundum ordinem regis iusticię factus est sacerdos. Unde manifestum est, quod sacerdotium Christi ab ordine regis iusticię ducit exemplum, quoniam et ipse Christus rex est iusticię, qui ab ęterne regnat, et regnabit in ęternum et ultra. Qui sacerdos dicitur

[419] In contrast for example, Chrysostom asserts against the Marcionites that only the humanity of Christ was anointed. Migne, P. G., LXIII, col. 29: "ὅτι ἡ θεότης οὐ χρίεται, 'αλλ' ἡ ανθρωπότης." Lancelot Andrewes seems to combine the thoughts of Chrysostom and the Anonymous. The way in which the (episcopal) *sacerdotium*, newly recovered in the English seventeenth century, was fused with the Stuart *regnum* in the heat of resisting the pressure of the Puritans is best represented in the writings of the Bishop of Winchester. Of all English writers examined who might have been influenced by our Tractate, he is significantly the most reminiscent of the Anonymous. Andrewes makes "Christus" preëminently a royal designation. Jesus was Christ because he was born in the royal line of David. Insofar as Jesus was the Christ he was human. "God cannot be anointed, man may." Yet in Heaven God is King and Christ his Eternal Heir. Thus in the Incarnation an Eternal *Christus* became incarnate in a human *christus*, Jesus of the line of David. Works, Anglo-Catholic Library (Oxford, 1841), I, pp. 76 ff. This is almost the phraseology of "De consecratione" in which Jesus Christ is in effect not simply a *Deus-homo* but a *Christus-christus*. Cf. Jerome quoted in the Anonymous' Appendix, below, p. 232, III, 20, x. Cf. n. 666 below.

[420] Jerome, De nominibus Hebraicis: "Melchisedec, rex iustus." Migne, P. L., XXIII, col. 826. Cf. Isidore, Etymologiae, vii, 6, 25.

in ęternum, non ultra. Neque enim in ęterno vel ultra ęternum sacerdotium erit necessarium.[421]

Forcing the texts, the Anonymous is insisting that Christ as the true Melchizedek, though King forever, will be Priest only up to eternity ("in ęternum") but not beyond into eternity ("non ultra"), on the ground that within eternity ("ęterno") the sacerdotal office will no longer be necessary.[422] In other words, even Christ's priestly rôle was provisional only. It was royal-priestly, the sacerdotality destined to be fully assimilated to royalty. Moreover, because this rôle pertained only to his humanity, Christ was regal in this respect by grace. The purpose in the Eternal Christ's being made (*factus*) *sacerdos* in Jesus the Man (who thereby became a *christus per gratiam*), and offering up this anointed humanity, as a Priest, was to redeem mankind, so that men might come to *rule* with him in the Kingdom above. Clearly, he a King did not become incarnate and die to make men priests in a heavenly *sacerdotium*, but to make them co-heirs and joint rulers with himself in the heavenly *regnum*. It was as Creator-King of the Universe that Christ descended as *sacerdos* to draw unto himself a *regale sacerdotium*.[423]

[421] J24/L4: 663, 8 ff. Cf. Jerome, Tractatus in librum Psalmorum: "Non dixit secundum ordinem Aaron, sed Melchisedech." Ed. by G. Morin, Anecdota Maredsolano, III: I, pp. 45, 7 f.; 201, 10 ff.

[422] This idea may be dependent upon a homily of Chrysostom: "Βασιλεὺς μὲν γὰρ ἦν ἀεί, ἱερεὺς δὲ γέγονεν, . . . ὅτε τὴν θυσίαν προσήγαγεν." Migne, P. G., LXIII, col. 103. The significance of Chrysostom's interpretation is pointed out by Giuseppe Martini, "Regale sacerdotium," Archivio della R. Deputazione romana di Storia patria, LXI (1938), 47. Chrysostom was preaching against various heretics who had seen in Melchizedek a theophany. Insisting on the fully human character of the priestking of Jerusalem, Chrysostom was at pains to distinguish between the bloody sacrifice of the Aaronic priesthood from the unbloody sacrifice according to the priesthood of Melchizedek. Martini carries the history of the interpretation of Melchizedek far beyond Bardy, but unfortunately when he comes to the eleventh century he feels it beyond the scope of his historic commentary on the sources of the Encyclical Quas primas (Christus Rex), 1925, to discuss "l'idea 'laica' del *regale sacerdotium*," as for example in the Anonymous, whom he mentions in passing. Pp. 179 f. It is to be noted further that Ambrosiaster's *tractatus* on Melchizedek makes much use of the concept of *per naturam* and *vicarius*. For further bibliography on Ambrosiaster see below, n. 584.

[423] J24/L4: 667, 14 ff.:
Qui etiam secundum quod rex est, [the Eternally Royal Christ] creavit omnia, regit omnia, et homines simul gubernans et angelos salvat; secundum vero quod sacerdos est, homines tantum redemit, ut secum regnare faciat. Hęc enim est tota intentio, qua sacerdos factus est, et se ipsum obtulit in sacrificium, ut homines

The Eternally Royal Christ as Creator-King becomes at several points in the Tractates indistinguishable from God the Father.[424] The Royal Christ, "non creatus, non inferior vel diversus a Patre, sed equalis et unus [425] cum Patre," is clearly distinguished from Jesus the *sacerdos*, a christ by grace through the Royal Christ's assumption of his humanity, "*factus* secundum ordinem Melchisedech et *creatus* et ideo minor Patre." [426] The Two *Christi* Christology of the Anonymous allows him to subordinate the historic Jesus Christ to God while seeming to be loyal to the Two Natures Christology of Chalcedon, for he insists upon the consubstantiality of the Royal Son and the Father. But in effect, the Eternal Christ has become the Father, or at least the superior, of Jesus Christ and the latter is expressly *factus* and *creatus* in-

---

regni sui et potestatis regię faceret esse participes. Regnum enim cęlorum ubique scripturarum promittit fidelibus, nusquam autem sacerdotium.

For Christ as Creator, cf. King Alfred's Dooms, F. Liebermann, ed., Gesetze, pp. 26 f.: "In six days Christ has made heaven and earth."

The Anglo-Saxon and Norse tendency toward Christocentricity is discussed and documented by William Chaney, Israel and England: Old Testament Influence on Anglo-Saxon England.

[424] The Father even takes on the "royal" function of Christ as Bridegroom of the Church. This may be an intended elaboration of Cyprian's formula about God as Father and the Church as Mother. J4/L3: 659, 37 f.: "Ipsa [the Church] etenim Dei Patris erat ac per hoc filiorum Dei mater merito debet nominari." Cf. J3/W: 221; J4/L3, n. 244; J22(26)/L2: 652, 44; J24/L4: 667, 5 ff. (quoted below, p. 177); J25/L1: 648, 2 ff.; J28/L5: 682, 32 ff.; 684, 11 ff.; 685, 31 ff. For a further discussion of the conflation of the Paternal and the Filial image, see below, p. 177.

A vivid impression of the distinction between the Exalted, Eternal Son and Incarnate Christ is gained by a glance in E. G. Millar, English Illuminated Manuscripts (Paris, 1926), p. 77, Pl. 24b. The illumination is discussed by E. Kantorowicz, "The Quinity of Winchester," Art Bulletin, XXIX (1947), pp. 73 ff. This illumination from New Minister in Winchester (dated circa 1012–1020), pictures the Father and the Eternal Son as identical, seated figures facing each other as in high converse while to the right of the Two is seated the Virgin Queen holding in her arms the Infant Jesus. Resting on her crown is the Dove whose head is haloed with a diminutive form of the cross-halo that surrounds the heads of the Father and the Eternal Son. In the mouth of Hell below the seated "Quinity" are Arius, Satan, and Judas in chains. Arius is there doubtless for having dishonored the Eternal Son, Judas for having dishonored the Incarnate Son, Satan for being the Adversary of God the Father.

[425] Version B has the more acceptable *unum*.

[426] J24/L4: 667, 10 ff.:

Christus enim Deus et homo, verus et summus rex et sacerdos. Rex est, sed ex eternitate divinitatis, non factus, non creatus, non inferior vel diversus a Patre, sed equalis et unus cum Patre. Sacerdos vero est ex assumptione humanitatis, factus secundum ordinem Melchisedech et creatus et ideo minor Patre.

Here follows the description of the rule of Christ the Creator-King quoted above, n. 423.

stead of the credal *natus* and *genitus*. The Anonymous' phrase, "tota intentio, qua *sacerdos factus* est,"[427] should be compared with Anselm's "cur Deus homo."

The extent to which the Anonymous succeeds in severing the "sacerdotal" Jesus of Nazareth from the Eternal Royal Christ is most apparent in his projection into the time of Jesus, of the relations between the bishop and the king which the Anonymous felt should obtain in his own century. That his Christology of the *Earthly* Jesus was "low" becomes astonishingly clear in a passage concerning the duties of subjects to their king. The Anonymous, regarding all kings who have been anointed as christs and even gods, is prepared to call also pagan kings *"christi,"* (perhaps supposing that they were anointed) as for example, the Roman emperors. With this in mind, it is instructive to learn what the Anonymous regards as the proper demeanor of Jesus, *christus per gratiam* and *sacerdos* according to the order of Melchizedek, over against the pagan emperor, also a *"christus" per gratiam*. Now inasmuch as the Eternal *Christus per naturam* was, according to the Anonymous, incarnate in Jesus, *christus per gratiam* we are a little unprepared for the Rouen divine's utter subjection of Jesus Christ to Tiberius *"Christus."* This the Anonymous grounds in Jesus' teaching and example.[428] Jesus enjoined obedience to Caesar, that is, to the office, not to the individual Caesar, who

---

[427] In contrast to this predominantly *royal*-priestly conception of the Atonement the Anonymous yields also one specimen of the exemplary theory of the Atonement, J31/B30: 485:
Passus enim pro nobis, reliquit nobis exemplum, ut sequamur vestigia eius, ut, si expedit, ponamus animas nostras pro fratribus nostris, quia ipse pro nobis animam suam posuit.

[428] The Anonymous discussing the tribute money, asks, J24/L4: 671, 30 ff.:
Annon et ipse [Jesus Christ], qui est caput totius ęcclesię et Petri magister et dominus et hostium ęcclesię et Petri magister et dominus et hostium cęlestis ovilis summusque pontifex, ostendit suo tam verbo quam exemplo regiam potestatem esse precellentem et omnes illi debere esse subditos? verbo quo dicit: "Reddite, quę sunt cęsaris cęsari et quę sunt Dei Deo"; exemplo, quia ipse cęsari tributum reddidit et Petro, ut hoc idem faceret pręcepit. "Reddite," inquit, "quę sunt cęsaris cęsari," non quę sunt Tyberii Tyberio. Reddite potestati, non personę. *Persona enim nequam, sed iusta potestas.* Iniquus Tyberius, sed bonus cęsar. Reddite ergo non personae nequam, non iniquo Tyberio, sed iuste potestati et bono cęsari quę sua sunt. Et ut hoc opere compleret, ait Petro: "Vade ad mare. . . . da eis pro me et te." "Da," inquit, "pro me et te, iuste potestati et bono cęsari, cui secundum hominem subditi sumus." . . . Iustum quippe erat, ut humana infirmitas divinę subderetur potestati. *Christus namque secundum hominem tunc infirmus erat, cęsaris vero potestas divina.*

might indeed be iniquitous; and he himself set an example [429] in submitting to Tiberius.

Previously the Anonymous had said that the humanity of Jesus Christ is *christus per gratiam*, while his divinity is from Eternity *Christus per naturam*. Here, while he does not hark back to this distinction, the Anonymous asserts by implication that the *christus per gratiam*, Jesus, was less than the emperor who was surely no more than a *christus per gratiam*. This subordination, the Anonymous declares, was justified insofar as Jesus was human (*secundum hominem*), but it is also *secundum hominem* that Jesus Christ was *sacerdos*. Therefore, Jesus must have been subordinate to Tiberius *christus rex* as a *christus sacerdos*. Jesus Christ on earth was by clear implication at this point only a *sacerdos*, having emptied himself of his royalty which was visible during the period of the Incarnation not in himself but in Tiberius! [430] In sum:

On the "high" Christology of the Eternal Christ, the Anonymous grounds the power of rulers. Thanks to his two Christologies the Anonymous' political theory, while seemingly *Christo*centric, will tend to be actually *Theo*centric, because the Person of the Humbled Christ has been reduced in significance and may no longer be said to exercise a predominant influence over the conception and image of the God of the Universe.

On the "low" Christology of the Humble Nazarene *sacerdos* who had put off or rather concealed his royal nature, the Anonymous bases clerical authority. But the dichotomy is not so simple as this schematization suggests, for in addition to their sacerdotal or sacrificial competence by virtue of their apostolicity, bishops possess also a derivative regal (*regere*) or jurisdictional power. To an analysis of episcopal competence and power we turn.

2. *Episcopal Authority*

In his opposition to papal encroachment, our high-ranking Norman publicist divine was giving expression to his major con-

---

The whole thought is dependent on Ambrosiaster (Pseudo-Augustine), Quaestiones Veteris et Novi Testamenti. A. Souter, ed., A Study of Ambrosiaster (Oxford, 1905), p. 63.

[429] Cf. the quotation from the Hibernensis (Jerome) in the Anonymous' Appendix below, p. 232, III, 20, x.

[430] The Anonymous acknowledges that individual Caesars were *membra diaboli*. J6/S: 130.

viction of the parity of all bishops,[431] for, as we have already had occasion to see,[432] he believed that all bishops have the authority of Peter, deriving it from Christ by virtue of their confession of faith in him, and by virtue of their standing in a spiritual succession with the Apostles whose office they discharge in the measure that they emulate their character and share their Apostolic faith. And the most Apostolic of all was the Apostle *par excellence*, Paul (rather than Peter).[433] Significantly, our author is devotedly and authentically Pauline, especially, as we shall presently note in his Christ mysticism, his adherence to the doctrines of election and freedom from the Law, and in his acclaim of love as the preëminent Christian virtue.

The Anonymous was ambivalent in his conception of the clerical office. He insisted that ordination conferred an indelible character upon the cleric, of which he might not be deprived,[434] but he was equally convinced that this indelible character should become visible, if not in saintliness,[435] at least in a markedly superior quality of Christian life:

Consecratio enim sanctificat et iustificat . . . mutat et efficit meliorem, et si non mutat nec efficit meliorem, non est consecratio.[436]

On the one hand the Anonymous trusts in the *ex opere* character of episcopal consecration, on the other hand he is distrustful of

[431] J2, J4, J5, J12, J23a, J24d, J29. Any legitimate differences as between bishops and archbishops is due to human necessity and not to divine institution, e.g., J23a/B23a: 476:
Unde etiam consequens est, ut episcopi qui vices Petri et omnium iuxta haec ipsa aequales esse debeant, quos divina institutio, sed necessitas tollendorum scismatum facit inaequales.
Cf. J4/L3: 660, 37 ff. where the blame for schism is placed on Rome: The source of this idea of inequality is Jerome. Cf. J2/B2: J4/L3: 660, 31 ff. But our Norman ecclesiastic sees no human reason for any ranks above archbishop like the primatial dignity. J2/B2: 445.
[432] See above, pp. 67 ff.
[433] J23a/B23a: 477, iii.
[434] J16, J17. In J11/B11 he says that obduracy on the part of a wayward cleric does justify suspension and unfrocking (p. 455, iii).
[435] There is indeed a slight tendency in the Anonymous to think of ordination as a saving sacrament with the consequence that to be ordained is to be more certain of salvation, for he is fully committed to the doctrine of predestination which explains for him the preponderance of reprobates who have been unaffected by the sacraments. J13a/B13a: 463: ". . . in populo pauci sunt electi, pauci membra Christi."
[436] J18/B18: 473, v. Cf. J14/B14: 468, iii. The writer is here talking of bishops.

episcopal power when it lacks the marks of apostolicity, namely charity and humility. In part his is the ancient problem of the relationship between official authority and charismatic power. He would like to make them one but finally resorts to the doctrine of predestination to explain theologically the discrepancy of which he is aware, between power and goodness. But his effort to make episcopal consecration with the chrism of the Holy Spirit at once "official," spiritual (in two senses), and elective (in two senses) is surely remarkable. Spiritual = 1) by the authority and with the sanction of the Holy Spirit through unction and 2) Apostolic, charitable, humble, other worldly, wanting in goods and external power. The first meaning is cosmic-sacramental, the second is ethical. Elective = 1) by the will of the duke or king or chapter and 2) by divine predestination or divine right, the very fact that one is a bishop being a presumption in favor of divine vocation.[437]

The distinctively Apostolic "unction" was spiritual (*unctio spiritualis*), God's bestowal of the grace of the Spirit.[438] It was invisible, whereas the "regal" aspect of episcopal consecration was indeed visible, the chrism. The Anonymous does not deny the significance of the Apostolic aspect of ordination, but its effect is secondary. In any event its presence is made known by the spirit of charity and its lapse is evident in a worldly spirit. In sum, the bishop's ordination is indelible insofar as it is regal, that is "messianic" or "christic." It is subject to impairment or extinction insofar as it is Apostolic, that is, dependent upon the maintenance of charity and humility.

The seeming ambiguities of the status and function of the *sacerdotium*, particularly the episcopate in our Tractates is not, if my analysis is correct, due to a heterogeneity of authorship, nor to a radical inconsistency in the author's mind, but to the fact that he has indeed two intersecting conceptions of the episcopal office, governmental (*regere*) and sacerdotal (*conficere Deum*).

---

[437] Cf. the later view of divine right kingship of say a Cranmer, according to whom royal birth is itself the manifestation of divine election to kingship, popular election being completely replaced by divine election. Here election as a redemptive concept (predestination to salvation) has given way to election as simple pre-ordination.

[438] See quotation below, pp. 181, 198.

The one depends upon anointment whereby the bishop becomes in effect a little christ, but by that token also as it were, a little king.[439] The other aspect of the episcopal office depends upon the possession and sustained expression of charity equated with apostolicity. It is spiritual. Love and humility bulk large in our divine's characterization of the sacerdotal rôle, since as we shall presently note his "laicization" and interiorization of sacrifice deprives the *sacerdos* of any distinctive sacrificatory function except that of bearing the image of the Humbled Christ. The efficacy of episcopal unction in its *jurisdictional* significance is seldom called into question. The fact that the words and forms used in the Primitive Church have most certainly been lost does not deprive the current ritual of potency.[440] For it is the *Eternal* Christ and the ever present Holy Spirit who impart the power to these consecratory *words*, not their quite dubious historicity. Their validation is not from the historic Christ working through the Apostles, but from the Heavenly Christ, acting through his temporal vicar in investiture and from the Holy Spirit working through the consecratory chrism. Although the *external* words used in consecration are undoubtedly different from the original Dominical and Apostolic benedictions, the Anonymous can appeal to the *inward, eternal* Word.[441] The Word of God (the Eternal Christ) effects the changes wrought in consecration, independent of the audible words of Apostolic tradition.[442] Christ bestows his

---

[439] The "royal" character of the episcopate will be enlarged upon in Section 8c below on the greater and the lesser king.

[440] J18/B18: 471:
. . . non his verbis consecratus est [the first bishop], quibus nunc consecrantur episcopi. Neque enim verba haec adhuc inventa erant, neque hic ritus consecrationis adhuc repertus erat, nec sacramentum olei et chrismatis adhuc institutum erat. Sed neque apostoli vel, qui ordinabantur ab eis, coronas adhuc gestabant in capitibus. . . .

[441] J18/B18: 471:
. . . quoniam verba illa, quibus apostoli in consecratione [the first] episcopi usi sunt, non ab homine neque per hominem, sed a Christo Deo et homine acceperunt, cuius verba omnipotentia sunt ad omnia, quae ipse vult efficiendum, quia non hominis tantum, sed etiam Dei omnipotentis verba sunt. . . . Quamvis et si Christi verba loquatur et dicat, non tamen eadem verba aliquid operantur, nisi per eum, cui Deus illa dedit. . . .
Cf. J24/L4: 667, 37 ff.

[442] J18/B18: 472, iv: "Sed si verba illa essent consecratio, pereuntibus verbis periret consecratio."

vicarial power efficaciously as he wills from on high to a particular person, otherwise consecration carries no power. Moreover the effects even of valid consecration vanish when God is no longer in the heart of a priest.[443] Thus, so it would seem, even the governmental or regal power of the bishop may be lost, no less than the sacrificatory, but all this is much clearer to the Anonymous when he is thinking of Rome or Lyons than when thinking of Rouen!

One of the important governmental functions of a bishop is his right to control the monasteries within his own diocese. Since, in general, the monks were loyal to Rome, we should expect the Anonymous to find good reasons to subject them to the control of the bishop, and this he does. He quotes Romans 13:1 ff. on obedience to the higher powers and his favorite combination, Matthew 10:40 and Luke 10:16, applying it to abbots:

Ex quibus verbis consequitur, ut abbates non recipiant Christum, si non recipiunt episcopum, et spernant Christum, si suum spernant episcopum, et tangunt pupillam oculi Dei, dum episcopum suum tangunt.[444]

Moreover, granting special exemptions to abbots, the Pope causes the (diocesan) *"regnum"* to be divided against itself.[445] The Anonymous appeals several times to the Mosaic injunction to observe filial piety. A daughter (a monastery) should show reverence toward her mother (the diocesan church). When the Pope interferes by means of privileges of exemption he fosters filial impiety. In this connection the Anonymous places the bishop in the same category as the royal *christus*, not only in ruling over a diocesan *"regnum"* but more significantly, in generating as a "spiritual father" monasteries through the Evangel of Jesus Christ.[446]

In this same important section of "De Romano pontifice," the Anonymous not only speaks of the bishop as a father, but in vindicating the bishop's right to rule the abbots of his diocese and

---

[443] Ibid., 473:
Sed si Deus esset consecratio, quicunque Deum non haberet vel eum perderet, consecrationem utique non haberet vel perdendo Deum illam sine dubio perderet, ac sic consecratus esse desineret.

[444] J28/L5: 682, 14 ff. The argument here is a deft application of Pseudo-Isidore. See above, n. 212.

[445] Ibid., 683, 13 ff. This appeal to Luke 11:17 is a hallmark of the Tractates.

[446] See quotation in following note.

to demand a profession of loyalty from them, the Anonymous grounds the episcopal authority in God the Father whom he tends here as elsewhere to assimilate to the Eternal Royal Christ. In this passage the Anonymous bases episcopal authority insofar as it is *regal* upon the same divine Person who, we shall see, also sustains the royal *christus*. He is asking rhetorically whether the abbots in maligning and disobeying their bishop are not doing the same to God the Father and Christ by the power of whose Evangel they have been [re-]generated.[447]

Since the *governmental* authority of the bishop is like that of the king grounded in the same Eternal Royal Christ virtually one with God the Father, and since the bishop is like the king a *christus* and a *deus*, on a lower scale generating churches (monasteries) and governing "kingdoms" (diocesan churches) like the Royal Progenitor of the Elect in Heaven [448] and the *christus Domini* on the throne, it will be presently our task to show how what we might style the diocesan *regulus et sacerdos apostolicus* is related to the national *rex et sacerdos*, for such is one formula for expressing in the thought of the Anonymous the age-long problem of the relationship between "Church" and "State." But before taking up this matter we shall want to know what happens to his episcopal theory when dealing with the Bishop of Rome.

3. *The Pope: Rome and Jerusalem*

Wanting a truly Apostolic character, an ecclesiastic, the Anonymous insists, need not be obeyed! Indeed, it is a meritorious act to resist the demands of spurious prelates who are in truth members of Satan: "Nam qui talibus irrogat contumelias, honorem Deo tribuit et gloriam." [449] In this mood our Norman cleric is a kind of neo-Donatist although the resistance which he advocates

---

[447] J28/L5: 682, 32 ff.
An non vero abbates patri maledicunt eundemque persequuntur . . . , dum verba dicunt et opus faciunt, quibus Dei Patris ordinationem sacratissimam et decretum cęleste et opus sanctum male destruere quęrunt, dum vicarium eius [God the Father's] episcopum, qui et ipse spiritualis pater est (quoniam per evangelium in Christo Iesu ipse eos genuit), potestate et vicibus, qua ei Christus tribuit, privare conantur, et illum, qui oculus Dei est, tangunt ac per hoc pupillam oculi Dei tangunt . . . ?
[448] See below, Section 5.
[449] J24d/W: 236.

is directed more against the jurisdiction of hireling bishops than against their sacerdotal ministrations. Popular resistance to episcopal jurisdiction is discountenanced.[450] Non-obedience is exclusively an *episcopal* (or royal) privilege over against pretentious primates and the Pope. For them to excommunicate an anointed bishop is to presume to make an Apostolic word undo the Word of God:

Quos cum excommunicat, apostolos Christi et christos Domini excommunicat et ita et unctionem et sanctificationem eorum in irritum redigit et ecclesiarum, quibus presunt, capita amputat, quod absque interitu corporum nequit fieri.[451]

Since Christ is the Supreme Pontiff, as long as a bishop obeys him he need not fear excommunication from the Pope:

Et si propterea aliquem [prelate] excommunicaverit, quod ei [the Pope] in talibus [the un-Christlike demands of the Pope] obediens non sit, si in aliis omnibus Deo obediat, non vereatur, sed audiat summum pontificem, qui omnibus sibi obedientibus dicit: "Ecce ego vobiscum sum omnibus diebus usque ad consummationem seculi." [452]

Anointment as a christ is the most valid claim to inviolability which a bishop can own. It imparts to him an authority which comes from the Eternal Royal Christ much more directly and palpably than does his purely sacerdotal competence from the Earthly Christ by way of an Apostolic succession which can be interfered with by the Pope.

The Anonymous does not deny the universality of the visible

---

[450] J13a/B13a: 463: "His [the people, most of whom are reprobates anyway] igitur invitis si detur episcopus, non est contra regulam veritatis vel decorem iusticie."

The Anonymous also holds that the disrespect of a serf for his earthly lord is irreverence for his heavenly Lord. J3/W: 220, *Sic et —**. At the same time the Anonymous is manifestliy distressed that "abjecti humiles contempti et sub colaphis potentium vivant." Ibid., p. 216, *Econtra —**.

[451] J28/L5: 684, 8 ff. Elsewhere he says:
A quo nulla excommunicatione poterit sibi obedientem separare. Sicut enim absolutione sua non potest efficere, ut membrum diaboli fiat membrum Christi, ita sua excommunicatione non potest efficere, ut membrum Christi fiat membrum diaboli. Ibid., 681, 39 ff

[452] Ibid., 36 ff. The quotation in n. 451 is a continuation of this passage.

Church [453] under the Pope as a kind of first among episcopal equals. But he holds that the Church of Rome falls into two assemblies: the Church of Satan, appearing to bulk exceedingly large and visible and the Church of Christ, to whom a kind of obedience is due out of love to God,[454] but he minimizes their authority over Christians outside of Rome to the point of extinguishing it by denying to the Pope the office of spokesmanship of even the Roman saints. Since it is not feasible to obey an entire Church, one must to be sure obey a person. But is the Pope to be obeyed as *papa* or as *homo*? This characteristic device of the Anonymous to distinguish between the office and the incumbent is a trick whereby he can either enhance an office and defend it even when the incumbent is personally unworthy (as he does in defending the goodness of Caesar despite the personal wickedness of Tiberius) or he can, as in the case of the papal office, speak respectfully of the Pope and yet boldly, if not brazenly, against the Gregorys, Urbans, and Paschals. In Tractate J1/B1, "An summus pontifex sit iuditio subiectus," the Anonymous distinguishes between the *pontifex*, the *homo*, and the *peccator*. He asseverates that, only the *peccator*, to be sure, can be judged, and he, by saintly Christians and that the *pontifex* may be judged only by his predecessors because "ab inferiori ordine nullatenus debet iudicare de ordine." [455] Elsewhere the Anonymous slyly cites I Peter on the dutifulness of Christians toward the emperor, and thus, it is Pope Peter and not the Anonymous who condemns the reigning Pontiff. In Tractate J29/L6, "De obediendo Romano pontifice," the Anonymous distinguishes between the Pope as *apostolus* and as *homo*. He should be obeyed as *apostolicus*, but that should mean *missus a Christo*. If the Pope's demands are

---

[453] Cf. J25/L2: 655, 10 ff.:
Cuius cumque nationis sint, cuiuscumque conditionis, in Christo unum sunt, id est unum corpus Christi, et unus cum eo spiritus, ac sic unus Christus, caput, corpus et spiritus sunt.
The Church as the universal Body of Christ is prominent in the Tractates.

[454] J30/L6: 687, 37 ff.:
Nos tamen paucis electis et sanctis filiis Dei qui sunt Rome, exhibere debemus reverentiam, sed qualem Pater noster qui est in celis precipit et vult, ut exhibeamus fratribus nostris in caritate, non in exactione, propter Deum, non propter seculi fastum.

[455] P. 437.

unapostolic they need not be heeded.[456] The Anonymous makes very cogent the argument for apostolicity. If the Pope claims to speak by Apostolic authority he should bear in mind the significance of *apostolus*. Such a one will always have among his most authentic credentials an Apostolic, that is to say, a charitable spirit.[457] The Anonymous haughtily denies the usefulness of the Roman "Apostle" in already Christian lands, since his sole legitimate activity beyond the diocesan administration of Rome, is missions, and suggests that he turn his attention to the pagans who are not in possession of the Scriptures.[458]

Obviously, to be truly Pope in the thought of the Anonymous, the Bishop of Rome must be so purely Apostolic in his way of life that his effectiveness is confined to moral suasion like the lowly Earthly Christ who was not of this world. Only insofar as he is Christlike in his injunctions, is the Pope authoritative and only as he refrains from giving instructions is he Apostolic! Like the later Spiritual Franciscans, the Anonymous decries the wealth and judicial presumption of the Papal Church. He would deprive it of both judicial power and possessions. Concerning possessions he says: " . . . membrum Christi non est qui . . . non renunciat omnibus, que possidet." [459] And concerning jurisdiction:

[456] J29/L6: 687, 7 ff.:
Ergo in eo, quod apostolicus est, obedientia illi exhibenda est, id est in eo, quod missus est, a Christo videlicet. Nam si ab alio missus est, nulla ei a nobis in hoc obedientia exhibenda est. Sed si a Christo missus, ad quid missus est? At enim ad hoc missus est, ut mandata Christi ad nos perferat et doceat nos, aut ad aliud, quod nescimus et quod ad Dei mandata pertinere minime videtur, in quo eum nec etiam audire debemus.

[457] J28/L5: 680, 17 ff.:
Romanus pontifex ideo apostolicus cognominatur, quod apostolorum vice et officio fungi creditur; quibus, si vere fungitur, consequens est, ut etiam apostolus nominetur. Qui si vere apostolus Christi est, a Christo utique *missus* est. Apostolus namque nostra lingua missus interpretur. Quod si a Christo missus est, Christi mandata adnuntiare, Christi gloriam querere, Christi voluntatem debet et ipse facere, ut Christi verus apostolus possit esse.

[458] J29/L6: 687, 12 ff.; quoted in part above, n. 269.

[459] Compare Ockham and Michael of Cesena's opposition to Pope John XXII who had insisted that he was justified in assuming royal prerogatives because Jesus Christ had been in possession of an *universale dominum omnium temporalium*. Ockham and Cesena argued that the Christian community represented a partial restoration of that society without force which had prevailed in Paradise. Under the Headship of the New Adam, the *sacerdotium* as the bearer of the Gospel and the embodiment of its principles, in a society only partly redeemed, should be without property and (regal) power. Cf. Dempf, op. cit., p. 510.

Tu [the Pope [460]] autem, o homo, qui in hoc mundo principatum desideras, non vis fieri sicut iunior et minister, sed vis dominari sicut reges gentium et sicut hi, qui potestatem habent super eo, beneficus vocari.[461]

The Anonymous immediately goes on to say that if the Pope exceeds his proper office by presuming to judge all Christendom, wanting as he does any Dominical authorization, he becomes a sinner and a member of Satan. His action against another prelate or a king is thus tantamount to a judgment by Antichrist of Christ himself [462] for the Pope presumes to make himself like unto the Most High which the Humbled Christ refused to do. Only to the Exalted Christ belongs the Judgment. The imitator of the Humbled Christ should not presume to go beyond the Nazarene exemplar. Whoever in pride judges the members of God presumes to judge God himself and is therefore Antichrist.

Rome, according to the Anonymous, can surely claim no spiritual preëminence as a place, Peter bestowed no more distinction on Rome than on Jerusalem and Antioch, nor could he have conferred his admitted Apostolic primacy among equals upon his successor unless he ordained him, which would have been impossible.[463] Before accepting her religion from Jerusalem she was indeed an evil city. She had nothing to glory in before the coming of the men of Jerusalem save her infidelity. He points out that the preëminence of Rome is due simply to the ancient political and

[460] Or the primate at Lyons, representing the Gregorian Reform.

[461] J31/B30: 483.

[462] J31/B30: 482:

Se quidem exaltat et spiritu superbiae invehitur, nam contra voluntatem Dei de membris eius iudicare presumit, immo de ipso Deo. Nam sicut . . . qui membra Dei audit et qui ea spernit, Deum spernit, ita qui ea iudicat, Deum iudicat. Qui autem Deum iudicat, eo vult superior fieri. . . . Antichristus in Christum se transfigurare nititur, dum ea, que Christi sunt, operari molitur.

[463] J23a/B23a: 476, ii. Note the characteristic device of distinguishing between person and place:

Sed videamus nunc, utrum privilegium, quod Christus Petro dedit, persone ipsius tantum dederit an et loco. Nam si personae tantum dedit, locus hoc nunquam habuit. Si autem loco et personae dedit, pares in hoc locum et personam fecit, quod tamen eum fecisse nusquam potest reperiri. Sed neque Petrus alicui loco privilegium suum contulit. Nam si alicui loco contulisset, illi utique contulisset in quo primum episcopus factus est et apostolatus sui exercuit potestatem [i.e., Antioch]. At vero locus ille privilegium hoc nunquam habuit vel habet. Sed hoc invenitur, quod beato Clementi hoc privilegium Petrus contulit, quem loco suo episcopum Romae ordinavit. Quem nisi episcopum ordinasset, hoc illi privilegium non dedisset.

military power of the city in which no Christian should take particular pride.[464] In another place, J12/B12, indeed, he pillories Rome for her ignoble past.[465] Here we observe not only a hatred of Babylon akin to that in the Book of Revelation but also a calculated enthusiasm for the Church of Jerusalem which in the very years in which the Anonymous composed his Tractates, was being freed by Norman Crusaders, his kinsmen.

The Anonymous is prepared to argue that of all earthly churches, that of Jerusalem should take precedence.[466] He is particularly eloquent in his praise of the Primitive Church and notes with satisfaction that though Peter may be called the Prince of the Apostles, he received this *magisterium* from a still higher prince of the Primitive Church, James, whom he feared and honored as bishop of Jerusalem.[467] He delights in his exegesis of Psalm 44:10 which makes Jerusalem *regina* standing at the right hand of Deity while the other churches, the *virgines* follow in her train, among them Rome — if not an adulteress! [468] When the Anonymous argues for Jerusalem over Rome, he is of course arguing for a regal Church over against a sacerdotal Church and this is true for three reasons. (1) An appeal to the primacy of the contemporary Patriarchate of Jerusalem, for the most part extinguished by the Mohammedans and currently being liberated by fellow Normans is not prejudicial to royal and ducal power, while it preserves a semblance of Ecumenicity and deference for Apostolic authority. (2) An appeal to the ancient Jerusalem also calls up the host of

---

[464] J4/L3: 660, 21 ff. The problem of the transfer of Dominical authority by Apostolic succession is prominent also in J18/B18 and J24d/W.

[465] J12/B12: 460:
Nam et si preteritos eius actus inspiciamus, inveniemus illam fuisse caput erroris, civitatem sanguinum, luxui et libidine deditam, purpuratam meretricam, demonibus prostitutam et omniformium viciorum plenissimam, nulla sancta persona, nullo sacramento, nullo miraculo, nullo Dei consortio sanctificatam, "in tenebris sedentem et umbra mortis" et a luce veritatis alienam. Sed facta est postea civitas lucis, urbs fidelis, quando suscepit fidem et doctrinam filiorum Jerusalem et caepit sequi vestigia sacerdotum Jerusalem et ambulare in lumine eius. . . .

[466] J4, J12.

[467] J12/B12: 461.

[468] J12/B12: 461:
Quoniam primitiva aecclesia est regina, de qua in pslamo ad Deum dicitur: "Astitit regina a dextris tuis," id est primitiva aecclesia in meliori parte tua. De Romana vera aecclesia et aliis subditur: "Adducentur regi virgines post eam," id est aecclesiae non adulterantes se post primitivam.

priest-kings of that city from Melchizedek through David to the Hasmonaeans, along with St. Stephen, patron saint of kings and deacons. And lastly, (3) to appeal to the Heavenly Jerusalem is to counter the claims of the papal *Pontifex maximus* with those of the Heavenly Melchizedek and the earthly *rex et sacerdos*.

4. *The Priesthood of all Believers and the Primacy of Baptism*

Since confession of the Petrine faith constitutes one a qualified successor of the Apostles, namely, a bishop, the Anonymous is prepared to acknowledge by the same token that in a sense every true Christian is a kind of *clericus*:

Facit etiam baptismus ut homo fiat . . . sors Dei, et quia sortitur a Deo sine visibile signo in spiritu et unitate *clericus* est Domini.[469]

Or again:

Hoc effectu [baptismatis] omnis fidelis spiritualis *sacerdos* efficitur, ut sacrificet sacrificium iusticiae et immolat sacrificium laudis. . . .[470]

Our author is intent upon eliminating the idea of laity which he relates to *publicani*,[471] from the Church, clearly espousing the doctrine of the priesthood of all believers and quoting I Peter 2:9 again and again for Scriptural support. He who puts on Christ in baptism, assumes His royal sacerdotal nature:

Nam et qui baptizatur summum sacerdotem induit, id est Iesum Christum, et stolam primam recipit et anulum fidei sanctitatis quoque amictu et vestimento salutis induitur.[472]

The spiritual altar, of which the stone altar is but the type, is the heart:

. . . cor ipsius fit altare illud spirituale, cuius hoc altare corporeum typus est et figura. . . .[473]

Or again:

---

[469] J24c/W: 234, * Facit — **.
[470] J14/B14: 465.
[471] J24c/W: 233, * At vero — **. Cf. Isidore, Etymologiae, vii, 14, 9.
[472] J24c/W: 234, * Nam — **; cf. J22/L2: 655, 1 ff.
[473] The reference here is to the heart of a priest, J11/B11: 455, but cf. also J24/L4: 665, 38:
Nam . . . et regis est sacrificare et immolare in spiritu.

Sacerdos . . . est omnis, qui exhibet membra sua hostiam viventem . . .
[Rom. 12:1], cuius etiam imago est ille, qui in lapideo templo immolat. . . .[474]

The fundamental sacrament whereby the interior sacrifice is
possible is, as we note, baptism. By passing through the Red Sea
of baptism, the elect are freed "de manu Egiptorum spiritualium." [475] More than that, by being reborn in Christ, they become
coheirs with him and sons of God, acquiring a higher nature. Indeed Christ in baptism causes his elect to be "divinitatis suę participes ac per hoc deos." [476] As Böhmer remarks, we have in the
Anonymous a lone Western survivor of the Old Catholic and Hellenistic concept and experience of salvation.[477] Since we have
elsewhere discussed the importance of baptism and the prominence of regal imagery in connection with clues and sources in
our Codex,[478] we need not develop the subject further.

[474] J22/L2: 653, 10 ff. It continues:
. . . et hostia, quę in illo immolatur, licet verum Christi corpus sit, huius tamen
hostię sacramentum, id est sacrum signum, esse perhibitur, ac per hoc in his
omnibus est veritas, in illis vero excepto Christi corpore typus et figura.

[475] J14/BL4: 466:
Vincit [baptism] enim et eicit foras principem huius mundi et exsuit principatus
et potestates [the angels of wickedness] et sicut Pharaonem et excercitum eius in
mari rubro, ita diabolum et satellites eius et omnem vitiorum exercitum demergit
in aquis Christi sanguine rubentibus et liberat filios Israel de manu Egiptorum
spiritualium.
The Anonymous, in striving to recover the full significance of the sacrament of
baptism, alludes to the atoning blood of Calvary, recovering thus the full ancient
meaning of baptism. Cf. Franz Dölger, Der Durchzug durch das Rote Meer als
Sinnbild der christlichen Taufe, Antike und Christentum II (Münster, 1930), p. 63;
Per Lundberg, La typologie baptismale, Acta Seminarii Neotestamentici Upsaliensis,
X (Leipzig and Upsala, 1942); Jean Daniélou, "Traversée de la Mer Rouge et
Baptême aux premiers siècles," Recherches de science religieuse, XXXIII (1946),
p. 402.
[476] J22/L2: 651, 40. Cf. ibid., 652, 40; J14/B14: 465 "divine naturae . . . participes;" J24c/W: 233, *Ab hoc — **.
The Anonymous suggests indeed both the royalty and the priesthood of all
believers, reborn in baptism as sons of the heavenly Rex et Sacerdos. Below, Section 5 and also n. 648.
[477] Kirche, p. 209.
[478] See above, n. 248.
The royal character of baptism and confirmation in the Eastern traditions is vividly
brought out by Thomas Michels, "Die Akklamation in der Taufliturgie," Jahrbuch
der Liturgiewissenschaft, VIII (1928), p. 85, where he says:
. . . dass der Gefirmte als in dignitate regali et sacerdotali positus ein Recht auf
die Akklamation hat. Dignus ist er aber nicht . . . wegen seiner persönlich-
moralischen Würdigkeit, sondern kraft der Würde, die ihm durch den sakra-

Of such sanctity and primordial greatness is baptism that all other sacraments including ordination are contained in it and derive from it.[479] Ordination is a secondary sacrament. It only qualifies one to administer the supplementary saving ordinances whereby postbaptismal sins are forgiven and the Christian is restored to his baptismal purity.[480] Thus the Anonymous does not entirely depreciate the Eucharistic office of the priest in trying to recover the full significance of baptism. Indeed, he ascribes the same deificatory potency to the Eucharist as to baptism. Christians eat and drink at the Altar that they may retain Christ within themselves, partaking not only of his grace "sed etiam divinę ipsius naturę." [481] In this, of course, he is not distinctive.[482]

---

mentalen Charakter zuteil wird. Die orientalische Kirche hat das mysterium dieser Würde, mit der eine wirkliche Gewalt verbunden ist, in seiner ganzen Bedeutung erkannt und im Symbol ausgedrückt, während die abendländische Kirche im sacramentum mehr die Verpflichtung sah, die der Christ mit seiner Eingliederung in die Kirche übernahm. Sie hat ja auch, soweit wir sehen, wohl allgemein die Bekleidung des Getauften mit dem weissen Gewande, nach Durandus noch in signum sacerdotii, angenommen, aber nur in einigen Gegenden die Auszeichnung des Gefirmten mit Kranz oder Krone in signum coronae regni vitae, quia ipse est membrum Christi, qui est rex et sacerdos.

Michels notes further that, according to Durandus, this Eastern feeling for the royal character of baptism survived in the Province of Narbonne.

Writing of the ordo of confirmation of the Coptic-Ethiopian Church of Alex-andria, Michels says:

Nach der Salbung mit dem hl. Myron wird der Getaufte und Besiegelte mit den weissen Gewändern bekleidet. Danach wird die Krone gesegnet, wobei das Volk den Segenswünschen des Priesters über die Krone durch das Amen zustimmt. Die Krone wird aufgesetzt mit den Worten: "In nomine Patris et Filii et Spiritus Sancti, Unius Dei, gloria et honore coronasti eum: Pater benedicit, Filius coronat, Sanctus Spiritus eum sanctificat et perficit. Dignus talis Christianus.

[479] J24c/W: 234, * Magna — **. Cf. J14/B14: 466:
Quare baptismus non est minus venerandus quam sacerdotium.
For another reason why baptism is superior to ordination:
Sed in hoc magna est differentia, quod sacerdotium nec dari potest nec aliquiɑ efficere sine baptismo, baptismus autem sine sacerdotio. Ibid., p. 465.
The Anonymous insists, moreover, that the efficacy of baptism rests not with the priest who ministers but with Christ who acts in baptism:
Nullus enim hominum habet baptizandi potestatem, nullusque baptizat, nisi Christus, quia hominis ministerium tantum exhibent baptizanti Christo, ille autem potestate sua baptizat. Ibid., p. 467.
[480] B14/B14: 465:
Nam et sacerdotii effectus ad hoc ipsum est institutus, ut efficiat hominem idoneum ministrum ad conficienda sacramenta, quae Deus condidit ad salutem humani generis, quae nichil aliud efficiunt, nisi ut emundemur a peccatis, quae post baptis-mum commisimus et renovemur in id, quod ex baptismo effecti fueramus.
[481] J22/L2: 654: 20 ff. Cf. J24/L4: 667, 1.
[482] Cf. Böhmer, Kirche, p. 209.

5. *Election Conceived as Divine Procreation*: *the Sanctification of Marriage*

The Anonymous is profoundly distressed that many, though baptized, reveal in their lives none of the marks of the Spirit.[483] He is convinced, indeed, that many take on Antichrist and become *participes demoniorum*.[484] He therefore resorts to the doctrine of predestination as the explanation for the manifest disparities between nominal and evangelical Christians, the former receiving only the water, the latter the Spirit.[485] Baptism in being thus spiritualized loses at one point expressly its sacramental character.[486] Baptism becomes in effect the type and provides the marital image of the divine procreation. For election is pictured as a kind of spiritual generation from Christ and his spotless Bride, the Celestial Jerusalem:

Ex coniugio enim Christi et celestis Ierusalem [quę sanctorum omnium mater est] tales nati sunt . . . quos suo divinitatis participes ac per hoc deos fecit, quos de Spiritu sancto genuit, quos sibi immaculata sponsa, sancta videlicet ęcclesia, immaculato partu in lęticia peperit.[487]

The Anonymous is feeling his way to a distinction between creation and generation (=procreation) [488] as functions of Christ considered as the fullness of Godhead. One is reminded of the

---

[483] J14/B14: 467:
. . . multi sacramenta percipiunt qui virtutem sacramentorum habere non pos‹ sunt.
[484] J31/B30: 489 f.; 492:
. . . conformes fiunt imaginis diaboli.
[485] Ibid., 468, iv.
[486] J14/B14: 468 f.:
Quoniam si tales creati sunt et formati, quales in libro viventium sunt scripti, et, quales electi sunt in Christo ante mundi constitutionem, preordinati et predestinati sancti prophecto [sic] et immaculati et filii Dei sunt *et non indigent baptismatis sacramento.*
[487] J22/L2: 651, 28 ff. The context in which this extraordinary passage occurs is the defense of clerical marriage. I have removed from it the phrases relating to legitimacy to make the image stand out the more clearly. The bracketed phrase is inserted from ll. 27 f. The cosmic nuptial image is represented in primarily historical coloration in J12/B12: 461:
Quoniam celesti sponso haec [primitiva aecclesia = Ierusalem, qui regina est, l.20] prima iuncta est et Dei sponsa prima effecta est, ac per hoc filiorum Dei prima mater est et prima sui parte cum Christo resuscita est. . . .
[488] On God the Father's procreation of the king at consecration see quotation below from Smaragdus, n. 536.

distinction between the created and the eternally engendered Son in the Arian controversy. The Anonymous suggests, as it were, an "Arian" relationship between Christ God and the *praesciti* (for they are only created) and a "Nicene" relationship between Christ God and his *electi* (for they are eternally engendered = procreated). This scheme lies, admittedly a little below the surface of the actual words of the Anonymous, but it is quite in keeping with his feeling for kings and bishops as *dii*. In effect he is saying that Christ creates many, a few he procreates as his own sons, these being elected to eternal salvation.

Our Rouen theologian effectively brings together Royal Procreation and election in commenting on I Peter 2:4 ff:

"Vos genus," inquit "electum," non de immundo et corruptibili carnis semine propagatum, sed de cęlesti et incorruptibili semine summi regis et sacerdotis procreatum, et ideo recte vocatur regale sacerdotium, sunt lapides vivi. . . .[489]

In most stark systems of election, it is God (the Father) who decrees election and reprobation and the Son who merely confirms by his death the salvation of those already predetermined thereto. In the Anonymous it is the Royal Christ who both creates and regenerates. Here we note again the propensity of the Anonymous to conceive of the Royal Christ as virtually preëmpting the rôle of the Father.

The Anonymous is thus able to hold to a high doctrine of election while preserving, nay enhancing the work of Christ. Be it noted, however, that this enhancement of the work of Christ is at the expense of the Priestly and Humbled Christ, for the Anonymous conceives of salvation as much more royal than sacerdotal.

Heavenly birth which is assimilated to election and sealed by baptism is placed over against illegitimacy, which is the problem he is primarily discussing in the Tractate from which we quote. It will be recalled that in the closely allied Tractate J25/L1 on clerical marriage, Fliche identified the technical language of the discussion of predestination as stemming from the school of Bec under Anselm.[490] Anselm's thought and language may be

---

[489] J22/L2: 655, 30 ff.
[490] See above, p. 26.

briefly stated for the sake of comparison.[491] By means of free will (*liberum arbitrium*) man distinguishes good from evil and makes a choice. By means of the divine commandment (*mandatum*) he is moved to do what is right. Grace (*gratia*) is the aid received without which the commandment cannot be fulfilled. God's predestination (*praedestinatio*) is really his prescience (*praescientia, praecogitatio*) which knows in advance the working out of man's free will and divine grace. Now according to Fliche, the Anonymous, while using the Anselmian language, does away with the significance of free will [492] and thereby converts the Anselmian theory into a rationale for the legitimizing of clerical marriage which Anselm himself, of course, vigorously opposed. For whatever is *in opere*,[493] be it good or bad, the Anonymous says, is predestined — so Fliche, confining himself to the one Tractate. But actually the Anonymous elsewhere insists that only what is good comes from God.[494] It would appear therefore that Anselm and the Anonymous differ not so much in their *a*scription of evil (Anselm: to the misuse of free will, the Anonymous: to Satan) but in their *de*scription of it. For Anselm clerical marriage, for example, is an evil. For the Anonymous it is a good (for those who have not received the gift of celibacy), since from it may issue predestined saints.

The Anonymous, be it said, is not countenancing illegitimacy but arguing with cogency for the efficacy of the cleansing waters of baptism, which the Hildebrandine Church seemed willing to jeopardize in its campaign against the ordination of priests' sons and for clerical celibacy. The children of legitimate marriage are, the Anonymous contends, no less and no more tainted with the sin of Adam than the offspring of concubinage.[495]

Sed et cum in Christo regenerantur, ex celesti et divina generatione equali libertate donantur, quia equaliter ad omni contagione originalium peccatorum liberantur.[496]

---

[491] De concordia gratiae et liberi arbitrii, Migne, P. L., CLVIII, coll. 521 ff.; discussed by Fliche, L'opposition antigrégorienne, pp. 22 ff.

[492] Ibid., p. 37.

[493] J25/LI: 647. For Dempf's interpretation of predestination in the Anonymous see quotation below, n. 522.

[494] See Tractate J21, p. 224 and n. 514.

[495] Ibid., 650, 33 ff.

[496] Ibid., 651, 8. He puts an "if" before the fundamental proposition of Pauline and Augustinian Christianity:

Sin is very real and pervasive for the Anonymous, but he tends as here, to neglect its corporate character. Instead he particularizes sin. Salvation is from the "contagione original*ium* peccat*orum*." With characteristic scriptural cunning, he cites the prophet-priest Ezekiel on individual responsibility for sins.[497] Moreover he prefers to ignore or open to question the traditional view that relates sex and sin:

. . . omnis hominum generatio sive multiplicatio legitima est et per naturam et benedicta a Domino.[498]

Departing from the customary view, the Anonymous indeed proclaims procreation as a great good, citing the biblical injunction to be fruitful and multiply, for only thus might the living stones of the Heavenly Jerusalem be shaped and fashioned. God is the author of life, parents are but his ministrants:

Deus . . . creat, non parentes. Parentes quippe non sunt auctores generationis filiorum, sed ministri. . . . Legitima igitur et bona est origo humane conditionis propter legitimum opus et bonitatem conditoris.[499]

Here as elsewhere we observe the Anonymous intent upon effacing the barrier that the Gregorian Reform would set up between the clergy and the laity, to the disparagement of the latter.

6. *Freedom from the Law, the Life of Evangelical Love, and Penitence*

The primacy of baptism with the Anonymous is emphatically no mere theological postulate with which to work out the doctrinal algebra based on the axiom of original sin. Baptismal salvation is

---

Si quid contagionis inest generationi hominum ex peccato, id commune est et generatis ex legitimo coniugio, et eis qui generantur ex non legitimo. Ibid., 650, 29.

[497] J22/L2: 651, 1 f.

[498] Ibid., 650, 14 f.

[499] Ibid., 650, 24 ff. Dempf, commenting on these passages, hails them as a sign that the divine and the natural order have been fused in the thought of "Gerard," making possible the rise of Realism in philosophy, for the radical dualism of God and Nature has been overcome in an affirmation of the world as created by God. Op. cit., p. 200. The whole of Dempf's exuberant appreciation of the significance of the Anonymous, whom he compares with Anselm, is suggestive though perhaps excessive.

for him freedom from bondage to sin by the royal fiat of the Heavenly King and freedom from the old law through rebirth as divine heirs who bear the image of the Ruler of Heaven.[500] Christian liberty is a royal freedom above the law. We are reminded of Paul and Luther. The Anonymous' contemporary, the author of Fliche's "second Norman version of Ulrich's Rescript," breathes the same spirit.[501] Our eleventh century divine recognizes, of course, that this Christian liberty does not eliminate the possibility of falling into sin and of making use of human law, but he specifically asserts that freedom from the bondage of the law can mean freedom from the strictures of canon law, wherever *ius ecclesiasticum* becomes restrictive of the evangelical spirit:

Ut ergo intrent in regnum celorum habundare debet iusticia illorum, et ab omni iusticia que non habundat, omnino illis est abstinendum, id est et *seculari* et ea que dicitur *canonum*. Nisi forte in ea parte que ex evangelio est et habundat. Est enim in parte evangelica et habundat, in parte nec evangelica est, nec habundat. Et ut verius fatear, perfectoria sunt precepta et meliora mandata iusticie scribarum et phariseorum, quam ea que sunt illius partis canonum.[502]

The Anonymous does not reject canon law as such but insists that it must derive from Scriptures, and particularly from the New Testament[503] or that a New Testament spirit be imported into the diverse and practical applications of canon law.[504] Lest one fall

---

[500] J22/L2: 651, 6 ff.:
. . . veniunt portantes obprobium antique prevaricationis et confusionem servilis conditionis, exeunt reportantes honorem divine generationis et celestis gloriam libertatis. Veniunt induti veterem Adam, . . . exeunt induti novum Adam, id est Christum. . . .
On the image of Christ in the baptized, see quotation below, n. 510.
[501] Noted by Fliche himself in L'opposition antigrégorienne.
[502] J9/S: 139 f. Cf. also above, n. 360. Ibid., p. 143:
. . . ex maxima parte de secularis iusticie fonte procedit [canon law].
[503] Ibid., p. 144:
. . . et iusticia *novi testamenti*, que *proprie Christianorum* est, nullus invitatur ad simile, sed omnes ad contrarium propter hoc quod dicitur: "Hoc est preceptum meum" usque "dilexi vos."
Ibid., p. 139:
Doctrina vero eius [Christi] est sanctum evangelium, id est novum et eternum testamentum in sanguine suo, cuius precepta perfecta sunt, et salutaria mandata.
[504] Ibid., p. 139:
Nam ut evangelica sunt [haec decreta] aut ex evangelicis prodeunt et nostre salute secundo in loco deserviunt, ut evangelica primo. Unde necesse est, ut de evangelicis primo, vel si res exigit, de canonibus secundo loco proferat omnis iudex sententiam.

into bondage to the law, our Norman Augustinian distinguishes (1) in Scripture, (2) in conciliar canons, and (3) in papal epistles between the *universale*, the *particulare*, and the *singulare*.[505] That which is "universal" is required of all regardless of age, sex, class, or nation. The ecumenical councils are universal in this sense though their several canons may relate to particular classes as for example, the clergy. That which is "particular" relates to a class, a sex or a region, for example the Councils of Toledo representing all of the Iberian Peninsula. That which is "singular" relates to a specific matter like Paul's instruction concerning a certain sinner in Corinth, the letter of Gregory I to Augustine concerning a temporary accommodation to the marital traditions of the Angles, or a synod embracing only a province of a larger unit, such as the provincial synods of Rouen. The Anonymous emphatically rejects the universalization of the singular and even, in the case of councils, the particular:

Unde sequitur, ut et Kartaginiensis et omnis Affricana sive Toletana sive alia [particularia] a nostris causis iure possit repudiari et sententia et persona.[506]

The Anonymous is several times pleased to apply Paul's anathema [507] to the canonists, insisting that in their adding to the evangelical righteousness the "pessimas traditiones hominum" they have imperilled it.[508]

The Anonymous would like to see the world ruled in love rather than by law, by goodness rather than power. The evangelical love which betokens membership in the Body of the Elect (just as Apostolic humility is the mark of the true *sacerdos*) is distinguished from another kind of love which attaches one to the world, making one a member of Satan. In this distinction the Anonymous

---

[505] Ibid.

[506] J9/S: 141. In practice, the Anonymous is willing to make more use of the "particular" and the "singular" than he here allows. But he surely displays a strong feeling for *domesticum* and *proprium iudicium* over against *alienum, peregrinum,* and *transmarinum*. Ibid., p. 140.

[507] Gal. 1:8; in the following form:
Si quis aliud annunciaverit vobis preter quod evangelizamus, licet angelus in celo, anathema sit. J9/S: 139.

[508] J31/B30: 483.

is following Augustine.[509] He indicates, however, that one may *make* oneself a member of Satan by allowing the *amor et concupiscentia huius mundi* to gain the ascendancy.[510] Although the Anonymous follows Augustine, it is at a distance, for his concept of divine election as heavenly procreation introduces a life-long uncertainty in that through misconduct one may abdicate from the royalty of the Christian life into which one had been born as a son of the Heavenly King. In the long Tractate "De charitate et obedientia," which at points has the character of a sermon, the Anonymous, abandoning for a moment his sophisticated exegesis, becomes almost ecstatic about the law of love, which must prevail among the members of the Mystical Body:

> Quoniam Christus verius et perfectius dilexit nos, quam aliquis sciat vel possit diligere aut se ipsum aut proximum. . . . Christus enim dilexit nos inimicos et, "qui longe eramus" . . . "ut unum simus cum eo et unus spiritus." [511] Et quamvis aequaliter idem facere nequaquam vel sciamus vel possimus, tamen, in quantum eum inmittari debemus. Sed ex hoc consequi videntur, ut aequaliter et uniformiter omnes tam videlicet patres, fratres, liberos, uxores, proximos, quam extraneos et alienigenas et inimicos diligere debeamus.[512]

For a while, as one reads, it seems that the law of love embracing even one's enemies might properly extend to the reprobate, but this possibility is suddenly cut short by the realization that no one

---

[509] J31/B30: 489 f., v:
Sed quia vere *cartitatis amor* non potest esse in his, in quibus regnat *amor et concupiscentia huius mundi,* audiamus et quae dentur nobis praecepta, ut desinamus esse amatores huius mundi. . . . Qui autem Deum negat et fidem respuit, non est in communione sanctorum, non est fidelis, non est catholicus, sed demoniorum particeps factus.

[510] The possibility of losing the image of Christ even after baptism is clearly stated in the following:
Hoc enim tantum reformatur in novitate sensus sui, induendo novum hominem, qui secundum Deum creatus est, id est dominum Jhesum Christum, in quo Patri bene complacuit. . . . Nam qui conformantur huic seculo, non reformentur in novitate sensus sui, sed Christi deponunt imaginem [after baptism]. Et celestis hominis forma spoliantur sicque Antichristum induunt et conformes fiunt imaginis diaboli. Ibid., 492 f.

[511] I Cor. 6:17 can be called the golden text of the Anonymous, found as it is throughout the Tractates.

[512] J31/B30: 486. The reference to children and wives might indicate that the Tractate is really a sermon.

may love the enemies of God, none may love the reprobate. As the Church of Rome is largely peopled by the reprobate, one glimpses immediately the limitations of the Anonymous' love.[513] Could we possibly extend our love to the sworn enemies of God, he asks rhetorically? Far from it, he exclaims in reply. Nevertheless the Anonymous is eager to make a distinction between the good in sinners which comes from God and the evil in them which takes its rise in Satan. Christians are enjoined to pray for the triumph of the vestige of the good in the reprobate. The Anonymous makes, moreover, the important distinction between our enemies and the enemies of God, however often one may be tempted to assimilate them to each other. It is to be observed, further, that the Anonymous does not regard evil, the sign of reprobation, as the will of God but rather as the will of Satan.[514]

The Anonymous often approaches Luther in discerning the paradox of the Christian life: "simul justus ac peccator." A chance use of the key text of the Reformation, Romans 1:17, illustrates the way in which our Norman divine, though he assimilates faith to charity, clearly ascribes to God the promptings to charity.[515]

---

[513] J31/B30: 487, v:
Sed nunc quaerendum est, utrum diligere debeamus membra diaboli et perditionis filios, qui filii Dei non sunt nec matrem habent Hierusalem caelestem, quos etiam nec fratres nostros dicere possumus et proximos, quia non habent nobiscum in Deo cor unum et animam unam, quoniam "sunt ex patre diabolo" et predestinati cum ipso in dampnationem sempiternam. Si enim hos tales diligere debemus, necesse est, ut diabolum quoque diligere debeamus, quia cum ipso unum sunt, quia eius menbra sunt, quia eius filii sunt et commune cum eo supplicium habituri sunt. Sed neque diabolum diligere debemus nec eius menbra. . . .

[514] J31/B30: 488:
Diligamus ergo inimicos nostros et oremus pro ipsis, ut fiant filii Dei, sicut et nos. Diligamus in eis naturam, odio habeamus vitia. Diligamus, quod eos Deus fecit, odio habeamus, quod eos diabolus fecit. Quod enim Deus fecit, bonum est, quod vero diabolus fecit, malum est. Nam bonum naturae nostrae proximum et Deo amicum est, malum vero a natura nostra extraneum est et Deo inimicum.

[515] J31/B30: 492:
Fides igitur nostra est, quae ex Deo nata est et vincit mundum et pugnat contra mundum et vincit ipsum. Et quia in Deo manet, non peccat. . . . "Et non potest peccare, quoniam ex Deo natus est. In hoc manifestati sunt filii Dei et filii diaboli. Omnis qui non est iustus, non est de Deo" (I Joh. 3: 9 f.). Non enim habet fidem. "Justus enim ex fide vivit" (Rom. 1:17). Qui autem fidem non habet et qui de Deo non est, filius est diaboli.

For allied expressions, see the first paragraph (possibly a separate sketch) of J3/W, especially: "Justus enim in principio accusator est sui" (Prov. 18:17).

In the long Tractate J3/W the Anonymous deals at length with the problem of forgiveness and penitence. The immediate problem may have been the suppression of sexual vices among the clergy.[516] The Anonymous holds that sin is at once an evil and a punishment for evil and in this he sees the greatness of God's rule,[517] while God's forgiveness is at all times possible if there is true contrition.[518] The sin against the Holy Spirit is interpreted as a want of true penitence and is understandably, therefore, the only sin that cannot be forgiven.[519] The Anonymous takes very seriously the Old Law and the New and insists that the God of the

[516] The discussions of the sins of Sodom (MS 22–6; cf. n. 219) and of the Church as spiritual mother suggest that this Tractate belongs, along with J25/L1, to the Norman publicist literature on clerical marriage which bulked large between the council of Rouen in 1074 and that of Lillebonne in 1080. Discussed by Fliche, L'opposition antigrégorienne, ch. ii.

The argument of this exegetical *tour de force* may be summarized thus: All sins may be forgiven, even Peter's disowning of Christ (MS, p. 16). Yet, in the Old Testament there are numerous examples of capital punishment meted out by the law for sin. Moreover, the discrepancies in the punishments exacted of Adam for disobedience, Cain for fratricide, Lot and the Sodomites for their sins, Lamech for murder, do not seem to be commensurate with the crimes (MS, pp. 19 ff.). But this is because we assume that death is the worst punishment. The Anonymous cites the discussion between Ruben and Judah with their father concerning Benjamin to prove that to carry guilt is worse than to be killed (MS, p. 30). And since God does not twice punish for the same sin (Nahum 1:9), it is really a lighter punishment to suffer in time rather than in eternity (MS, p. 24). Mortal punishment in the New Dispensation is, of course, replaced by penance as a kind of spiritual death to one's former sins (MS, pp. 33 f.). God was willing to spare Sodom if there were but ten good people in the city. Ezechiel says that the sins of Jerusalem are worse than the sins of Sodom (MS, p. 24). Now the very worst sin of Jerusalem was to crucify Christ, yet Christ forgave Jerusalem (MS, p. 25). Therefore Sodom is also forgiven as Jesus says expressly in reference to Capernaum (MS, p. 26).

The only unforgivable sin is that against the Holy Spirit defined as *inpęni-tentia sive desperatio** (MS, p. 38) which sounds almost Lutheran. The Anonymous suggests without clearly articulating it that God's righteousness is vindicated for both the Old and the New Dispensations since, by earthly trials, capital punishment, or the sacrament of penance, equal degrees of sin have been equally punished. And as for those sinners who, despite God's more merciful provisions for his children (MS, p. 32), will suffer eternal and hence *equal* punishment for diverse sins which to human eyes appear to be of *unequal* magnitude, is not the equality of punishment, *infinity*, to be understood as the consequence of their common offense to an *infinite being*, the Holy Spirit, by having neglected or distrusted or despaired of His sacrament of penance?

[517] J3/W: 214 * Illud — **, also 214 * Ecce — **.

[518] The word itself is not used in J3/W.

The author emphasizes Peter's tears after denying Christ thrice: "Lacrimas eius lego, satisfactionem non lego." Cf. J11/B11: 453: "Paenitentia autem voluntatis est, non necessitatis."

[519] Ibid., p. 221, * Remittentur — **.

Old was not cruel, but that in the New Dispensation penitence aided by the Holy Spirit replaces capital punishment.[520] He is convinced of the efficacy of the penitential system but characteristically emphasizes *caritas*, citing Matt. 25:41 ff., as a sure guide to the proper manifestation of love to Christ and a turning away from evil in true penitence.[521]

7. The Christian Rôle of the King

Having considered some of the more prominent doctrines and convictions of the Anonymous as we try to extract them from the *oeuvres de circonstance* of the Codex, we may now turn to his conception of the Christian rôle of the king which constitutes the heart of his writings.

a. Rex messias est.

It is the conviction of the Anonymous in some of his Tractates, based upon his tripartite periodization of history,[522] that Jerusalem

---

[520] Ibid., p. 218, * Apud — **; 219, * Et ideo — **.

[521] Ibid., p. 221.

[522] See above, pp. 12 f., in connection with the contribution of Alois Dempf. We have elsewhere noted Dempf's observation that "Gerard," as he calls the Anonymous, anticipated philosophical Realism in bringing together the natural and the supernatural (above, n. 499). He continues (the page references are to Libelli de lite, III):

Zu diesem vollständig 'aristotelischen' Realismus kommt nun aber eine noch ebenso freie und souveräne Beherrschung der Paulusbriefe und des Symbolismus, d.h. einer Einordnung der Weltgeschichte und der Offenbarungsstufen in das Reichsbewusstsein. Voluntas enim est et praedestinatio dei lex aeterna est, in qua omnium rerum decursus decretus est, et paradigma est, in quo omnium saeculorum forma depicta est (648). Damit die gegenwärtige Kirche vermehrt, das himmlische Reich aufgebaut und die Zahl der Erwählten erfüllt werde, vollzieht sich der vorher geordnete Ablauf der Jahrhunderte.

Die paulinische Dreizeitalterlehre wird mit einer genialen Wendung im Dienst des Königtums nach der Zukunft hin verschoben. Statt der Äonen des Naturgesetzes, des mosaischen und des neutestamentlichen Gesetzes sind die drei Äonen Gerhards das alttestamentliche, vorbildliche Gottesreich mit einem nur vordeutenden Königtum und Priestertum von Adam bis Christus, das neutestamentliche Saeculum von der ersten bis zur zweiten Ankunft Christi mit dem wahren, allgemeinen Priestertum und mit dem wahren Königtum und Priestertum Christi und das dritte Reich des ewigen Jerusalem ohne Priestertum.

Die Offenbarungstufe des Neuen Testaments ist, vor allem seit es ein christliches Königtum gibt, schon vorbildliches Gottesreich des ewigen Jerusalem. Jam quippe mysterium regni operatur, heisst es in kühner, positiver Wendung des apokalyptischen mysterium iniquitatis, des transzendenten Wirkens des Antichrist im corpus diaboli.

Das Teufelsreich wird nun völlig von "dieser Welt" und besonders vom irdischen Staate abgetrennt und nur das amoralische und sündhafte Leben gewissermassen als Unterwelt unter dem positiven Reichsbewusstsein eines wirklichen Gottesreiches

has almost descended, that the Kingdom of Heaven is partly realized within history through the progressive achievements of the royal *christi*, who are, in a sense, messianic kings exercising by anticipation the judicial and royal functions of Christ at his Second Advent.[523]

In an exceedingly important passage where the Anonymous, drawing upon the rich treasures of the Edgar Ordo, first discusses the coronation sword in its interior as well as its exterior efficacy, the thought moves rapidly through a remarkable series of parallelisms in which two images, one explicit and the other implicit, are fused in such a way that the king is praised not only as a true Solomon but also, curiously, as a John the Baptist. As *Johannes redivivus*, who in the first century was himself looked upon as *Elias redivivus*,[524] the king is thought of as preparing the whole of his kingdom bodily and spiritually for the coming of Christ, or rather, as leading the Church-Kingdom of the earthly elect to their Heavenly King. As the new Solomon, he is also himself the proclaimed *rex pacificus*.[525]

---

auf Erden aufgefasst. Augustin selbst wird mit seinen positiven Aussagen über das Königtum zum Kronzeugen dieser Zeitalterauffassung gemacht, da er sagt, unter den Christenverfolgern coepit impleri quod scriptum est: et adorabunt eum omnes gentes (ep. 185).

Die Kirche ist ja schon frei per inhabitantis in se spiritus sancti praesentiam, sie ist das allgemeine, priesterliche Königtum und das christliche Königtum und darum ist das Reich dieser Freien figura coelestis regni et libertas eorum figura futurae liberatatis, quae est summum bonum civitatis dei nostri (673).

Man wird bei dieser kühnen Wendung an Hegels "germanisches Reich" des allgemeinen Priestertums und der innerweltlichen Sittlichkeit in der Substantialität des Staates als objektivem Geist erinnert.

Nie ist Kühneres und mystisch Tieferes über das christliche Könitgum gesagt worden als Gerhard tut. . . .

[523] Augustine had interpreted conversion and baptism as a first resurrection and hence as Christ's Second Advent for the individual Christian soul. De civitate, XX, 6 f. As we shall presently see, the royal consecration is a kind of second baptism and hence a "second coming" of Christ.

[524] For an interesting later application in England of the eschatological significance of Elijah in connection with John Oldcastle and Richard II see Elhahami liber metricus de Henrico quinto, "Rolls Series," XI, pp. 151, 158.

[525] J24/L4: 674, 10 ff.:

Gladius quippe eorum [anointed kings], etsi per materiam corporeus est, sed per virtutem sacramenti Spiritus sanctus est, ut quos materia corporis per iusticiam *exterius* interficit, sacramenti virtus per Spiritum sanctum *interius* vivificet. Hac enim de causa gladium portant, ut in eo feriant peccatores et vindicent iniuriam domini Sabaoth, et de "regno eius tollant omnis scandala" et ascendant ad predam, quasi leo contra hostes Domini, et diripiant fortitudinem inimicorum eius, et "vox" eorum tanquam leonis "clamantis in deserto." Et si queris, quid clamet, "parate,"

In this fused imagery the king is hailed as the harbinger of the Kingdom of which he is also the Messiah. One might have expected the Anonymous to liken the consecrating pontiff to John, but this does not seem to be the case. Perhaps the Anonymous is picturing the king as a new John the Baptist, bearing each purified generation of chosen ones heavenward where they enter the Kingdom of Christ. Whether the movement is one of ascent or descent is scarcely clear. Clear, however, is the conviction that the king is the shepherd of a royal flock who have been cleansed in baptismal waters and as one people are nourished by a heavenly food, for at the table of the New Solomon, the faithful partake of the solid food of the Pacific One.[526]

b. Rex sanctus est.

Royal unction has a manifold significance for the Anonymous. We have just mentioned its messianic implications. It constitutes the king a *christus* and *deus* for his people. This we shall discuss in the next subsection. As a kind of divine epiphany,[527] consecration is, moreover, at once a baptism and a coronation, a reënactment of the baptism of Christ by John the Baptist, the central motif of Epiphany. Since liturgically, Epiphany brings together

---

clamat, "viam Domini, et rectas facite in solitudine semitas Domini nostri."
Hoc enim clamat *rex iustus* voce, clamat opere.
Clamat verbo, clamat examplo.
Clamat minis, clamat blandimentis.
Clamat legibus, clamat edictis.
Clamat imperio, clamat iudicio.
Ideo in republica omnipotentis Dei, i.e. in sancta ęcclesia sive in hoc mundo, tenet solium summi regiminis,
    solium glorię et pulchritudinis,
    solium iusticię et fortitudinis,
    solium iudicii et equitatis,
    solium regni et imperii,
    solium misericordię et pietatis,
    solium gratię et decoris,
    solium modestie et dilectionis,
    solium propitiationis et reconciliationis,
    solium David et filii eius pacifici Solomon,
    solium Christi et Dei,
    solium quod neque par habet neque prestantius in sedibus huius seculi.
The reference to the king as a lion, which is not from the Ordo, cannot be connected with Merlin's prophecy of Henry I as the lion of justice. Geoffrey of Monmouth had not translated Merlin into Latin until well along in Henry's reign.
[526] See below, p. 171.
[527] See below, p. 162.

not only baptism and Christ's appearance to the Gentiles (Magi) but also the related themes of nativity and marriage (Cana), the Anonymous is pleased to think of the coronation as the royal nuptials of the Church, whereby the king is solemnly joined to his Bride, the Church-Kingdom. We have previously considered the nuptial aspects of coronation [528] and baptism.[529] Our immediate task is to show that this nuptial coronation-baptism is a rite of sacramental purification, constituting the king a *sanctus*.[530]

Throughout the earlier sections of the "De consecratione" the Anonymous discusses the king and the bishop together as *christi*. At the beginning of the argument he is determined to show that anointment, be it the ordination of a bishop or the coronation of a king, is truly sacramental, transforming the consecrated one into a different kind of person, "quod vir unctus oleo sancto et divina benedictione sanctificatus mutetur in virum alium, id est in christum domini." [531] However much the Anonymous spiritualizes the other sacraments, he desires to show that the royal, like the episcopal consecration is a sacrament operative *ex opero*, leaving an indelible effect.[532] He describes with some vividness, drawing upon the language of the royal *ordo* the change wrought within the consecrated king as the chrism penetrates into his inner being:

[528] See above, pp. 77 ff.

[529] See above, Section 5.

[530] And possibly, by implication, consecration also constitutes the people a *gens sancta*, since there is an implied representative or vicarious principle in liturgical coronation.

[531] J24/L4: 664, 34 ff.

[532] Peter Damiani, as we have already noted, accepted royal unction as one of the sacraments on the same level with baptism. (See above, n. 239.) It was Pope Gregory VII who first challenged the indelible character of royal anointment by claiming the right to depose anointed kings. Schramm observes that Henry IV's most cogent argument against the Pope was to point out the danger he incurred of invalidating all sacraments in attempting to overturn one. Only in the twelfth century were the scholastic resources available for undergirding the sacraments in such a way as to eliminate royal consecration as an eighth without jeopardizing the seven decided upon by the Church. Even in the next century Grosseteste had to tread warily as he remained loyal to the Church while explaining to his king the significance of the latter's royal unction. Scholastic reasoning eventually distinguished between *sacramenta ordinis* and *sacramenta in characterem imprimentia*. Admirably discussed in connection with Grosseteste on royal unction by P. Schramm, *English Coronation*, p. 128.

Hęc est Dei "sacratissima unctio," quae nulla reperitur sacratior. Hęc "super capud eius defluit et *ad interiora* descendit et cordis illius intima penetrat." . . .[533]

The king is felt to be almost physically[534] transformed into a *sanctus* by the holy chrism in which flows the cleansing potency of the Holy Spirit. A ritual ablution preceded the coronation, reminiscent of Solomon's descent to the running waters of Gihon for his consecration at the hands of Nathan and Zadok.[535] Purified by a kind of second baptism,[536] a magnificent confirmation[537] as it were, inducted by a special form of ordination into *la religion*

---

[533] J24/L4: 677, 26 f. The Anonymous is here quoting the Edgar Ordo, which at this point is dependent on the Frankish Ordo of 877 attributed to Hincmar.

[534] Hellmut Kämpf shows how the French publicist, Pierre Dubois combining Aristotelian-Stoic anthropology with sacramental notions of royal unction, considered the French king as having a special *physis* and as being by virtue of his status of *christus rex*, prototype of a perfected humanity, a representative of the human race and as such entitled to the cure of souls within France and the spiritual leadership of Christendom. Pierre Dubois, und die geistige Grundlage des französischen Nationalbewusstseins um 1300 (Leipzig and Berlin, 1935), especially pp. 42, 95, 105.

[535] The running waters of Gihon (II Chron. 32:30) in or at which Solomon was consecrated king (I Kings 1:45) and referred to in the Edgar Ordo, were identified with Gihon, one of the four rivers of Paradise (Gehon in the Vulgate: Gen. 2:13). Thus the Anonymous could ascribe paradisiac purity and sin-freeing potency to all consecratory waters — those of baptism (see above, n. 248) and those of the coronation ablution.

[536] Smaragdus in his foreword to the Via regia similarly considered royal unction as a kind of baptism:

Deus omnipotens te, o clarissime rex [Louis the Pious], quando voluit, et ubi voluit, de regali nobilique genere nobiliter procreavit, et misericorditer ad lavacrum regenerationis perduxit: caput tuum oleo sacri chrismatis linivit, et dignanter in filium adoptavit. Constituit te regem populi terrae, et proprii Filii sui in coelo fieri jussit haeredem. — Migne, P. L., CII, col. 933.

Cf. F. Kern, Gottesgnadentum, pp. 79 f. and n. 143.

In Byzantium the sacring of Emperor Tzimisces was expressly interpreted as a special sort of cleansing baptism which purified the ruler of his guilt in instigating the murder of his predecessor. Wrote Theodore Balsamon: "Since the unction of holy baptism eliminates all sins previously contracted, however serious they may have been, in like manner the imperial unction wipes away the sins contracted by Tzimisces, especially his blood guilt." Migne, P. G., CXXXVII, col. 1156. The religio-political background is discussed by Joseph Cardinal Hergenröther, Photius, Patriarch von Constantinopel. . . . (Regensburg, 1869), III, pp. 718 f.

[537] Cf. the biographer of Alfred the Great, Asser, who seems to assimilate confirmation to consecration when he writes: "Leo papa . . . infantem Aefredum . . . ordinans unxit in regem et in filium adoptionis sibimet accipiens confirmavit." The reference is to a Roman pilgrimage of Alfred at the age of five. Leo IV granted him the insignia of a Roman consul and confirmed him. There is no hint of a consecration after his accession to the throne. See Schramm, English Coronation, p. 15.

royale,[538] the king has impressed upon him an indelible saintly character. There is no problem here for the Anonymous, as in the case of clerical ordination, concerning Apostolic humility and goodness as the marks of authenticity, for the divine authentication of kingship is power, itself an inestimable good. Of royal power there can scarcely be too much, so holds our publicist of a feudal age, for power creates order and in order there is peace. It is as *rex pacificus* that the king is likest God. Through coronation, conceived as a purificatory act, the king becomes indeed a *sanctus*, morally qualified to rule a holy people.

Sancta quippe est potestas regiminis, sanctum et regimen ipsum, nec ad illud accedere quisquam iure, nisi *sanctus*.[539]

The royal *unctus* is a *sanctus* in the sense of one set apart from the world. Indeed it is not primarily a moral distinction. The primary principle of royal sanctity is otherness. Only secondarily is the concept schematized morally.[540] *Sanctus* means *hagios* which in turn means "quasi extra terram." [541] Hence kings (and *sacerdotes*) are "extra terram et extra mundum segregati inter Deum et populum mediatores effecti." [542] Having their habitation in heaven, they are qualified to rule their subjects on earth, for only a *sanctus* may properly rule the *gens sancta*.[543]

For the Anonymous intuitively feels that the king's people are

---

[538] In France, Jean Golein in his Traité du sacre describes the cleansing effect of the royal sacring upon Charles V in 1372, who chose to be anointed with the Holy Oil from Heaven on the Feast of the Holy Trinity, as though to symbolize the participation of all Three Persons of the Trinity in his anointment, likened thereby to that of Christ in the Jordan. Golein distinguishes first between ordinary oil and the Holy Chrism of St. Remigius that descended from heaven for the use of royal French anointments.

Et quant le roy se despoille, c'est significance qu'il relenquist l'estat mondain de par devant pour prendre celui de la *religion royal*; et s'il le prent en tele devocion comme il doit, je tieng qu'il est telement *nettoié* de ses pechiez comme celui qui entre nouvellement en religion esprovée, . . . Printed by M. Bloch, op. cit., p. 483.

[539] J24/L4: 668, 44 ff.

[540] Cf. Rudolf Otto, The Idea of the Holy. . . ., tr. by J. Harvey (London, 1928).

[541] A privitive + γῆ J24/W: 227. The argument of this whole section is that *sanctus* is applied in the Old Testament to things, animals, and acts devoted to God, quite apart from ethical considerations.

[542] J24/L4: 669:9 ff. The whole passage is quoted below, n. 580.

[543] On the basis of his doctrine of the priesthood of all believers, the Anonymous thinks quite naturally of the whole baptized people as a *regale sacerdotium* and hence as a *gens sancta*.

sanctified with him as a *gens sancta* in the essentially corporate act of royal consecration (= a second baptism and collective confirmation of the original baptism whereby both they and their prince become a *regale sacerdotium*). Thus the whole trend of the thought of the Anonymous is to make the national *populus christianus* consubstantial, as it were, with the Royal Christ and as such inviolable against any papal ministrations which are not strictly "Apostolic," i.e., derivable solely, by way of the Apostles, from the lowly *Christus sacerdos per gratiam.*

Coronation is thus understood as an *ex opere* sacrament capable of fusing power and righteousness, which is to proclaim the messianic dream an historical reality.[544] The Anonymous fails to see the danger of royal absolutization through his doctrine of the sacramentally secured perfection or at least sacrosanct otherness of the wielder of political power.

c. *Rex christus et deus est.*

The Anonymous wrote in an age when it was possible for so eminent a churchman as Lanfranc to gain credit at the hands of his biographer for his having gently rebuked (and thereby manifested a superior discernment) a certain cleric on the occasion of a royal banquet when the latter, beholding the splendor of King William I exclaimed: "Ecce Deum video." [545] The Anonymous, like the overwhelmed cleric at the royal feast — though with greater subtlety — declared that he too beheld God in the king. The deification of the ruler as a consequence of unction, the Anonymous held, is etymologically clearer in the Greek than in Latin, for here "consecration" is called "apotheosis." [546] That into which the

---

[544] Reinhold Niebuhr, Nature and Destiny of Man (New York, 1941), II, p. 27: The real issue [in the history of the Kingdom] is between the highest form of Messianism (according to which history culminates in an age which resolves the problem of justice by combining power and goodness in the person of a Messianic king), and the insight of prophetism according to which all nations and people are involved in rebellion against God.
The prophetic element in the Anonymous is confined to his denunciation of papal self-absolutization.

[545] Migne, P. L., CL, Vita Lanfranci, col. 53.

[546] J24/L4: 665, 30 f.:
Nam et si Greci sermonis utaris ethimologia, id est apotheosis, sonabit tibi deificatio.

consecrated person changes through the sacrament of unction is a christ and a god.[547] The Anonymous cites Psalm 82:6, "I have said, Ye are gods," and Exodus 22:28, "Thou shalt not revile the gods, nor curse the ruler of thy people," and concludes that kings (as also priests) are therefore gods and christs.[548]

Our Norman publicist prelate is able to identify his anointed, purified and saintly king with the Lord, the more readily for the reason that the baptism of Christ in the Jordan was also a kind of coronation, his adoption as the Son of God:

Regis vero unctio instituta est ad exemplum illius quem [Filium suum primogenitum] Deus Pater unxit [ante secula] prę omnibus participibus suis.[549]

The Anonymous draws the parallel between the consecration of the Son of God and that of the king from the Edgar Ordo of 973 which he uses to such great advantage throughout "De consecratione." The coronation is indeed an epiphany. Just as the Roman *imperator* in the celebration of his triumph was Jupiter,[550] so at the

Böhmer suggests that the Anonymous may have drawn upon Pseudo-Dionysius or John Scotus, revived during the Berengarian Controversy, as a source for the idea of *deificatio*. Kirche, p. 210, n. 1.

[547] Ibid., 676, 36 f. Writing of the royal and episcopal rites of consecration, he says:
Consecrant enim et sanctificant immo deificant, alia regem, alia pontificem.

[548] J24/L4: 665, 18 f. Bede may very well be one of the sources of the theory of the royal and sacerdotal *christi*. In his Expositio Actuum Apostolorum et Retractio he writes:
Porro Christus regiae sive pontificalis appellatio dignitatis est; namque pontifices et reges per legem oleo sancto ungi et ob id xpistoi nuncupari solebant, in figuram nimirum eius qui 'oleo laetitiae,' id est, spiritu sancto prae consortibus suis a deo unctus rex nobis et sacerdos magnus fieri dignatur est; sacerdos videlicet ut hostia nos suae passionis emundet ab omni peccato, ut ad dexteram dei positus etiam-nunc interpellet pro nobis, rex autem ut devictis omnibus adversariis nostris ad regnum nos immortale perducat. — M. L. W. Laistner, ed. (Cambridge, Mass., 1939), p. 405.
For a valuable discussion of Clement of Alexandria's use of θεοί for Christians who through perfection have reached the heavenly state, see Friedrich Andres, "Die Engel-und Dämonenlehre des Klemens von Alexandrien" (Fortsetzung), Römische Quartalschrift, XXXIV (1926), pp. 131 ff. On bishops as *dii*, see above, n. 214.

[549] J24/L4: 669, 31 f. The *ante secula* is absent in Version B which has the preferable reading, since only *secundum divinitatem* is Christ consecrated *ante secula*. *Filium suum primogenitum* is inserted from 1.36. Cf. Smaragdus quoted above, n. 536.

[550] Cf. Franz Altheim, A History of Roman Literature, tr. by Harold Mattingly (London, 1938), p. 237; also Lily Ross Taylor, The Divinity of the Roman Emperor, Philological Monographs, I (Middletown, Conn., 1931), p. 45.

descent of the Holy Spirit in the unction, this liturgical reënact-ment of the scene at Jordan, the Christian king was in that solemn moment Christ for the realm.

As Berges points out, in the New Dispensation the image of God, long overlaid by the sin of the Fall of Adam, is recovered through baptism, while in consecration, conceived as a representa-tive and collective form of baptism, the image of God is intensified in a unique way so that the king becomes for his people the figure of Christ in their midst, the purified image of the Second Adam, the perfect Man, the restored likeness and image of God.[551] We may call the coronation corporate, vicarious, and representative because through it the Church-Kingdom succeeds in elevating its head to the level of full "consubstantiality" with the King of Glory, the better to resist the encroachments of the waxing Papal Monarchy which was ascribing ever more exalted ecclesio-political preroga-tives to the Vicar of Peter, whose authority, however, could be shown to stem solely from the Earthly Christ.[552]

To be sure, the Pope as an *episcopus* and all *episcopi* (as well as their Old Testament counterpart, the *sacerdotes*) are also, by virtue of their consecration christs and gods. It is only in the final sections of "De consecratione regum et pontificum" that the Anonymous insists that the royal recipients of the chrism are su-perior to the others. For the nonce, while elaborating his thoughts concerning the general effect of the chrism itself, the Anonymous is for the most part willing to consider king and bishop on a parity.

As the Anonymous makes some distinction between the Old and the New Dispensation, our consideration of the king as a christ and a god will fall naturally into two parts.

In the Old Testament the king and the priests were anointed that they might thus, bearing the image and holding the place of the Lord, rule the people of Christ, "in regendo populo Christi Domini figuram vicemque tenerent et in sacramento [unction] preferrent imaginem." [553] At the moment of unction, according to the Anony-mous, the Spirit of the Lord as a deificatory power leapt into the

---

[551] Op. cit., p. 27, n. 1.

[552] Innocent III was the first Pope to assume also the title of *vicarius Dei*. Jean Rivière, op. cit., Appendice VI, "Vicarius Dei," especially p. 439.

[553] J24/L4: 664, 19 f.

men of God, transforming them into "viros alios." [554] The anointed king became forthwith a "gemina persona," remaining as he was by nature with his own peculiarities, but becoming also another person by grace, embued with spirit and power, exceeding all others.[555] At once a person and a personage, the king was a veritable *deus-homo*:

In una quippe erat naturaliter individuus homo, in altera per gratiam christus, id est deus-homo. Et una quidem unicuique propria erat, altera communis.[556]

One immediately asks in what way the *Deus-Homo* of the New Testament differs in the mind of the Anonymous from a Davidic *deus-homo* of the Old Covenant.

According to one view of the Anonymous, the Old Testament *christi* were anticipations and types of the Christ who came in the fullness of time. In one passage he says specifically that the kings of the Old Covenant prefigured the *Christus regnaturus*, which is to say, the Royal Divinity of the *Christus-christus*. The Old Testament priest, in contrast, prefigured the sacerdotal humanity of the *Christus-christus*:

Prefigurabat etiam sacerdos, quod Christus ad oram esset passurus mortem et traditurus semet ipsum in oblationem et "hostiam Deo Patri, in odorem suavitatis." Rex autem prefigurabat, quod regnaturus esset in eternum et sessurus in solio et sede celesti.[557]

We have already noted that even in discussing the Old Testament, the Anonymous makes a distinction between the Royal Eternal Christ, whose full nature was yet to be revealed, hence *regnaturus* and the Humbled Earthly Jesus, hence *passurus*. Old Testament kings were proleptically the vicars of the Eternal Christ who had yet to reveal his royalty at the Ascension.

[554] The idea may have first occurred to the Anonymous in examining the Hibernensis. See below, p. 218, item III, 23.

[555] Ibid., 664, 26 ff.:
Itaque in unoquoque gemina intelligitur fuisse persona, *una ex natura, altera ex gratia*, una in hominis proprietate, altera in spiritu et virtute. Una, qua per conditione nature ceteris hominibus congrueret, altera qua per eminentiam deificationis et vim sacramenti cunctis aliis precelleret.

[556] J24/L4: 664, 30 f. This extraordinary assertion, which is all the more striking in Böhmer's edition of the text through being capitalized, is absent from Version B. But cf. a similar thought in Pope John VIII above, n. 169.

[557] J24/L4: 666, 3 ff.

In general the distinction between an Old Testament king and Jesus Christ is, according to the Anonymous, that between a *christus Domini* and the *incarnatio Domini*. The Old Testament christ was not an incarnation of the Lord, although the unction and the leaping of the Spirit upon him changed his nature. But in one important respect the change wrought in the Old Testament king by unction made him superior to the Earthly Christ, for the royalty of the former was visible, while in Jesus Christ it was for the most part suppressed in discharging the priestly office which belonged to his humanity. Since the Old Testament royal *christus* prefigured the *Christus regnaturus*, that is Christ in Majesty after the Ascension, rather than the lowly Christ of Nazareth, the Old Testament *christus rex* was in effect tacitly superior to the *christus sacerdos*, Jesus. David was thus more manifestly a *deus-homo* than was the concealed and humbled *Deus-Homo* of faith. The Old Testament king was a *christus Domini*, but since the Lord of the New Testament is projected back into the Old by virtue of the doctrine of the Eternity of Christ, the Old Testament king was clearly, no less than the anointed Christian monarch, a *christus Christi*. It was the Eternal Christ, as Lord, who anointed the kings of old.[558]

The fact that a prophet-priest performed the unction, the Anonymous is careful to point out, should not be construed as a recognition of any superiority on his part, who remained throughout the operation the mere conduit of divine power. The fact that it was a prophet-seer rather than a simple priest who poured the vial of oil on Saul and later David remained, all the same, a little disconcerting for the royalist Anonymous, who, though well prepared to show how the Christian *sacerdos* is subordinate to the Christian king, could only countervail the clear preëminence of the prophet in the Old Testament as a man of God by styling the king also a prophet, and by making the king the recipient not only of the oil of unction, which he shared with priests, but also of the *Ruach*, by which he was touched as was the prophet. This he does by citing I Samuel

---

[558] J24/L4: 665, 14 ff.:
Unxit ergo Dominus Saul, unxit et David, sed per Samuelem, qui fidelis propheta erat in domo Domini. Et propter hoc uterque iure vocatus est christus Domini et habuit in se spiritum Domini, immo, quia "Domino adherebant, unus cum eo erant spiritus." Unde et in lege etiam *dii* vocati sunt.

10:6 where the spirit of prophecy passes to Saul as by contagion from the prophet band after his unction at the hands of Samuel:

Post unctionem vero insilivit in eum spiritus Domini et propheta factus est, et mutatus est in virum alium, ut etiam sacerdotale ritu immolaret hostias pacificas.[559]

Saul was a *christus*, king and priest by unction, and a prophet by inspiration. The fact that anointment was extended to priests in the Old Testament did not undermine the conviction of the Anonymous that unction was primarily a royal rite.[560]

Under the New Dispensation the fullness of Jesus Christ is known, not simply anticipated, as under the Old Dispensation. Therefore the Christian king and the Christian priest are christs and gods in a way that their counterparts in the Old Testament could not have been. Whereas, the Old Testament *christi* were figures of the *Christus futurus* (*Christus regnaturus* and *passurus*) but not expressly of *Deus*, the New Covenant kings and priests are figures and images of both. Now that Christ has come and sent also the Holy Spirit, it may be said that both Christ and the Holy Spirit operate in them. Kings (and *sacerdotes*) of the New Covenant are in even a profounder sense than under the Old Dispensation *dii* and *christi*:

Sunt enim et ipsi unum cum Deo et Christo eius, sunt et dii et christi per adoptionis spiritum, et in eis etiam loquitur Christus et Spiritus sanctus, et in eis vices suas perficit et operatur; in eis sacrificat et regnat et regit populum suum. Unde et uterque in spiritu et christus et deus est, et in officio figura et imago Christi et Dei est.[561]

"Figure" and "image," "Christ" and "God," may be used synonymously or there may be intended here a distinction between Jesus (*Christus per gratiam*) and Christ (*Deus, Christus per naturam*), for the Anonymous goes on to say that the priest is the image and figure of Christ the Priest, the king the image and figure of Christ the King: "Sacerdos inferioris officii et naturę, id est humanitatis,

---

[559] J24/L4: 665, 2 ff. The status of the anointed king as a prophet, as also a priest, is a basic principle of the coronation Ordo. But see below, n. 567.

[560] Old Testament scholarship, of course, sustains the Anonymous, questioning the historicity of all priestly unction prior to the Exile.

[561] J24/L4: 667, 5 ff.

rex superioris, id est, divinitatis." But a Christian king is *rex et sacerdos*, therefore the image and the figure of both Christ (insofar as he was simply Priest) and God (insofar as he is eternally King) that is to say, of *Christus per gratiam* and *Christus per naturam*. The Christian king is more than an image of Christ-God, he is also the image (like the priest) of Christ-Man:

. . . rex Deus et Christus est, sed per gratiam, et quicquid facit non homo simpliciter, sed Deus factus et Christus per gratiam facit. Immo ipse, qui natura Deus est et Christus, per vicarium suum hoc facit, per quem vices suas exsequitur.[562]

d. *Rex sacerdos est.*

Since the king is an image and vicar of the *Christus-christus*, the *Deus-homo*, the *Rex-sacerdos*, it remains for us to discuss the distinctively sacerdotal or quasi-sacerdotal functions of the king. These are in part the prerogatives deriving from our Norman divine's doctrine of the priesthood of all believers doubly secured by a second "baptism" in the form of royal consecration. But behind the Anonymous lies also that whole cycle of Merovingian and Carolingian thinking about the king as Melchizedek, *rex et sacerdos*.[563] Inasmuch as the same sacramentally potent oil (*res*)[564] is used for both king and bishop, the Anonymous contends, the effect thereof cannot be diverse for the royal and the sacerdotal

---

[562] J24/L4: 667, 35 ff.

[563] Venantius Fortunatus had addressed Childebert I as "our Melchizedek, by right king and priest." Gregory of Tours wrote of the king as a "good priest." These and numerous other examples are cited by Voigt, op. cit., p. 292.

The Anonymous grounds many of the royal prerogatives in the Church by appealing to this mysterious figure. J24/L4: 663, 7 et passim; in another connection, J12/B12: 458. Gustave Bardy points out that Ambrosiaster upon whom the Anonymous draws represents a peculiar, ancient heresy, vigorously opposed by Jerome, according to which Melchizedek, without father and mother, king of justice and priest of peace (Salem), was none other than the incarnation of the Holy Spirit. "Melchisédech dans la tradition patristique (fin)," Revue Biblique, XXXVI (1927), 26 ff. Now the Anonymous, it is true, never goes so far as to make the king, concerned for peace and justice, expressly an embodiment or vicar of the Holy Spirit, nor, make the king the vicar of Christ and the bishop (with his emphasis upon *vita aeterna* and on *spiritualia*) the vicar of the Holy Spirit. But there are elements of his thinking that suggest a Spiritual kingship.

[564] J24/L4: 665, 21 ff.

Habet itaque rex et sacerdos communem olei sancti unctionem et sanctificationis spiritum et benedictionis virtutem et Dei et Christi commune nomen et rem communem, cui merito debetur hoc nomen. Nam nisi rem haberent, falso designarentur hoc nomine.

recipient. Therefore the king must become a priest at his consecration and the *sacerdos* (bishop) a king during investiture:

Et quicquid pręrogat vel tribuit, sive rex episcopatum, sive sacerdos regnum, iam non homo pręrogat et tribuit, sed deus et christus Domini. Et si verum fateri volumus, et rex sacerdos et sacerdos rex, in hoc quod christus Domini est, iure potest appellari. Nam et sacerdotis est in spiritu Christi regere populum, et regis est sacrificare et immolare in spiritu.[565]

The sacrificial act of the king is the oblation of his contrite heart.[566] There is a distinction between the king's *regere* and *immolare in spiritu*, for in ruling he is the figure of the King of Glory, while in the immolation of his royal heart he is the image of the suffering Christ. The Anonymous calls his sacrifice royal and beholds its prototype in the priestly work of the Priest-King Melchizedek, himself a type of Christ. Let us consider the sacerdotal functions ascribed to the king as the image of the royal-priestly Christ of the Cross.

Reaching back into the Old Testament to a passage which we have already cited, the Anonymous observes that Saul was a prophet by inspiration from the band of dervishes coming out of the town, and a priest and king by unction. Moreover, in I Samuel 10:8, Saul is bidden to meet Samuel to make burnt sacrifices and peace offerings (so, the Vulgate).[567] The king is thus understood

---

[565] Ibid., 34 ff. The Anonymous continues:
Ipsius etenim est exhibere "se ipsum hostiam vivam, hostiam sanctum, hostiam Deo placentem," et immolare Deo "sacrificum laudis," sacrificium iusticię, sacrificium spiritus contribulati, quod totum significatum est per carnale sacrificum, quod sacerdos offerebat iuxta ritum visibilem sacramenti.

[566] "Nam . . . regis est sacrificare et immolare in spiritu." J24/L4: 665, 37 f. Cf. the Antiphonae de susceptione regum of the so-called Gregorian Liber responsalis of the ninth century, especially the following responsory: "Elegit te [the king] Dominus sacerdotem sibi, ad sacrificandum ei hostiam laudis." Migne, P. L., LXXVIII, col. 828A/B. For the possibly Gallican element here, cf. Reinhard Mönchemeier, Amalar von Metz: sein Leben und seine Schriften: Ein Beitrag zur theologischen Litteraturgeschichte und zur Geschichte der lateinische Liturgie im Mittelalter, Kirchengeschichtliche Studien, I: 3 & 4 (Münster, 1893), pp. 28, 90 ff. Amalar endeavored to recover a good text of the Roman antiphonaries which he found in Corbie and by collation with the texts available in Metz. The critical history of the resultant text is discussed by H. Leclercq, "Antiphonaire," D.A.C.L., I: 2 (1907), coll. 2454 ff.

[567] Modern criticism, however, construes Samuel as the sacrificer. In any event the Anonymous conveniently overlooks I Sam. 13: 13 f. where Saul is deposed from the kingship for presuming to perform priestly sacrifice.

to be qualified to offer sacrifices by virtue of the same unction which made him a king.[568]

Much better than Saul as an example of the royal possession of sacerdotal prerogatives was Solomon, *rex pacificus* and *merito eccelsiastes*, who by virtue of his unction was a type of the future Christ both regal and sacerdotal, building the Temple, instituting a new liturgy, praying, and consecrating.[569]

Appealing to the Edgar Ordo, the Anonymous argues that the Christian king, by virtue of the same unction that makes every baptized man a "cleric," can in his turn perform the Christian "sacrifice" of bread and wine, and what is still more important, "forgive" sins in imitation of Christ:

Ad exemplum quippe illius [Jesus Christ] est unctus et deificatus [the king], et ideo illum sequi potest in omnibus. Quare et peccata *remittere*, et panem et vinum in sacrificium potest *offerre*, quod utique facit in die quo coronatur, precipue videlicet solennitatis.[570]

We shall consider the royal offering (*offerre*) first. The power to offer bread and wine in sacrifice is a reference to the medieval practice of the royal presentation of the elements at the Coronation Mass. The king of England, for example, like the Byzantine and Holy Roman Emperors, after the coronation came *within* the sanctuary and presented the bread and wine for his own communion.[571] It is quite possible that the Anonymous in the foregoing passage is endeavoring to assign to the king a representative rôle in the presentation of the elements whereby the "collective" significance of the Eucharist is recovered. Gregory Dix observes the expiration of the primitive "collective" Eucharistic liturgy by the eleventh century, although this liturgical revolution was "virtually

---

[568] J24/L4: 664, 38 ff.

[569] J24/L4: 666, 34 ff.
Solomon quoque pacificus rex ipse tot sacramentis Christi et ęcclesię refulsit, ut ecclesiastes merito vocaretur. Ipse, quod nulli sacerdotum concessum fuit, *domum* Domino *ędificavit* novumque *sanctuarium construxit*, novum sacrificandi ritum institutit, sacerdotum numerum ampliavit, *templum* Domini *dedicavit* et omnia interiora eius *sacravit*, *solemnitatem dedicationis fecit*. Et sacerdotali more orationem ad Deum fudit et populum benedixit. In his igitur omnibus per figuram christus Domini fuit et Christi futuri vices exercuit.

[570] J24/L4: 678, 18 ff.

[571] Cf. Gregory Dix, "The Idea of 'The Church' in the Primitive Liturgies," The Parish Communion, edited by A. G. Hebert (London, 1937), pp. 116 f.

completed by the end of the fifth." This revolution is what he calls, deploringly, the "clericalization" of the Eucharist, a process in which the Body of Christ becomes a "hieratic object" rather than continuing to be understood as the Christian people (a royal priesthood) themselves. It is quite possible that the Anonymous' explication of the Edgar Ordo represents an effort to restore the collective Eucharistic offering in the person of the consecrated king.[572] Nevertheless, however worthy the effort of the Anonymous to reassert the primitive conception of the corporate character of the Eucharist, he actually imperils the conception of the Church as the Body of Christ, for by making of the king a representative communicant, the Anonymous merely puts over against Eucharistic sacerdotalism an equally defective royalism.[573]

In another striking passage the Anonymous alludes to the high responsibilities of the king as enumerated in the coronation Ordo, among them the nurturing of the Church and he concludes:

. . . qua propter necesse est, ut sanctam ecclesiam pascat cibo celesti. . . .

Again, after an ecstatic recounting of the king's messianic prerogatives which the "eloquia Dei et misticae verba consecrationis [the Edgar Ordo] docent," he concludes:

[572] Ibid., pp. 116, 131 ff. Dix does not hold Rome responsible for the early phases of the clericalization of the Eucharist, but rather the Carolingian theologians (pp. 133 f).

[573] Dix observes further:
There are indications everywhere in the history [of eucharistic practices] of a subtle and (to me) unexpected connection between three things which at first sight might be supposed independent questions. 1. The conception of the Church as a whole, and not the 'celebrant' as the priest of the eucharistic offering. 2. The practice of frequent and general communion by the laity. 3. The extent to which the Church, regarding herself as a particular creation of God distinct from the world into which she was created, *vindicates her own freedom in choosing her hierarchy in independence of the secular power.* . . . I think it will be found that wherever and whenever that right has been effectively lost to the secular ruler . . ., there and then with a curious precision it will be found that the practice of frequent and general communion by the laity rapidly declines, and the "collective" character of the eucharistic sacrifice is soon lost sight of.
Ibid., p. 135, italics mine. I am pleased to quote these words at length because they well illustrate the bearing of Christology (in its eucharistic aspect), upon the relationship of Church and State and furthermore give expression to a conviction similar to my own concerning the proper relationship. The Anonymous in opposing clericalization unfortunately falls into another extreme, that of regalization.

Nos dico, qui nutriti sumus in lacte non tantum Petri, sed etiam Christi, qui sedimus ad mensam veri Salomonis et vidimus cibos mensę eius et de soliditate gustavimus ciborum pacifici.[574]

In the foregoing passages the Anonymous alludes both to the Coronation Mass and also (perhaps more particularly) to the solemn festal meal following the coronation, which is taken as a kind of Messianic Banquet. The fact that it is the table of "the True Solomon" carries one into the realm of realized eschatology, for the Kingdom of Peace has already come and the Eucharist established by Christ and administered by Peter and the dutiful Roman hierarchy as a memorial feast until he come again is for a moment, transcended.

We turn now to that second sacerdotal prerogative conferred upon the king by virtue of the coronation Ordo, namely, the power to "remit sins" (*peccata remittere*). We seem to have in this passage [575] a theological allegorization of the amnesty granted by the king at his coronation. Funk noted with some relief that the word *remittere* is found only in Version A, being in Version B replaced with *destruere*, which more nearly comports with what could be expected of a Christian monarch bent upon the suppression of evil. But, as Funk was obliged to acknowledge, in a second passage, which is admittedly curious, the Anonymous again mentions the sacerdotal prerogatives of the king consequent upon coronation:

Fit ergo summus rector et quo superior nullus est et pacificus *propitiator* populi Christiani, qui est ecclesia sancta et templum Dei vivi, per quod vices Christi potest exequi in *remittendis peccatis et reconciliatione peccatoris*.[576]

---

[574] J24/L4: 674, 25 ff. A contemporaneous description of the royal repast that followed upon the coronation of Edgar himself is printed by Schramm, "Die Krönung bei den Franken und den Angelsachsen." Schramm notes that some of the material in the "De consecratione" concerning the royal repast is derived from other sources than the Ordo, pp. 231–3. Further material on the coronation meal in the period of the Anonymous is found in William of Malmesbury, edited by Stubbs, "Rolls Series," XC, I, 146; Symeon of Durham, edited by Th. Arnold, "Roll Series," LXXV, I, 68, and F. Liebermann, The National Assembly in the Anglo-Saxon Period (Halle, 1913), p. 52.

[575] Above, p. 168.

[576] J24/L4: 677, 21 f. The last two phrases are found only in Version A. Similar phrasing is found in a quotation from the Edgar Ordo, ibid., 678, 36 ff.:

Qui 'tali benedictione glorificatus' est, 'ut Davitica teneat sublimitate *sceptrum*

It is clear from the words of consecration, the Anonymous argues, not only that the king propitiates for the sins of his people, but also that "he is consecrated and deified" in order to justify his people before God in both body and soul:

Sed per hec omnia ostenditur, quod ipse per gratiam sibi a Deo collatam potest *iustificare* et *salvare hominum corda et corpora* ac per hoc fit iustificator hominum et salvator.[577]

Funk observes that the power "to justify and save heart and bodies" [578] has been commonly ascribed to kings in all mirrors of princes since The Twelve Abuses of Pseudo-Cyprian (the Scotus Anonymus).[579] As propitiators and saviors of their people, kings (like priests) are mediators between God and the people.[580] While the Anonymous includes the bishop with the king as mediator, the king, in the mind of the Anonymous, is preëminently such, because of his representative rôle in the Church-Kingdom.

It is appropriate at this point to observe the manner in which the Anonymous adapts his sources and presses them to yield an even more eloquent testimony to royalism than they contain. For example, the foregoing ascription of mediatorial power to the king

---

salutis et *sanctifice propitiationis munere* reperiatur locupletatus.' Unde et *animas salvare* et *peccatis hominum propiciari,* ut sanctificentur, videtur esse idoneus.

Similar tendencies are found in Pierre Dubois. Cf. H. Kämpf, op. cit., p. 40. By virtue of his coronation, the French king, might, according to Pierre Dubois go beyond the coronation oath in the exercise of his spiritual prerogatives:

. . . regia maiestas, cuius generaliter interest propter se et propter publicam salutem . . . videre potest dominus rex *oves suas* pereuntes, *animas* et *bona perdentes* cum ipsius principis preiudicio et incommodo temporali *contra* consuetudines *antiquas regni,* quas ipse servare promisit. . . .

The fourth century Ambrosiaster is much more sober than the Anonymous on the matter of the princely rôle in salvation, but see his commentary on Rom. 13, 4 c. where kings are "omnibus velut paedagogi," using force lest their subjects "in poenam incidant futuri judicii."

[577] J24/L4: 677, 13 ff. Basing his thought upon H. M. Chadwick, The Cult of Othin (Cambridge, 1899), F. W. Buckler in "Barbarian and Greek" Church History, XI (1942), p. 19 suggests the possibility of the persistence of Germanic notions of the king as a self-sacrificing savior of his people. Cf. Williamson and Murray above, n. 401.

[578] The idea is developed further in Section 8e (1).

[579] So-called by John T. McNeill, Christian Hope, pp. 35 f.

[580] J24/L4: 669, 8 ff.:

Ideo igitur consecrantur sacerdotes et reges et sanctificantur, ut nullis negotiis vel actibus, qui ad Deum minime pertinent, occupentur, sed sancti sint, id *est extra terram et extra mundum* segregati, *inter Deum et populum mediatores* effecti, et in celis conversantur et in terris subditos moderentur.

and the bishop is based upon the Edgar Ordo which has taken over the "Designatio" containing this phrasing from the German Ordo of Mainz, c. 960.[581] In the Edgar and German *ordines*, however, the key phrase is the prayer that Christ as "mediator Dei et hominum" make the king in his realm "mediatorem cleri et plebis."[582] Thus the Edgar (and before it the German Ordo) went no further than to compare the mediatorial rôle of the king between the people and the clergy to that of Christ between man and God. The Anonymous, however, goes much further and, combining the two terms, boldly styles the king himself a mediator between the people and God, a function which the priests are said to share with him on a smaller scale.

To sum up, the Anonymous is able to effect this daring transposition of terms by virtue of his confidence in the representative and collective significance he attaches to the coronation unction interpreted as a vicarious purification and regalization of the nation. In the baptism-coronation all within the nation-Church are elevated to the status of royal co-heirs with *Christus* (at once the earthly monarch and the Eternal King). In view of the strong sense of communal solidarity native to the medieval mind, it may be said without exaggeration that the anointed king is thought of by the Anonymous as a real propitiator and savior of his people, by virtue of his sanctified headship of the *regale sacerdotium*. And because his consecration is royal, "christic," and divine, rather than sacerdotal, Apostolic, and human, the national Melchizedek is endowed with a more visible soteriological power than the Vicar of Peter.

Having examined this royal *princeps presul*[583] *et summus* as the

---

[581] Cf. the Ordo as printed by Schramm with several fonts to show the sources, "Krönungen bei den Franken und Angelsachsen."

[582] From Robert's Benedictional, op. cit., p. 147:
Sta et retine amodo status quem hucusque paterna suggestione tenuisti hereditario tibi iure delegatum per auctoritatem dei omnipotentis et per presentem traditionem nostram omnium scilicet episcoporum ceterorumque dei servorum; et quanto clerum sacris altaribus propinquiorem prospicis, tanto ei potiorem in locis congruis honorem impendere memineris, quatinus *mediator dei et hominum te mediatorem cleri et plebis* in hoc regni solio confirmet et in regno aeterno secum regnare faciat, Jhesus Christus Dominus noster. . . .

[583] J24/L4: 667, 30, 678, 29. This title is unique to the Robert Benedictional in Rouen. See above, p. 39. The Anonymous himself apparently adds *et summus*. It is of interest to note that this title or one of the several variant readings is ultimately derived from the *ordo* used by Pope John VIII in the coronation of Louis II in 878.

antitype of the *Pontifex maximus*, head of the international *sacerdotium*, it is now our task to discuss the relationship of the national *rex et sacerdos* to the national or provincial *sacerdotium*.

8. The Relationship between the Regnum and the National or Provincial Sacerdotium

Four "christological" arguments variously meet the needs of the Anonymous in his regalization of the Church and his subordination of the national *sacerdotium* to the *regnum*. (a) He may derive the authority of the king from the royal, divine nature of Christ and the authority of the bishop as *sacerdos* from the sacerdotal, human nature of Jesus Christ. (b) He may distinguish the unction of the king and the bishop and construe the one in imitation of the anointment of Christ, and the other, in imitation of the lesser benediction of the Apostles. (c) He may subordinate the *sacerdotium* to the *regnum* by interpreting the king as the primary reflection of, and participation in, the nature of Christ: the bishop as a secondary reflection of, and participation in, the nature of the king — all three being *Christi*. The first and the last patterns constitute the major and minor themes of the Anonymous' political theory. But two subsidiary theories are distinguishable. (d) He may show that the king is *rex et sacerdos*, *presul princeps et summus*. We have already discussed the king's sacerdotal function. It remains to relate him in this capacity to the national or provincial hierarchy. Allusions to the quasi-sacerdotal character of the king are, as it were, the grace notes of the Anonymous. They are destined to be taken up much later and transposed as the *leitmotif* of the Henrician and Lutheran ecclesio-political symphony. Finally, in addition to these four "christological" variations and arrangements there are (e) several fine specimens of pure royalist counterpoint.

The Anonymous seems always able to draw levies from a Pope with which to assail the Pope. In this case, he was doubtless ignorant of his indebtedness. See Schramm's edition showing sources, "Krönungen bei den Franken und Angelsachsen." The implications of this title are brought out more fully below, Section 8d.

a. The King Reflects the Divine Nature of Christ and the Sacerdos, *the Human.*

Unlike his contemporary Hugh of Fleury, and in distinction to Ambrosiaster [584] and Cathwulf and others in the tradition who conceive of the king as the image of God and the bishop as the image of Christ, the Anonymous is strictly Christocentric in respect to both the king and the bishop. The king, no less than the bishop, is the image of Christ, although in maintaining this position, the Anonymous, as we have several times noted, virtually equates the Eternal Christ and God the Father.[585] Fundamentally this coalescence takes place in the thought of the Anonymous because of the recession of the concept of the sacrifice and the atoning work of Christ, in consequence of which the Son has no rôle distinct from the Father's. This conflation of the Filial and Paternal images obliges the Anonymous to distinguish between Christ as a divine King and Christ as a human Priest, and eventually between the Heavenly and the Earthly Christ, in order to accomplish that which the publicists in the line of Ambrosiaster have worked out by the distinction between *Deus* and *Christus.* Berges, having observed that the doctrine of the king's divine image will tend to be replaced by the doctrine of the king's divine vicariate in the High Middle Ages, suggests that this shift may be explained as the replacement of an ontological by a more

---

[584] The Commentaria in duodecem epistolas B. Pauli (Hebrews is not included), traditionally ascribed to Ambrose is published in Migne, P. L., XVII, coll. 47 ff.; the Quaestiones Veteris et Novi Testamenti, formerly attributed to Augustine, in C. S. E. L., L. Ambrosiaster's formulas permitted Greco-Roman ruler worship to survive in an acceptably Christianized version according to which it is God in the ruler or represented by the ruler that one reveres and not the ruler himself. Berges raises the question as to what extent Ambrosiaster actually transposed and Christianized such pagan religio-political words as ἐπιφανὴς θεός, υἱὸς θεοῦ, *praesens numen.* Op. cit., p. 26, n. 3.

For the identification of Ambrosiaster see Germain Morin, "La critique dans une impasse: à propos du cas de l'Ambrosiaster," Revue Bénédictine, XL (1928), pp. 251 ff. Here he recounts his four earlier attempts to identify Ambrosiaster. For commentary see A. Souter, A Study of Ambrosiaster (Cambridge, 1905). For the most recent evaluations see Gustave Bardy, art., Dictionnaire de la Bible, Supplément I (Paris 1928), pp. 225 ff. and C. Martini, Ambrosiaster: de auctore, operibus, theologia, Spicilegium pontifice athenaei Antoniana, IV (Rome, 1944).

[585] For the discussion of this conflation, see above, p. 130.

juridical conception of the divine likeness of royalty.[586] The Anonymous held, of course, to the ontological conception connected with the older feeling for the Kingship of Christ as distinguished from the Kingship of God, despite the general tendency to abandon the former emphasis.[587] The Anonymous writing at the end of the eleventh century and at the beginning of the twelfth espoused the *Gottesebenbildlichkeit* rather than the *Gottesvikariat* of the king, to use Berges' terms, but when he said *Deus* he pictured Christ in Majesty. The Anonymous was not wanting, however, in a supplementary doctrine of a *Gottesvikariat*, again conceiving as virtually identical, God the Father and the Exalted Son.[588]

Thus, although the Anonymous belongs in a general way in the line Ambrosiaster — Cathwulf — Hugh of Fleury, his terminology is distinctive. Where they alike contrast *Christus* and *Deus*, the Anonymous contrasts Jesus the Man, *christus sacerdos per gratiam* with Christ as God, *Christus Rex per naturam*. And the king takes not simply the place (*vices*) [589] of the Royal Christ as vicar and his bishops that of the Humble Christ, but he and they, are an image and likeness of the Lord (*imago, figura*),[590] yea more than that, a divine presence which is greater than merely a divine representation, because in them (*in eis*) [591] Christ and the Holy Spirit sacrifice and rule, in them the divine potency is manifest (*Christi naturę imitatio sive potestatis emulatio*),[592] participant

---

[586] Op. cit., p. 27:

Hier ist schliesslich, wenn auch nicht genau, zwischen 'Gottesebenbildlichkeit' und 'Gottesvikariat' des Königs unterschieden — eine Unterscheidung zwischen der ontologischen und der mehr juristischen Qualität der Gottähnlichkeit, die der synonyme Gebrauch der Worte später aufhebt.

[587] Berges observes, "dass der Christus König-Gedanke nicht immer so lebendig war wie die Vorstellung des Gottkönigs. Gegen Ende der 'romanischen' Kunstperiode schon sind ja auch die Darstellungen des Gekreuzigten mit Königskrone selten geworden." Ibid., p. 26.

[588] As Böhmer notes, there is some ambiguity in the Anonymous as to whether royal deification takes place *ex gratia* or *per participationem divinae gratiae et naturae*. But Böhmer would have it that *ex gratia* (= Berges' *Gottesvikariat*) prevails over *per participationem* (virtually equivalent to Berges' *Gottesebenbildlichkeit*).

[589] J24/L4: 664, 13.

[590] Ibid., 664, 19.

[591] Ibid., 667, 7.

[592] Ibid., 667, 24.

as they are in the divine grace and nature (*participes diviṇe gratiẹ atque naturẹ*).[593] Christ co-rules with kings (and bishops) (*conregnare*) in this world.[594]

For the subordination of the sacerdotal christ to the royal christ, the most important passage is the following. Here the bearing of the Anonymous' Two *Christi* Christology on the relationship of the *regnum* and the *sacerdotium* receives its clearest statement. After reasserting his conviction that both kings and priests are *christi* and *dii*, he goes on:

Unde et uterque in spiritu et Christus et Deus est, et in officio figura et imago Christi et Dei [or Christi-Dei, Version B] est. Sacerdos sacerdotis, rex regis. Sacerdos inferioris officii et naturẹ, id est humanitatis, rex superioris, id est divinitatis.[595]

A few lines before, the Anonymous had first announced the ecclesio-political significance of his christological distinction in discussing Old Testament priests and kings:

Sacerdos [of the Old Testament] quippe aliam prẹfigurabat in Christo naturam, id est hominis, rex aliam, id est, Dei. Ille [596] superiorem qua ẹqualis est Deo Patri, iste [596] inferiorem quẹ minor est Patre.[597]

Here the Anonymous makes the crucial distinction between priest and king which had remained below the surface of the Tractate until this point, expressly distinguishing the *christus patiens* (inferior to the Father), to whom we have been referring as the Humbled or the Earthly Christ, and the *Christus regnans* (equal with the Father) to whom we have referred as the Eternal Royal Christ or Christ in Majesty. The *Christus patiens* of Good Friday hanging on the Cross, "King of the Jews," and even this same Christ on Palm Sunday was, in the thought of the Anonymous, in effect less a showing forth of the *Christus regnans* than any anointed king of the Old Covenant. Only in Glory,

[593] Ibid., 667, 4 f.

[594] Ibid., 664, 9.

[595] Ibid., 667, 8 f. The continuation of this passage, dealing with the two natures of Jesus Christ, is given above, n. 426.

[596] The copyist has reversed *ille* and *iste* or perhaps the Anonymous himself nodded.

[597] J24/L4: 666, 1 ff. The continuation of this passage is quoted and discussed above, p. 164.

following the Ascension, was his eternally royal character recovered. Now it is in Jesus, *sacerdos, christus per gratiam* that
the Anonymous grounds the power of the clergy insofar as their
competence is sacerdotal, i.e., sacrificatory. Such power based
upon Jesus the Suffering Servant, the Anonymous argues, is clearly
inferior to that of a Christian prince, for the latter bears the
image of, and mystically participates in, the royal divine nature
of the Eternal Christ, discharging on earth a rôle like unto his
above.

Moreover, since Christ, as the Gospels proclaim, became incarnate as Priest to establish among the faithful, not a *sacerdotium
cęlorum* but a *regnum cęlorum*, an additional argument is provided for the contention that the royal power in Christ was
superior to the sacerdotal as, indeed, the royal power is among
men.[598] Therefore every bishop is properly instituted by the
royal power.[599] Just as the Jesus of Calvary was made a *sacerdos*
by the (incarnate) royal nature and was as such subordinate to
his Heavenly Father (even though Christ was equal to the Father
by reason of his hidden royalty, recovered at his Ascension), so
the bishop should be invested with his episcopal dignity (that is,
in this instance, his jurisdictional competence) [600] by the king.

Moreover, since Jesus Christ restored the Adamic unity of the
spiritual and the earthly in his own Person, it is appropriate

[598] J24/L4: 667, 19 ff.
Hinc igitur apparet maiorem esse in Christo regiam, quam sacerdotalem potestatem, et pręstantiorem, tanto scilicet, quanto divinitas eius maior est humanitate
atque pręstantior. Quare et a quibusdam estimatur ut in hominibus similiter maior
sit et pręstantior regia potestas, quam sacerdotalis, et . . . . rex maior et pręstantior, quam sacerdos, utpote melioris et pręstantioris Christi naturę imitatio
sive potestatis emulatio.

[599] The omitted *inquiunt* is explained above, n. 223. J24/L4: 667, 24 ff.:
Quapropter non est . . . contra Dei iusticiam, si sacerdotalis dignitas instituitur
per regalem vel ei subdita est, quia in Christo ita actum est, ut sacerdos fieret per
suam regiam potestatem et subditus Patri sit per sacerdotalem, cui est equalis per
regiam.

[600] It would be more logical here for the Anonymous to maintain that the king
bestows episcopal jurisdiction on the *consecrandus* but not his sacrificatory competence which he already possesses by virtue of priestly ordination. This indeed is
the theory delineated in Subsection *b* below. But here the Anonymous is really
claiming more for the king than the bestowal of jurisdictional authority. As *rex et
sacerdos* he bestows not only "royal" (jurisdictional) authority but also royal-
sacerdotal power, that is sacrificatory competence in the spiritual, Melchizedekian
sense.

that his Body Corporate,[601] the Church, maintain the unity of his two natures and offices in such a way that the king reflect his divine nature and the priest, his human nature. And just as Jesus Christ was one Person and not two, so his Church-Kingdom must be one body and not two, and this unity of *regnum* and *sacerdotium* — as though stuck together *in glutino Dei* [602] — must be set forth in the deportment of Christ's representatives, the royal and the sacerdotal *christi*, who should bear the harmonious and unified relationship to one another that once prevailed in the mingling of the divine and human natures (=*christi*) in the historical Jesus Christ. And since the Church-Kingdom is the *corpus regale* [603] of the glorified, no longer suffering, sacerdotal Christ, the royal power properly prevails over the sacerdotal order in Christian society, lest this *regale sacerdotium*, this *regnum Dei* be divided against itself and not stand.[604]

The Christian world is, to be sure, ruled by the two Gelasian principals, the *regalis potestas* and the *sacerdotalis auctoritas*, but this world is no longer half pagan, it has become the *gens sancta*, the *ecclesia*:

Mundum hic [Gelasius] appellat sanctam ęcclesiam, quę in hoc mundo peregrinatur. In hoc igitur mundo habent principatum sacri regiminis sacerdotalis auctoritas et regalis potestas.[605]

The relationship in a redeemed community is the reverse of that which perhaps properly obtained before society had been christianized. The royal power is now superior to the sacerdotal authority, not as in the Old Dispensation because of the primacy

---

[601] F. W. Buckler, proponent of "Barbarian" Christianity, formulates well the transition from the natural to the corporate body of Christ: "In passing from the Gospels to the Church we pass from the *Regnum Christi Regis* to the *corpus regale Christi Regis*." "Barbarian & Greek and Church History," *Church History*, XI (1924), p. 12.

[602] J24/L4: 669, 4 ff. After "showing" that his view is completely in accord with the Gelasian *dictum*, the Anonymous concludes the section:

Ideo igitur consecrantur et benedicuntur sacerdotes et reges, ut sanctę gentis et seminis benedicti, sancti sint rectores et benedicti et sanctę potestati sanctoque regimini sancti cohereant, et ministri et sanctorum decens sit copula et in glutino Dei unita conventio.

[603] This term is Buckler's, above, n. 601.

[604] "Regnum in se divisum desolabitur" is a recurrent theme throughout the Codex.

[605] J24/L4: 663, 27 ff.; cf. 668, 32 ff.

of the temporal [606] but because at length the Kingdom of God has become more visible in a christianized liturgical kingship than in an imperialized papalized *sacerdotium*. Pope Gelasius had, of course, clearly given as the reason for the separation of the royal power and the sacerdotal authority that only Jesus Christ had as God-Man combined these offices perfectly and that He, discerning the proneness of man to sinful excess, ordained for the welfare of mankind that never, as under the Old Covenant and among the Gentiles, should these two powers be brought together in a single hand.[607] But the Anonymous has nullified the Gelasian precaution and circumvented his strictures by insisting on the Christlikeness and deity conferred on the king during liturgical consecration, which in restoring the supra-lapsarian divine image, secures for him a sacramental sanctity that "legitimizes" his exercise of combined religious and political power in emulation of the Heavenly Melchizedek.

b. The King has the Unction of Christ, the Bishops the Benediction of the Apostles.

Although the Anonymous would seem to have succeeded fairly well, on his own premises, in subordinating the *sacerdos* to the king, making one the image of the human nature of Christ, the other of the divine, nevertheless, he seems unwilling to rest his case solely upon this argument and at one point in the "De consecratione" entertains the notion that the unction of bishops is after all fundamentally different from that of the king. Although, he says, the outward forms of royal and episcopal unction may seem alike, according to the inner grace they differ.[608] The one repeats the Consecration of the Son of God at Jordan, while the

---

[606] Thomas Aquinas was later to contrast in this sense the priestly kingdom (Ex. 19:6) of the Old Covenant and the royal priesthood (I Peter 2:9) of the New.

[607] A. Thiel, ed., Epistolae Romanorum Pontificum (Braunsberg, 1868), pp. 567 f.

[608] J24/L4: 669, 23 ff.

Si vero ad exempla divinę rationis, iuxta quę unguntur et sanctificantur, maior regis quam sacerdotis et unctio et sanctificatio et potestas. Etsi enim secundum materiam olei et visibile sacramentum eadem sit unctio et sanctificatio sacerdotis et regis, sed *secundum interiorem gratiam et veritatem invisibilis et spiritualis unguenti* et maxime secundum exemplum filii Dei, ad quod instituta est, maior et sanctior videtur unctio et sanctificatio et potestas regis quam sacerdotis.

other is instituted in imitation of Moses' setting apart of Aaron
and of Christ's blessing of the Apostles:

Nam unctio quidem et sanctificatio sacerdotum ad exemplum Aaron instituta est, quem Moyses uncxit et sanctificavit, et quod maius est, ad
exemplum apostolorum, quos uncxit Deus Pater unctione spirituali et
gratia Spiritus sancti. Regis vero unctio instituta est ad exemplum illius,
quem "Deus" pater "unxit" ante secula "pre omnibus participibus suis,"
Iesu Christi Domini nostri.[609]

These parallels enable the Anonymous to think of the king as related to the bishops he has elected as Christ to the Apostles whom
He chose, for just as Christ was anointed above all his fellows
(Hebrews 1:9 and the Edgar Ordo) so must also the king, whose
consecration repeats that of Jesus Christ, be superior to all fellow participants in sacred unction, namely bishops, priests, and
indeed all who are christened.[610] He continues:

Quapropter sicut melior est Filius Dei apostolis suis, et sanctior unctio
eius unctione apostolorum et potestas eius sublimior potestate illorum,
ita melior videtur rex sacerdotibus et sanctior unctio eius unctione illorum et potestas eius illorum potestate sublimior.[611]

Bishops, to be sure, follow Christ no less than the king, but they
do so "interposita vice et immitatione apostolorum." [612] With
these excellent arguments he concludes:

Unde et regis potestas et ordinatio episcoporum potestate et ordinatione
sublimior esse cernitur, et si non sublimior, non tamen esse videtur inferior.[613]

One is surprised to encounter this final admission of uncertainty,
for the Anonymous has given throughout the appearance of
utter confidence. Even as he temporarily demotes the bishop as
a mere imitator of the Apostles and by implication deprives the

---

[609] A continuation of the foregoing excerpt. The same parallel is repeated more
briefly ibid., 677, 24 ff.

[610] Ibid., ll. 33 f.

[611] Ibid., 670, 5 ff.

[612] Rex enim principaliter sequitur Christum, id est ex eius vice et imitatione,
episcopi vero, etsi secuntur Christum, hoc tamen faciunt interposita vice et immitatione apostolorum.

[613] Continuation of the foregoing quotation.

bishop of the status of a true *christus*, he shows evidence of a loss of nerve in his otherwise daring assault upon the papal citadel. Perhaps he feels that he may have gone too far toward undermining his own clerical position. How our Norman ecclesiastic restores to the national episcopate what he has taken from the international *sacerdotium* in insisting upon its Apostolicity is the subject of our next Subsection.

c. Royal and Episcopal Christi, *the Greater and the Lesser King.*

The ambiguity of the Anonymous' utterance on the relationship of the bishop to the king and the seeming hesitancy evidenced in the foregoing quotation may be explained satisfactorily as follows — although never quite so clearly articulated by the Anonymous himself!

Insofar as his purely sacerdotal (sacrificial) function is concerned, the bishop is not a *christus*. The Anonymous, even when most "unctuous" could never think of the earthly Christ surrounded by twelve lesser christs. To be christs, the Anonymous would probably have said, had he been pressed, the Apostles would have had to be bishops, and to be bishops they would have had to be under a king, which the Apostles were not since the royalty of their Master was concealed except to the eyes of faith. The functions of the Apostles were therefore solely spiritual [614] and their unction spiritual.[615] Bishops too have Apostolic, spiritual, evangelical functions, but in addition administrative or jurisdictional responsibilities. Bishops at investure become kings, just as kings at their consecration become priests.[616] They are *reguli*, as it were, in the measure that they are *christi*. The former term is not found in the Anonymous, but the thought is

---

[614] Of course, one day they will be seated at the right hand of the Lord to judge the twelve tribes. This the Anonymous recognizes (e.g., J31/B30: 481) and because of his half-realized eschatology, bishops as the successors of the Apostles may judge, though the Apostles themselves had been restrained therefrom.

[615] See quotation above, p. 181, and the discussion of spirituality, pp. 134 f.

[616] The Anonymous puts it thus: "rex sacerdos [est] et sacerdos rex." See full quotation given above, p. 168. Cf. also below, n. 620 and another quotation given below, n. 650: ". . . episcopi . . . sunt . . . reges . . . "; also n. 652: ". . . reges regnant et sacerdotes sanctificant et *utrique iudicant*."

there. After comparing the powers bestowed on the bishop and the king in their respective *ordines*, he concludes:

Unde sequitur, ut etiam e duobus alterum dicamus, videlicet, ut aut sacerdos sit etiam rex, aut rex sit etiam in hac parte sacerdos. Sed quodlibet horum verum sit sive utrumque, negare non possumus, quin sit in hac parte una eademque utriusque potestas, et in toto misterio et virtute unum virga regalis et episcopalis.[617]

Or again, of the Pope, the Anonymous says "et ipse summus pontifex est, in quantum rex est."[618] Compare also the following:

Quod si quis dicat, quod etiam sacerdos rex sit — omnis enim, qui regit rex iure potest appellari — hic pro eis melius facere videtur, ut rex instituatur per regem, minor per maiorem.[619]

It is not clear to whom he here alludes, probably a curialist arguing that the emperor or king can be set in office only by a higher ruler, an axiom that would conform with what would seem clerically rational. The point is that with an important reservation the Anonymous is prepared to grant that the Pope or any bishop is a *rex* [620] in the measure that he heads a diocesan *regimen*. The bishop in his administrative capacity is a lesser king under a greater. We might put it this way: The bishop as *sacerdos* receives at consecration a reinforcement of the Apostolic spiritual unction which was already his on becoming a *presbyter*. And as we noted under Subsection *b*, the bishop as *apostolicus* is inferior to the king as the Apostles were to Jesus Christ. But the bishop

---

[617] J24/L4: 675, 1 ff.

[618] Ibid., 679, 24 f.

[619] Ibid., 667, 27 ff.

[620] Cf. J24/L4: 672, 28 f.: "Et hec . . . gratia communis est regum et sacerdotum, in quantum et ipsi [sacerdotes] reges sunt." Cf. ibid., 663, 23 ff.: "Ad hoc ipsum [regnum] etiam et episcopalis ordo instituitur . . . ut et ipse regat sanctam ęcclesiam secundum formam doctrinę . . ."

The idea that the bishop is a kind of king the Anonymous perhaps derived from the Pseudo-Isidorian epistle of Pope Clement (actually of course the Pseudo-Clementine Recognitiones) from which he took other material (cf. above, n. 212):

Aaron crismate compositionis perunctus, princeps populi fuit et tamquam rex primitias et tributum . . . accepit . . . et . . . plebem iudicabat. — Hinschius, op. cit., p. 53.

Francis Accursius (thirteenth century) in a "harangue" declared that an archbishop, particularly, was a kind of *rex*, because he was obliged to rule (*regere*) his province. E. Kantorowicz and George L. Haskins, "A Diplomatic Mission of Francis Accursius," E. H. R., LVIII (1943), p. 436 and n. 3.

as *episcopus* (overseer, ruler of the Christian people of his diocese) receives at consecration-investiture a "christic" unction of
viceroyalty. In this capacity the bishop is inferior to the king
as a satrap to the great king.[621] The royal and the episcopal
christi differ thus in the scope of their *regimen* but not in their
legal title.[622] The jurisdictional powers of bishop and king are
regal; they are equal in quality, but in quantity the king's is
superior. Ultimately the reason for their "equality" in title if not
in scope is their common source in the Eternal Christ. Hence in
very truth the "world" is governed by two powers, the Anonymous avers, speciously appealing to Pope Gelasius' dictum, after
assimilating *mundus* to *ecclesia*. Therefore a king may invest a
bishop and a bishop consecrate a king without either being thought
inferior to the other, for in both consecratory acts it is Christ-
God who bestows the jurisdictional grace:

Quod quidem sequitur, ut regis et sacerdotis communis sit huius regiminis principatus, in quo etiam et paris privilegii videtur esse sacerdotalis
auctoritas et regalis potestas et rex et sacerdos equales in principatu
sacri regiminis. Quare non magis videtur absurdum, si rex hęc pręrogat
homini qui futurus est episcopus, quam si eam pręrogaret episcopus,
presertim cum neque rex neque episcopus ei pręrogant, sed eorum caput,
id est Christus Deus, in cuius sacramento, immo in quo, non sunt duo,
sed unus Christus.[623]

Be it noted here that the Anonymous affirms of the *Heavenly*
Christ that he is one. He has previously said that the historic

[621] For an interpretation of the Arian Controversy in terms of the Oriental great
king and satraps, see F. W. Buckler, op. cit., also "The Re-emergence of the Arian
Controversy," Anglican Theological Review, X (1927/28), pp. 11 ff.

[622] Berges, who does not draw the distinction I have made between the spiritual
(Apostolic) and the "christic" consecration of the bishop, says that the Anonymous
distinguishes the bishop from the king by reason of their office, not their legal title:
Op. cit., p. 28:
. . . seit Christus kann es nur ein "regale sacerdotium" geben, und wenn man
weder dem König noch dem Bischof die besondere Christusebenbildlichkeit ab-
sprechen will, bleibt allein übrig, in beiden diesselbe "gratia" . . . wirksam zu
sehen und den Unterschied zwischen beiderlei Christusebenbildlichkeit statt in den
Rechtstitel in das *Amt* zu legen.
This comes close to what we are saying here in Subsection c. The text for the common grace is J24/L4: 665, 21 ff. But Berges overlooks another place which was the
basis of Subsection b where the Anonymous says that the interior graces of royal
and episcopal consecration are in fact different. Ibid., 669, 26.

[623] J24/L4: 668, 33 ff.

Jesus Christ was in a sense two Christs, one by nature, one by grace. Here he is at pains to say that the consecratory grace which empowers both kings and bishops to rule is from the Royal Christ. Neither the consecrating archbishop (at a coronation) nor the officiating king (in episcopal investiture) is superior, the one to the other, for in either rite it is the same Royal Christ *per naturam* who effects the sacramental change through his ministrant, either an episcopal or a royal *christus per gratiam*:

Nec puto, quod aliquis iustius debeat ea prerogare quam Christus ex natura per Christum ex gratia, sanctus ex natura, per sanctum ex gratia.[624]

Both king and bishop by virtue of the common chrism are qualified to institute [625] the other and each to rule, for one in mystery and power are the royal and the episcopal *virga*.[626] Such is the tentative contribution of the Anonymous to the solution of the investiture problem. The royal power is at least not inferior [627] to the episcopal.

d. The King as Presul Princeps et Summus.

"At least not inferior," the Anonymous breathes heavily, as he comes momentarily to rest on the shoulder of the royalist peak, but further up, haloed in clouds of glory, he descries the royal

[624] J24/L4: 668, 39 ff. Cf. following note.

[625] This verb is used in preference to "invest" because the consecration of both the king and another bishop is performed by the *sacerdos*. To emphasize the coördinate relationship of the king's essential but non-liturgical function in episcopal election-investiture-consecration and that of archbishop at the royal consecration-investiture, the non-liturgical word *instituo* is used of both. For example:

Quapropter si rex instituit sacerdotem, vel sacerdos regem, non homo instituit hominem, sed sancta Dei potestas, sancta virtus, sancta sapientia et istum instituere et illum alium per alium."

[626] J24/L4: 675, 4 f.: ". . . et in toto misterio et virtute unum virga regalis et episcopalis."

[627] Ibid., 670, 8 f.

In insisting on the "royalty" of the episcopate while enhancing that of the king the Anonymous may be likened to Robert Sanderson, bishop of Lincoln. In the seventeenth century, the problem of strengthening *de jure divino* the governmental (*regere*) authority of episcopacy over against the challenge of the Presbyterians to both king and episcopate without at the same time derogating from the ecclesiastical competence of the king was an acute one for the Stuart divines. The very title of Sanderson's Episcopacy (as Established by Law in England) not Prejudicial to Regal Power, written in 1648 but not published until 1661 was symptomatic of the problem confronting Anglicanism in that parlous century.

summit itself. For him, the mystery of kingship is that the lesser elevates to office the greater, John baptizes Jesus,[628] and suffragans consecrate their metropolitan. Cardinals who elect the Pope, he pointedly remarks, are not superior to him whom they elevate to power. Surely the *presul princeps et summus* is not inferior to the archbishop who consecrates him.[629] Nay more, it is he who completes the hierarchy above the metropolitans.

This feeling for the superior dignity of the king over the Church (which is both his and Christ's Kingdom) is due to the fact that the king is not only the image and vicar of *Christus Deus*, but also in a unique way co-ruler with him. In the sacramental-cosmological sense the royal *christus per gratiam* is Christophorous supplying the human vehicle or nature for a political or perhaps we should say, simply a royal incarnation [630] of the Eternal *Christus per*

[628] Cf. the antiphon in the Manuale Ambrosianum, II, in Epiphania Domini, p. 91, l. 20:
Hodie . . . vino laetantur convivia:
baptizat miles regem, servus dominum suum,
Johannes Salvatorum: aqua Jordanis stupuit,
columba protestatur, paterna vox audita est: Filius
meus hic est, in quo bene complacui; ipsum audite.
This antiphon is dependent upon the Oriental rite, F. C. Conybeare, Rituale Armenorum (Oxford, 1905), pp. 426, 28. We have already noted the fondness of the Anonymous for a related antiphon in Epiphany, above p. 77. The survival of this essentially Eastern feeling is discussed by E. Kantorowicz in Laudes, p. 142 and at greater length in his "Epiphany and Coronation."

[629] J24/L4: 679, 19 ff.:
Nec ideo minor est dicendus [presul princeps et summus, l.19] pontifice, quia consecrat eum pontifex, quia plerumque fit, ut minores consecrent maiorem, inferiores superiorem, ut cardinales papam et metropolitanum suffraganei. Quod ideo fit, quia non sunt auctores consecrationis, sed ministri.
See the note on the source of this title, above, n. 583.

[630] An interesting later parallel to this kind of thinking is found in Plowden, the English lawyer, c. 1550, concerning the king's two bodies. His "Christology" of the royal person reminds one at once of Chalcedon:
So that he [the king] has a body natural adorned and invested with the estate and dignity royal, and he has not a body natural distinct and divided by itself from the office and dignity royal, but a body natural and a body politic together indivisible, and these two bodies are incorporated in one person and make one body and not divers, that is, the body corporate in the body natural et e contra the body natural in the body corporate. So that the body natural by the conjunction of the body politic to it (which body politic contains the office, government, and majesty royal) is magnified and by the said consolidation hath in it the body politic.
The formula is perhaps not so lapidary as the one in Leo's Tome, but this royal Two *Bodies* doctrine is an interesting parallel to the Anonymous' Two *Christi* doctrine. It is the basic text in Frederic W. Maitland's "The King's Two Bodies," Selected

naturam, once incarnate as *Sacerdos*. This exceedingly important doctrine of *condominium* is introduced by a passage, ascribed by the Anonymous to Gregory Nazianzenus.[631] On the basis of it he concludes:

Rex enim Christo *conregnat*. . . . Magnum ergo et divinum munus est et cęlestis investitura, quod rex Christo *conregnat* et in regno Christi quę sunt humana dispensat, et quod ab illo et vito venia et mortis potestas indulta est, gladius datus est, ut non tam operetur, quam ut comminetur.[632]

This Byzantine conception of rulership [633] was rejected by Charlemagne who held that the Apostolic intention in II Timothy 2 on co-rule with Christ was in the realm of faith only.[634] A political construction of the passage was for him inadmissible. Charlemagne's authority seems to have been more theocentric than Christocentric. The whole thought of the Anonymous is, in its peculiar way, Christocentric. In marked contrast to the Gelasian dictum that Christ had expressly severed the regal and the priestly powers out of a recognition of the danger of their abuse when united in any but the divine, the Anonymous asserts the divinity of kings by consecration, the fusion of two natures, divine and human, and hence the king's Christlike competence in both the temporal and spiritual realms. The Anonymous holds that the Celestial Christ so far approves of the rejoining of the royal and sacerdotal functions that the king, by virtue of the apotheosis,

Essays, ed. by H. D. Hazelton (Cambridge, 1936). On the constitutional significance of the distinction, see E. Kantorowicz, "Christus-Fiscus," Synopsis: Festgabe für Alfred Weber (Heidelberg, 1948), esp. pp. 225–229. While the second royal "body" is the nation and the cosmic dimension has been lost, nevertheless the parallel with the Anonymous is closer than would appear, for also the Anonymous intuitively feels that the king's people are sanctified with him as a *gens sancta* in the essentially corporate act of royal consecration.

It will be recalled, moreover, that the Anonymous delights in that kind of analysis which divides the Pope into *pontifex, homo, peccator*, J1/B1, or Rome into *locus, lapides, fideles*, and *reprobati*.

[631] Cf. Oratio xvii, cap. ix, Migne, P. G., XXXV, col. 976.
[632] J28/L5: 685, 15 ff.
[633] Cf. E. Kantorowicz, Laudes, p. 50, n. 127 and "Synthronos." Back of this lies the ancient Eastern cycle of religio-political thought traced by Arthur Darby Nock, "Σύνναος θεός," Harvard Studies in Classical Philology, XLI (1930), pp. 1 ff. See also Peter Charanis, "Coronation and its Constitutional Significance in the Later Roman Empire," Byzantion XV (1940/1), pp. 49 ff.
[634] M.G.H., Leges, III, II, Supplement, Libri Carolini, pp. 8 ff.

may be said to co-rule with Him. Moreover, by the glorious rite of royal consecration (here, *investitura*), the Royal Christ commits to the king the *sacerdotes* [635] who — to complete the thought of the Anonymous for him — are to be related to their national priest-king, in the same way that the national, royal *christi* of Christendom are related to the Eternal Christ. As the king becomes one with Christ during his consecration, so does the bishop become one with his king in investiture-consecration:

Cum autem hanc investituram rex tribuit, non laicus, sed christus Domini tribuit, christus videlicet Domini per gratiam ei conregnans, qui Christus Dominus est per naturam, et quia isti Christo conregnant simul, quę ad regnum suum pertinent, ambo simul tribuunt, ambo simul execuntur. Et qui hos ab hoc opere dividere nititur,[636] id efficere conatur, ut domus Dei cadat, et regnum Christi desoletur. . . . Verumtamen Christus iste per gratiam, id est rex, servit Christo per naturam.[637]

The Anonymous knows very well, of course, that the king bestows "neque ordinem, neque ius sacerdotii" [638] on a bishop but only the "dominationinem et tutelam ecclesię et potestatem regendi populum Dei," [639] for the bishop's sacerdotal-sacrificial

[635] J28/L5: 685, 33 ff.: "Et hęc quidem sublimis et gloriosa investitura [=here, royal consecration] est, qua Deus [the Eternal Christ] imperatorem sive regem investit, ut . . . celorum via largius pateat, et terrestre regnum celesti regno famuletur, et ut manui suę sacerdotes suos Christus committat et eisdem etiam dominari concedat."

[636] By challenging the right of the king to invest his bishops. Cf. nn. 604, 649.

[637] J28/L5: 685, 33 ff. Another phrasing of the *conregnare* is found in J24/L4: 663, 21 ff.: ". . . ideo enim regnant in ecclesia, que est regnum Dei et Christo conregnant, ut eam regant, defendant." See also 664, 9.

[638] Canon law makes the following distinctions:
I. *Potestas jurisdictionis.*
  A. *Jurisdictio fori.* External ecclesiastical matters.
    1. Legislative, including the power of defining and enforcing doctrine.
    2. Judicial.
    3. Coercive.
  B. *Potestas poli.* The relationships between man and God: dispensations from vows, etc., based on the sacrament of penance.

II. *Potestas ordinis.* The power of conferring grace through the sacraments.

According to canon law only a *sacerdos* (here, priest or bishop) can exercise the *potestas jurisdictionis.* The Anonymous, writing of course at a time before these distinctions were formulated with their present clarity, may be said to have preëmpted for the king the *jurisdictio fori* and to have seriously undercut the significance of the *potestas poli* and the *potestas ordinis.*

[639] J24/L4: 667, 42 ff. He is perhaps even more emphatic on this point in the generally more sober J28/L5: 685, 40 ff.:

competence comes to him only in Apostolic succession. What the Anonymous aims to accomplish is to establish the non-lay character of the king, meaning thereby more than the concession of the *temporalia* or even his investiture of bishops. The king is himself a minister of Christ and as such *presul princeps et summus*.

Nay more, he is so high "ut nulla potestas Deo sit propinquior." In appealing to a Pseudo-Isidorian preface to a council, the Anonymous characteristically exploits a verbalism, this time a textual corruption (?) and writes: "Ex qua videlicet perpendere potestis, quantum imperator prelatus sit pontificibus et erectus usque ad c̨elum [=zelum] per Dei providentium. . . ."[640] On the basis of a unique text, the Anonymous goes on to an assertion of even greater exaltation of the king:

Propter quod usque ad c̨elum a domino Iesu Christo erectus esse dicitur. Ad c̨elum, inquam, non utique istud corporeum quod videmus, sed incorporeum quod non videmus, id est invisibilem Deum. Usque ad Deum [=c̨elum!] quippe est, quia ei in potestate ita coniunctus est, ut nulla potestas Deo sit propinquior, imperatore sublimior, sed omnis sit alia inferior. Quia summi et c̨elestis imperatoris et secundi terrenique una eademque potestas est, sed principaliter, terreni secundarie.[641]

The foregoing passage, which precedes a long citation of the precedent of the kings of Spain and their authority over bishops, councils, and doctrine,[642] serves us well in concluding our inquiry into

---

Investiture dico huius regiminis videlicet et dominationis in populum et possessionis temporalium rerum, non sacerdotii et sacerdotium gratiarum. In his enim numquam audivi investituram nominari.

Anton Scharnagl characterizes the position of the Anonymous in comparison with his contemporaries: Ivo of Chartres, he says, stood for the freedom of the Church and the substitution of the *Eigenkirchenidee* by the *Protektionsidee* reducing investiture to *concessio*. Op. cit., p. 88. Elsewhere (p. 120) he writes:

Am weitesten geht der Anonymus von York, der auf Grund seines theokratischen Systems, für die Fürsten die volle Investitur des Eigenkirchenrechts beansprucht. Ihm steht am nächsten Hugo von Fleury, der die Investitur zwar auf die Temporalien beschränkt, aber auch ein Ernennungsrecht des Königs verteidigt.

[640] J24/L4: 676, 1 ff. Hinschius, op. cit., 283: "Dominus noster . . . imperatorem erexit ad *zelum* qui undique sacerdotum pontifices ad se convocavit. . . ."

In fairness to the Anonymous it should be noted that the Gonzales Collectio canonum, i.e., the pure Hispana, also gives *ad coelum*. Migne, P. L., LXXXIV, col. 163.

[641] Ibid., 10 ff.

[642] Ibid., 16 ff.

the bearing of a Royal Christology upon the relationship between the *regnum* and the *sacerdotium*. The Preface to the Acts of Chalcedon intended no more than to empower the Emperor to call a council in order that peace might prevail and doctrine be not altered, a provision allegedly of Jesus Christ himself, foreseeing future doctrinal strife. The Anonymous exploits *zelum*, identifying it with *coelum* and the "invisible God." God is styled "Emperor," and it is then asserted that the power of the Heavenly and the earthly is one and the same. In consequence of the exaltation of the emperor and the identification of his power with that of God, it is natural for the Anonymous to write:

Unde manifestum est reges habere sacrosanctam potestatem ęcclesiastici regiminis super ipsos etiam pontifices Domini et imperium super eos, ut et ipsi [in their turn as satraps] pie fideliterque regant sanctam ęcclesiam, inmaculatam sponsam immaculati sponsi, dignam digni, divinam Dei, cęlestem cęlestis.[643]

The Church is of course the Immaculate Spouse of the Exalted Christ. The meaning of the entire commentary on *ad cęlum* is therefore that the power of the Exalted Christ and the emperor/ king is one, for God has drawn the reigning monarch to himself "ad cęlum." [644]

The Anonymous' ecclesio-political theory is Christocentric, but the Christ whom his king imitates and whose power he shares is the Royal Exalted Eternal Christ, for whom the Crucifixion was but an incident to be pondered over by priests. Christology has become almost completely regalized.

e. Lesser Reasons for the Superiority of the King to the Bishop.

Apart from investiture the king has other, as we should say, spiritual (rather than, as the Anonymous is somewhat awkwardly obliged to say, sacerdotal) functions.

[643] J24/L4: 676, 27 ff.
[644] Allied to the Anonymous' feeling for the participation of the king in Godhead, is the idea expressed in the Capitula Pistensia, probably from the hand of Hincmar (H. Schrörs), that the king participates in the *numen* and *nomen Dei*, M.G.H., Capit., II, p. 305.

(1) *The King Rules the Hearts as Well as the Bodies*
of His Subjects

Arch and canny as ever, the Anonymous points out that there can be no proper exclusion of the king from ecclesiastical affairs on the ground that the king has competence only in matters pertaining to the body, while the Church is concerned with the soul, for according to the credal faith in the Resurrection, both the body and the soul are to be saved. One is reminded of Richard Hooker's indignation [645] against those who assert that God ordained kings for no other end and purpose than to mast up men like hogs:

Necesse est . . . si bene regantur corpora, bene regantur et animę et e converso, quoniam utraque ideo reguntur, ut in *resurrectione* simul utraque salventur.[646]

The earthly kingdom under its *rex et sacerdos*, tends to replace the *ecclesia* as the instrument of salvation.

Another argument for the king's superiority to the bishop is connected with the foregoing. It is a reinterpretation of the common assumption, Gelasian and Imperial, that the king rules the bodies of his subjects. It reminds one of the sophistry of Portia's distinction between flesh and blood. By appealing to a passage ascribed to St. Ambrose [647] the Anonymous argues as perfectly self-evident that the king who admittedly controls the bodies of Christians, controls also what these redeemed bodies display, namely, the royal-sacerdotal dignity.[648] The Anonymous moves on to reinforce his point by appealing to a favorite textual argument that the Kingdom of Christ cannot be divided against itself

[645] Laws of Ecclesiastical Polity, VIII, iii, 2.

[646] J24/L4: 663, 29 ff. He continues:
Veruntamen si rex haberet tantum principatum regendi corpora christianorum, nonne etiam haberet principatum regendi templum Dei quod sanctum est?
Cf. ibid., 677, 13 ff. quoted above, p. 172 and J28/L5: 684, 43 ff. The Edgar Ordo makes reference to the king's proper concern for both *corpora* and *corda* of his subjects. Cf. the citation of Isidore by Deusdedit (II, 160), ed. Glanvell, pp. 267 f.

[647] I have not located it. Cf. De mysteriis, vi.

[648] J24/L4: 663, 38 ff.:
"Nam et ideo christianorum corpora in baptismate sanctificantur, et post unctionem mistica veste induuntur, ut regia simul et sacerdotali dignitate potiantur," sicut dicit beatus Ambrosius. Quę cum ita sint, manifestum est, quod rex habet principatum regendi eos qui sacerdotali dignitate potiuntur.

without falling. For this reason too the king should not be separated from ecclesiastical affairs.[649]

(2) *The Royal* Christus *as Principal Bearer of the Keys*

The king is also superior to the bishop by virtue of the royal character of the Keys, defined as the power and government of the kingdom, itself an honor proper to kings and not to priests except insofar as they too are kings.[650] The ascription of the power of the Keys to the king is based, as so frequently in the "De consecratione" upon the Edgar Ordo. In the Edgar Ordo (here dependent upon the German Ordo) at the bestowal of the *virga* the bishop prays that He, "qui est clavis David et sceptrum domus Israel, qui aperit et nemo claudit, claudit et nemo aperit, sit tibi [the king] adiutor, qui educit vinctum de domo carceris sedentem in tenebris et umbra mortis, ut in omnibus sequi merearis eum." The king is here bidden simply to be worthy of his Heavenly Lord. The Anonymous goes much further. In the first place he interprets the Isaianic passages to mean opening by grace the Kingdom of Heaven, freeing from sin, and transporting into the realm of light and life.[651] He goes on to apply the great Messianic passages

---

[649] J24/L4: 663, 41 ff.:
Non ergo debet excludi rex a regimine sanctę ecclesię, id est populi christiani, quia ita divideretur regnum ecclesię et fieret desolatum. . . . Non est igitur bonum ut regnum sanctę ęcclesię desoletur, quia et ipsa ęcclesia carens regno cito desolaretur. Carebit autem regno, si reges ab eius procuratione et tuitione separentur. Sed et corpora christianorum minime regentur, si regalis potestas ab ęcclesia divideretur. It will be recalled that the Anonymous himself uses the same divided kingdom text to defend the realm of the bishop from papal encroachment by way of special grants to the monasteries within a diocese.

[650] J24/L4: 672, 15 ff.
Quia igitur et episcopi christi sunt et reges, claves regni cęlorum accipiunt, quę magis ad regiam potestatem pertinent, quam ad sacerdotalem. Regni enim cęlorum claves dicimus, non sacerdotii cęlorum, per quod sacerdotes signantur fore etiam reges. — Cf. also ll.30 f.
Archbishop Cranmer also held that the King whom he served so dutifully possessed in addition to the sword, the Keys. Answering the examiner Martin during the trial under Mary, Cranmer said in part:
There is no subject but to a king.
The pope is contrary to the crown. I cannot obey both: for no man can serve two masters at once, as you in the beginning of your oration declared by the sword and the keys, attributing the keys to the pope, and the sword to the king. *But I say the king hath both.*
Miscellaneous Writings and Letters of Thomas Cranmer, ed. by J. E. Cox, Parker Society Publications (Cambridge, 1846), p. 213.
[651] J24/L4: 672, 25 ff.

(Isaiah 22:22; 42:7) to the earthly vicar of the Exalted Christ. Moreover, the plural is only a manner of speech, the Anonymous maintains. Actually there is but one Key, for there is but one power, which the earthly king manipulates and, only by his leave, the bishops.[652] The Anonymous is at pains to assimilate the Keys of Peter to the Key of David and to insist that the power of the Key is one for kings and bishops in the degree to which the bishops at investiture share in the royal nature. The Keys of Peter have been transformed into the Key of David without having lost, however, their power to loose and bind.[653] They have been regalized and returned to the bishops by royal grace. Such, at least, is my interpretation of the following projection backwards into Apostolic times:

Nam et Petrus et ceteri apostoli, priusquam sacerdotio fungerentur [which was possible only after Calvary] sed tamen iam cum Christo regerent discipulos Christi, claves regni cęlorum acceperunt a Christo. Quę res indicio est, ut non sacerdotibus debeantur claves istę sed regibus.[654]

For "disciples" we read "laity," for "Peter and the other Apostles" we read "bishops" and learn that they exercise their sacerdotal function, as it were, by their human "Apostolic" nature, but that their power to rule and to save — for such is the Anonymous' definition of the power of the Key(s) — is bestowed upon them by Christ (through the instrumentality of the king) at investiture.[655]

[652] Ibid., 37 ff.:
. . . quia non est nisi una eademque clavis regni cęlorum et David, id est regis cęlorum. Non enim est nisi una eademque potestas et virtus et sapientia Dei, per quam reges regnant et sacerdotes sanctificant et utrique iudicant.

[653] Theodolph, bishop of Orleans, in a remarkable poem with imagery akin to that of the Edgar Ordo, ascribed to Charlemagne the power of the Keys, which Peter bestowed upon him on earth, having as it were, another set for himself in heaven:
Caeli habet hic claves, proprias te iussit habere,
Tu regis ecclesiae, nam regit ille poli.
Tu regis eius opes, clerum populumque gubernas,
Hic te caelicolas ducit ad usque choros. — M. G. H., Poet. lat., I, 524.

[654] J24/L4: 672, 35 ff.

[655] In interpreting the passage as a projection backwards, we need not be confused by the fact that the Gospel accounts required the Anonymous to consider Jesus before his sacrificial death as a king, even though elsewhere when generalizing on the whole of Jesus' earthly ministry, he characterized him as *sacerdos*, making Calvary stand for the whole of his life.

(3) *The Royal* Christus, *the Door,*
through which the Pastors of the Flock Enter the Fold

By virtue of his being the primary image of Christ, the king is clearly the one door through which the shepherds of the flock may pass. Without his consent to their consecration, bishops are not shepherds, but robbers. The staff bestowed upon the king at his anointment is the symbol of both his function as gate and chief shepherd, the imagery being conflated. Only as bishops acquiesce in the power of the king do they become lesser shepherds of the flock. The Anonymous identifies the sheepfold with the Kingdom of God and the Kingdom of God with the Realm. The Door in Heaven is Christ, the door on earth the second christ.

Quare et sanctissimi sacerdotes subditi sunt regibus tanquam Christo, eisque obsequium prestant, quia in regibus eim regnantem intelligunt et dominantem omnibus. Ac per hoc denique dum per reges intrant in ovile ovium, id est in potestatem regiminis, per hostium id est per Christum intrant, et pastores sunt ovium. Rex enim per potestatem Christus est et Christus hostium. Quicunque igitur per regis potestatem intrant, per Christum intrant. Ac per hoc intrant per hostium et pastores sunt ovium.[656]

As proof of the correctness of royal or imperial instatement of a bishop, the Anonymous cites a letter of Gregory the Great to the sister of the Eastern emperor in which he speaks of the Emperor as having elevated "an ape into a lion." [657] Apparently before the granting of the princely permission for consecration as a lesser *christus* and a lesser pastor, the *consecrandus* in his purely Apostolic state is a mere caricature of power.

We cannot leave the subject of the king as door and shepherd

---

[656] J24/L4: 672, 5 ff. Cf. J24/L4: 675, 6 ff.
. . . Non est contra Dei ordinationem . . . si rex, si sanctus, si consecratus, cuius totum est et virge sacramentum et virtus et potestas, illi [bishop-elect] dat quod suum est, cuius neutrum, est, et qui horum nichil habet. Sanctus enim in hoc non sancto, consecratus non consecrato, habens non habenti committit sanctitatis et virtutis ministerium, et secum intrare facit per hostium sibi apertum. Christus enim est hostium primum rex autem secundum, quia post Christum est hostium, quia alter Christus per adoptionem post Christum, qui Christus verus vices suas credere dignatur et regnum. Ideo igitur et qui intrat et cui committitur a rege, per hostium intrat et pastor est ovium. Alioquin fur potius esset et latro.
[657] Ibid., 675, 17 ff. The original was a pun on Leo I.

without some reference to the view of F. Kampers concerning the Shepherd King.[658] Kampers noted that Alcuin styled Charlemagne not only David but also royal shepherd. Combining the biblical idea of Melchizedek (*rex et sacerdos*) with what Kampers regarded as the essentially oriental idea of the Shepherd King, the Carolingian bishops thought of their ruler as the religio-political ruler-redeemer of a non-Roman *Oikoumene*, the threat of which Rome checked in full career with her more congenial theory of the *translatio imperii*, foisted upon Charlemagne. Voigt has rejected Kampers' theory of a Byzantine source and the excesses of his inference from Carolingian royal appellations.[659] But whatever the ultimate source, the feeling for the king as shepherd-redeemer described by Kampers crops out in "De consecratione." Though its language may be largely explained by the prominence of the Johannine pastoral image in the Gregorian controversy and by the Edgar Ordo, much of which was Carolingian in origin, nevertheless the very *élan* of "De consecratione" would seem to make of it a late survival of the kind of cosmic royalism [660] Kampers has described.

(4) *The King as* Doctor Ecclesiae

In view of the messianic, pastoral, and redemptive claims for the king already made, his right to control doctrine seems quite natural and not at all spectacular. Yet in the first part of "De consecratione" the Anonymous had ascribed doctrinal rule in the Church to the bishop. In the latter part of the same Tractate the king's competence in this specialized area is recovered in connection with the already discussed conception of the *condominium* of Christ and the king.

Sed christiani reges gentiles ab ęcclesia reppulerunt, hereticos condempnaverunt et eorum prava dogmata in sinum ecclesię penitus extinxerunt;

---

[658] "Rex et sacerdos," Historisches Jahrbuch (1925), pp. 495 ff. Fritz Kern held to a similar opinion. "Rex et sacerdos," Festschrift für Dietrich Schaefer (Jena, 1915). Kern, though holding to the preponderating influence of the pagan as distinguished from the biblical element in shaping Carolingian ideas of kingship, points out that it was Christian representations of the ancient Melchizedek in art that set the style for the coronation robes. Op. cit., p. 2.

[659] Op. cit., p. 359.

[660] An allied interpretation in the field of Old Testament research is the unfinished work of Hugo Gressmann, Der Messias (Göttingen, 1927).

Christo enim conregnabant, immo in Christi regno christiana jura dispensabant.[661]

More explicit and widesweeping than the foregoing which after all does not go much beyond what had already obtained in the Anglo-Saxon and Carolingian Churches,[662] is the assertion and the inference therefrom that the emperors were supreme over the first Four Councils. As these are likened by the Fathers themselves to the Four Gospels, the Anonymous may imply that the king and duke have authority both in local councils and over the Gospels.[663]

The Anonymous also quotes at length from Action I of the Council of Chalcedon at which Emperor Marcian was styled Teacher of the Faith.[664] Like most of the other powers of the king considered as superior to the bishop, the suggestion for the control of doctrine is derived from the Edgar Ordo with its prayer that the king "ecclesiam . . . doceat . . . et instruat."

(5) *A King Superior to the Bishops even though Not Anointed*

That the Anonymous truly believed in the *ex opere* effectiveness of royal unction, there can be no doubt, and yet for all his earnestness there juts up at one point the underlying royalist substratum unadorned by any theories about unction and chrism. The erosion

---

[661] J24/L4: 664, 7.

[662] Alcuin had declared that Christ gave Charlemagne to his people as *doctor et rector*. M.G.H., Ep. 41. Against the Adoptionist Elipandus of Toledo, he wrote of Charlemagne as "catholicus in fide, rex in potestate, *pontifex in praedicatione*, iudex in aequitate, philosophus in liberalibus studiis." Quoted by Kampers, op. cit., p. 49. Remigius had defended his consecration of Clovis against three bishops who were dismayed by the priestly character implied in the ceremony by stating that the king was a veritable *praedicator* as well as *defensor ecclesiae*. Referred to by Voigt, op. cit., p. 241. Adilbert of Milan referred to Charlemagne as illuminated by the Holy Spirit. Ibid., p. 357. On royal or imperial unction as an act of the Holy Spirit constituting the royal *christus* a *doctor ecclesiae*, see Philipp Oppenheim, "Die sakralen Momente in der deutschen Herrscherweihe bis zum Investiturstreit," Ephemerides Liturgicae, LVIII (1944), p. 45.

[663] J24/L4: 675, 24 ff.: "Cęterum quanta sit imperatorum sive regum auctoritas congregandi concilia eisque preessendi, testatur sanctorum patrum et sacerdotum auctoritas, quę de quattuor principalibus conciliis sicut sancta IIIIor evangelia omnibus fidelibus amplectendis ita dicit. . . ."

Here follows the preface from Pseudo-Isidore which introduces the Councils under the presidency of the four emperors. While the consequences concerning doctrine and the Gospels were not expressly drawn by the Anonymous, they were much later by the first Protestant King.

[664] Cf., on the Carolingian development of the term, K. Voigt, op. cit., p. 75.

of liturgical kingship set in somewhat more than a century after the time of our writer. The great versatility of this inclusive theorist of Christocentric kingship is vouched for in the fact that he has also left us an expression of that Divine Right kingship which was destined to supplant his own more characteristic doctrine.

His sense of the possible inadequacy of the appeal to unction in sustaining his royalism is evidenced by the fact that the Anonymous appeals to the ancient Christian argument for priestly subordination to pagan emperors *regardless* of their status as the anointed of the Lord. He points out also that Paul as a Roman citizen appealed to Caesar and quotes the words of Paul and Peter concerning obedience to those in authority. He then observes further that in the Old Testament Moses who was not anointed nevertheless had authority over Aaron.[665] With these words the Anonymous reveals that he is prepared to abandon even his favorite argument of the *ex opere* effectiveness of chrism in making a man into a king. For his loyalty to the prince is more profound than even his convictions about unction. With these words we behold a first fissure in the Anglo-Frankish institution of Davidic or Liturgical kingship.

It is not hard to visualize his nod of assent to Bishop Lancelot Andrewes of Winchester's distinction between "unctus" and "christus" in the interests of Stuart absolutism [666] and to overhear

[665] J24/L4: 666, 24 ff.:
Sed de Moyse quid dicemus, qui *non fuit rex unctione* sacratus, *non fuit sacerdos,* sed dux tantum populi fuit? Nonne et ipse super sacerdotes potestatem habuit et imperium? Nonne Aaron et filios eius uncxit et *consecravit* in sacerdotes et levitas et tabernaculum et altaria et omnia vasa eius *sanctificavit* et totum *dedicavit sanctuarium?* Quę nulla ratione facere potuisset, nisi illi super hęc omnia Dominus et potestatem dedisset et imperium, qui nichil iniuste agit vel iniquum.
We have already mentioned the importance of this text as an evidence of the concern of the Anonymous to defend also the right of ducal investiture in Normandy. See above, pp. 52 ff. and 105.

[666] Andrewes, who may have derived some of his extraordinary christological ideas from our Tractates, felt the necessity of distinguishing between the "rex *christus*" and the "sacerdos *unctus.*" Works, IV, p. 45, 50, 54. Andrewes was so convinced of the potency of royal chrism that he spoke of the Spirit accompanying its use in coronation as the True Olive, corresponding to the True Vine. Ibid., p. 84.
Andrewes virtually dechristianized the office of the royal *christus Domini.* Especially interesting in view of the possible dependence of Andrewes upon our Tractates is his discussion of the relationship of the *sanctus* and the *christus.* Andrewes says: "Omnes Sancti non sunt christi, at Reges christi; we cannot say of all Saints they

his approval of Cranmer's address to the boy king Edward in which the humble Archbishop disavowed any special authority accruing to himself by virtue of his function at the coronation, holding as the Reformer did that kings "be God's anointed, not in respect of the oil which the bishop useth, but in consideration of their power which is ordained, of the sword which is authorised, of their persons which are elected by God, and endued with the gifts of his Spirit for the better ruling and guiding of his people." [667]

(6) Obedience to the King a Foretaste of Heavenly Liberty

In some ways the most remarkable passage of the entire "De consecratione" is that in which the Anonymous describes the rewards of utter obedience to the king as the meaning of Christian liberty. Conformance to the will of the *christus per gratiam* is made equivalent to heeding the will of God. Rarely could one find such a daring identification of Christian freedom and obedience to the temporal power. With the king in the possession of the Keys and the other attributes of spiritual sovereignty he and his priests can together, sharing a common grace, reinforce each the special competency of the other that the Church might be fully Catholic, chaste, and free.[668] Freedom from sin and wickedness, this is the common goal of priest and king, ruling with Christ! Obedience to them is a foretaste of heavenly liberty:

---

be christs, of Kings we may." Sanctity does not make a *christus Domini*. Tyrants as well as devout rulers are all alike *christi*. "Then," he continues, "if religion makes them not, heresy will not unmake them." Andrewes has in this assertion completed the dechristianization of the conception of the royal *christus*, while insisting all the more vigorously upon his divine right and the sacriligious character of any kind of resistance to him. As in the Anonymous resistance to the king is sacrilege, regardless of the sanctity or orthodoxy of the monarch. Similarly the *christus Domini* has complete authority over his priests and prophets. Andrewes cites the banishment of Abiathar by Solomon and the declaration of Samuel that all the tribes of Israel including Levi, and hence the *sacerdotium*, were placed under Saul. Cf. n. 419 above.

[667] Miscellaneous Writings and Letters, ed. by J. Cox (Cambridge, 1846), p. 126.

[668] J24/L4: 673, 5 ff.:

Catholica per fidem et communionem sanctorum, *casta* per sobrietatem et continentiam, *libera* per inhabitantis in se Spiritus sancti presentiam. "Ubi" enim "spiritus Domini, ibi *libertas*." *Libera* sit, inquam, ut nulli turpitudini serviat, ut non regnet peccatum in suo mortali corpore, ut non obediat desideriis et concupiscentiis carnis, ut non obsequatur spiritibus immundis . . . ut propter suam libertatem cum Christo regnet in ęternum. Hoc enim est propter quod reges regnant et regunt ecclesiam, ut cum Christo regnent in ęternum.

Iam quippe misterium futuri regni operatur, et *ipsi sunt primitię cum Christo in futuro regnantium*. Regnum enim eorum figura est cęlestis regni et *libertas eorum futurę libertatis*, quę est summum bonum civitatis Dei nostri.[669]

9. Summary

We have now come to realize the full significance of the anointed and invested bishop as *regulus*. In marked contrast to Wyclif, whose doctrine of Election and Dominion strengthened the royal but also the centrifugal, *feudal* powers at the expense of the ecclesiastical, the Anonymous in his devotion to the royal power had the astuteness to *preserve* and even to enhance the episcopate as a means of reinforcing that royal power. He strengthened the king in proving the indelible character of unction as it effected the bishop, insisting, however, that the unction imparted a royal or a royal-priestly rather than a purely Apostolic sacerdotal power, and that as the king was the recipient of the same unction in a more representative way than any of his bishops, he was both more royal and more priestly than were they.

Secondly, he undergirded the king by insisting on the hierarchical principle in respect to the clergy *below* the archiepiscopal dignity and by demanding the obedience owed the local bishop by the regular clergy. At the same time he asserted with even greater conviction that the hierarchy is properly completed *above* the archiepiscopal rank, not by a primate and the Pope, but by the sacerdotal king who is no layman, but *rex et sacerdos* and *presul princeps et summus*.

The king as vicar of the Celestial Melchizedek and antitype of the Pope provides the religio-political unity upon which the Anonymous insists. In a notable passage already cited [670] he excoriates as pagan all organismic conceptions that divide the unity of the Kingdom of Christ, which is to say, the kingdom of the vicar of Christ. Any hierarchy above the archbishop must terminate in

---

[669] A continuation of the foregoing.

[670] The elaboration of the hierarchy above the rank of Archbishop, the Anonymous half seriously remarks, is a return to polytheism with its system of *flamines* and *archiflamines*, each priest authorized to sacrifice to the god appropriate to his sacerdotal level, J2/B2, 444, viii.

Christ's royal vicar. It is this unity which makes the worship of Christians unified and directed to the One God, for each bishop, holding the place of Christ, offers the sacrifice of praise to Christ, who is present for each people preëminently in their king. The king is, as it were, one facet of the Eternal Christ turned toward a given Christian people. If one wishes to avoid the paganism of worshiping demons, one must refuse to accept the Hildebrandine universal hierarchy. But the Anonymous falls into another idolatry, that of worshiping the king, or what comes to the same thing, of worshiping the Universal Christ through the ruler of one's country.[671] One may compare the thought of the Anonymous with that of Archbishop Laud who warned against religio-political sectaries. They were, he said, breaking English Christianity into a kind of polytheism.[672]

In opposing the Gregorian recovery of what the Anonymous would regard as a spurious (he says pretentious or Satanic) universalization of the Church in its extrication from feudal involvements and particularizations, our writer struggles against the Hildebrandine identification of the *ecclesia* with the internationalized *sacerdotium* and the consequent secularization, or as he says, laicization of the *regnum*.

In a typically "Protestant" manner our ecclesiastical publicist of Rouen directs his most impassioned criticism not against the State but rather against the Church of Rome and the executors of its policy in France, particularly the primate in Lyons. He sees not at all the dangers inherent in a monolithic society. His Christocentric theory of royal authority leaves no place for criticism except homiletical exhortation to greater Christ-likeness on the part of the wielder of power. At the same time the Anonymous is an Old Catholic in his mystical sacramentalism. He is a conduit

---

[671] More extreme even than the Anonymous is the author of the Norwegian Speculum regale described by Berges. Op. cit., 159–84. With the introduction of chrismatic coronation into Norway, God, Christ, and king, became almost interchangeable. The worship of the king was made equivalent to the worship of God.

The Speculum is translated by Lawrence Larson as The King's Mirror (New York, 1917).

[672] "No man can rend the Church into sects, but he would have many Gods." Works, Anglo-Catholic Library, I, 132. For both Laud and Andrewes, the Church and State were so much one that political faction, no less than sectarianism, was construed as imperiling *monotheism* as symbolized in the anointed monarch.

through which pass ancient Oriental feelings for the mystery of kingship. His utter confidence in the *ex opere* character of the royal sacring is so great that he really believes that the king has become an *alius vir* by virtue of sanctifying consecration. Thus in sanctifying a *singulare* as the head of regional or national *particulare* (to use terms from his own Tractate 9) in conceiving the national Church to be a tribe of the *genus electum* and an autonomous branch of the *regale sacerdotium*, and in hallowing the entire *regnum* as the earthly counterpart of the divine in opposition to the Gregorian sanctification of a universal class (the *sacerdotium*) our Norman divine belongs at once to two opposed trends in the political history of the West: 1) to that which endeavors to bring the civil community under Christian judgment and to infuse into it a Christian ethos and 2) to that other which leads to the absolutization of the State. Dempf was right when he saw in the Anonymous a medieval analogue of Hegel.[673] McNeill [674] and Gavin [675] were also right in interpreting the Anonymous as a prophet of Christian hope for a Christian Society. To be sure, we today who have witnessed and participated in the demonic fury of the sanctified *particularia* of race, class and nation are disposed to be critical of the Anonymous' hallowing of the *particularia* of diocese and realm. But in his age (and here, with Brackmann),[676] when the *sacerdotium* was the *particulare* which purported to be *the* divinely instituted *universale* and as such threatened to dechristianize the laity and its chief institutions (the State and the family), the Anonymous of Rouen discharged what appears to have been an obscure and unheeded rôle of priest-prophet,[677] calling his fellow Christians back to the ideal of a hallowed society and turning their eyes forward to the anointed of the Lord, in his late eleventh century De Monarchia — "On the Consecration of Bishops and Kings."

In the Anonymous' spirited defense of the laity, meaning

---

[673] See above, p. 10 and n. 522.

[674] See above, p. 17.

[675] See above, p. 21.

[676] See above, p. 13.

[677] The prophetic function is at once radical and conservative. It looks back to the ideal covenantal relationship or, as in this case, to the Davidic kingship under Charlemagne. It looks forward to the divine realization of this relationship under a messianic king. The Anonymous was both a radical and a conservative.

thereby for the most part the king, but to a lesser extent also all baptized Christians, we have heard an authentic voice of fierce protest against the rise of a clerical empire that seemed to him and to many of his contemporaries, ruthlessly bent upon making the Kingdom of Christ a universal Papal Monarchy. Insofar as the Anonymous perceived in the Roman clergy the pride of domination, his reproach of Gregory and his successors deserved attention. But he remained utterly oblivious to the equally great peril of royal and national absolutization for which he provided the theological apologia.

It would appear from our analysis of some thirty Tractates that the Anonymous' conception of Christ and of his Church had considerable bearing upon his final utterances concerning the rôle of the State, which, as we have seen, was for him no mere power structure without cosmic and indeed specifically Christian sanctions. But by depreciating the ministry of the earthly Christ and grounding the authority of the king over his Church-Kingdom solely in the grace of the Eternal Royal Christ, the Anonymous took from the Church its distinctive office in the divine economy; for, being the Body of Christ, the Church has corporately a royal, priestly, and prophetic function. Therefore the Church can never be assimilated to the kingdoms and societies of this world. A royal and priestly people, the Church has both in its corporate character and in its individual Spirit-driven spokesmen a prophetic duty to rebuke, an office of which it cannot acquit itself when beholden to any ruler of this world. It was for this reason gathered from the world, the better to discharge its function for the world. Its direct involvement in, or association with, government deprives it of even that modicum of objectivity to which the children of light may aspire. By corrupting the Gelasian principle in the interests of an Anglo-Norman Territorial Church, the Anonymous threatened the very heart of Christianity in the measure that he may have been influential in reducing the Faith to the proportions of a merely ethnic religion, a religion of the *polis*, whose chief usefulness is to serve as the cement of society and to provide the latter with the appropriate solemnities for its own glorification. To be sure, Christianity as a Religion shares, within self-imposed limits, these same functions with the ethnic and in our day the politically inspired pseudo-religions of blood, soil, and class; but the Church as the bearer of Revelation ceases to be the universal Church of Christ whenever it supposes her principal office to be discharged therein.

AN APPENDIX CONTAINING
HITHERTO UNPUBLISHED PORTIONS OF MS 415

Preceded by a List of All the Tractates of the Codex and the Titles as Given in the Old but Not Ancient Table of Contents, along with an Indication of the Places where the Pieces are Severally Published

    J = the numeration in M. James, Descriptive Catalogue, II.
    L = Libelli de lite, III.
    B = Böhmer, Kirche und Staat, "Beilagen."
    A = Lemarignier, op. cit., Pièce justificative, IV.
    H = Hellmann, op. cit., I, 121 ff.
    S = Scherrinsky, op. cit., "Anlagen."
    W = Williams in the following Appendix.

CONSPECTUS OF THE "TRACTATES" OF MS 415 [678]

Page in C.	No. and Publication	21 Codex Superscriptions		17 "Contenta" Titles of 15th or 16th Century
1	J1/B1	*An summus pontifex sit iuditio subiectus.*	1	same
3	J2/B2	*De una ecclesia et de Romana ecclesia* — possibly a preliminary sketch of J4/L3.	2	same
16	J3/W	Cum de homine negat Petrus.		
39	J4/L3	*Quod Rothomagensis ecclesia non est subiecta Romanae* — "Apologia archiepiscopi Rotomagensis" in L.d.l.	3	. . . non subiecta sit ecclesiae R.
			4	Quod Hierosolymitana ecclesia prima est et.; reference to p. 93 (J12)
50	J5/B3	*De privilegiis peculiaribus.*	5	same
53	J6/S	*De temperandis legibus.*	6	same
55	J7/W	Cum aliquis in iudicio de crimine reus convincitur — theme similar to that of foregoing.		
56	J8/B8	Si mercennarius et qui non est pastor.		
57	J9 I&II/S	Omne iudicium aut in ecclesiasticis situs est negotiis aut in secularibus.		
85	J10/W	*De potestate sacerdotali et regia* — breaks off; may be connected with foregoing.	7	same; reference to p. 219 (.;.) which is part way through J24B.
86	J11/B11	*De canonibus et decretis,* later superscription.	8	De canonum paritate
93	J12/B12	*De ecclesia Romana et Hierosolimitana.*	(4)	Quod H. ec. prima sit
100	J13/B13a	*De electione pontificis.*	9	same
101	J13/B13b	Si nullus potest fieri episcopus.		
102	J14/B14	*De baptismo et eucharistia.*	10	same
108	J15/S,J [679]	*De nuptiis* — see above, p. 28	(11)	same
113	J16/B16	*De depositione sacerdotis.*	11	De n. et dep. sacerdotis — the latter indicated as beginning on p. 113, but the title thereof is on the otherwise blank p. 112
114	J17/B17	*De benedictionibus.*	(12)	
			12	De b. & de verbis consecrationis [680]

---

[678] Italicization indicates a title. The initial words of unentitled Tractates are given in regular type. Variations in the wording of the seventeen titles of the "Contenta" are indicated.
[679] The fragment of J15(II) is printed by M. James, Descriptive Catalogue, II, 184.
[680] *Consecrationis* looks like *transeuntibus.*

CONSPECTUS OF THE "TRACTATES" OF MS 415 (*continued*)

Page in C.	No. and Publication	21 Codex Superscriptions	17 "Contenta" Titles of 15th or 16th Century
114	J18/B18	*De consecratione corporis Christi.*	
118	J19/B19	Christus factus est sacerdos diaconus subdia[co]nus — unfinished.	
120	J20/B20	In passione domini.	
121	J21/S W	Si deus omnia regit et moderatur — largely a transcript of Augustine's Enchiridion, 10–14.	
128	J22–J26/L2	*Apologia pro filiis sacerdotum.*	13 same; reference to p. 247 (J26)
139	J23a/B23a	*De equalitate ministrorum.*	(14) referred to as beginning on p. 139
142	J23b/B23b	Agnus Dei qui cotidie immolatur.	
143	J24A/L4 & H & W	*De consecratione pontificum et regum.*	14 same, combined with foregoing; reference to p. 145 (which is not, however, the beg. of J24) and to p. 171 where the *regnum Anglorum sive Saxonum* appears in the *ordo.*
204	J24B/L4	Sancta ecclesia sponsa Christi est.	
235	J24c/W	Laicus et christianus.	
237	J24d/W	D. n. Iesus Christus si Petro soli contulit claves.	
239	J25/L1	*An liceat sacerdotibus inire matrimonium.*	15 matrimon*ia*
247	J26 = J22/L2	Apologia pro filiis sacerdotum et concubinarum.	
264	J27/AS	Sanctorum patrum auctoritas.	
265	J28/L5	*De Romano pontifice.*	16 same; reference to p. 273
279	J29/L6 (I) & B29 (II)	*De obediendo Romano pontifice.*	(16) same; combined with foregoing
284	J30/L6 (III)	Considerandum est de Romana ecclesia.	
285	J31/B30	*De charitate et obedientia.*	17 same

TRACTATE J3

On Punishment and Penitence [681]

I. (P. 16) Cum de homine negat Petrus in filium negavit hominis ut remitteretur ei non in Spiritum sanctum. Tercio quoque interrogatus ait: *Nescio quid dicis.*[682] Hoc est, sacrilegia vestra nescio. Sed nos excusamus, ipse non excusavit. Non enim sat est involuta responsio confitentis Jhesum sed aperta confessio. Quid prodest verba involvere si videris denegasse? Et ideo Petrus non de industria sic respondisse inducitur quia postea recordatus est et tamen flevit. Maluit enim ipse suum accusasse peccatum ut iustificaretur fatendo quam gravaretur negando. *Iustus enim in principio accusator est sui.* Et ideo flevit. Quare flevit? Quia culpa obrepsit ei. Ego soleo flere si culpa mihi desit, hoc est si non me vindicem, si non obtineam quod inprobe cupio. Petrus doluit et flevit quia erravit ut homo. Non invenio quid dixerit, invenio quod fleverit. Lacrimas eius lego, satisfactionem non lego. Sed quod defendi non potest, ablui potest. Lavent lacrimę delictum, quod voce pudor est confiteri. Et venię fletus consulunt et verecundię lacrimę sine horrore culpę loquntur. Lacrimę crimen sine offensione verecundię confitentur. Lacrimę veniam non postulant et merentur. Inveni cur tacuerit Petrus, ne tam cito venię petitio plus offenderet. Ante flendum est sic precandum. Bonę lacrimę quę lavant culpam. Denique quos Jhesus respicit plorant. Negavit primo Petrus et non flevit, quia non respexerat Dominus. Negavit secundo non flevit quia adhuc non respexerat Dominus. Negavit tercio et respexit Jhesus. Et ille amarissime flevit. Respice, Domine Jhesu, ut sciamus nostrum deflere (p. 17) peccatum. Unde etiam lapsus sanctorum utilis. Michi nil nocuit quod negavit Petrus, profuit quod emendavit. Petrus inter Iudeos negavit. Salomon contubernio gentili deceptus erravit. Flevit ergo et amarissime Petrus. Eodem momento, eodem tempore. Respicit te Christus si in aliquo fortassis laboras quia secretorum tuorum testis adsistit. Respicit ut recorderis et fatearis errorem. Imittare Petrum dicentem alibi tercio: *Domine tu scis quia diligo te.*[683] Etenim quia tercio negaverat tercio confitetur. Sed negavit in nocte, confitetur in die. Hęc autem ideo scripta sunt, ut sciamus neminem iactare se debere. Nam si Petrus lapsus est quia dixit et si alii scandalizati fuerint, ego non scandalizabor, quis alius de se presumat? Denique et David quia dixerat: *Ego dixi in mea habundantia non movebor in ęternum* eam sibi iactantiam obfuisse profitetur dicens:

---

[681] For a summary, see above, n. 516.
[682] Luke 22:60.
[683] Cf. John 21:15 f.

Avertisti faciem tuam et factus sum conturbatus.[684] Unde te evocem,
Petre, ut doceas me quid flens cogitaveris? Unde inquam te evocem de
cęlo ubi iam choro insertus es angelorum? An etiam de cumulo quia non
putas iniuriam et ibi esse unde Dominus resurrexit? Doce nos quid tibi
profuerint lacrimę tuę? Sed docuisti ilico. Nam qui lapsus es antequam
fleres postquam flevisti electus es alios regere qui te ipse ante non rexeras.
Habebat ergo lacrimas Petrus pio quas fundebat affectu, non habebat
proditor fletus quibus culpam ablueret sed tormenta conscientię quibus
sacrilegium fateretur. Ut dum suo reus iudicio dampnatur. Et sponta-
neo supplicio facinus expiatur pietas Domini qui se ipse nollet ulcisci
et divinitas probaretur qui conscientiam mentis (p. 18) invisibili potestate interrogaret. *Peccavi,* inquit, *quod tradiderim sanguinem iustum.*[685]
Et si cassa est pęnitentia proditoris quia peccavit in Spiritum sanctum
est tamen ullus in scelere pudor culpam agnoscere. Et quamvis ille non
absolvitur Iudeorum tamen inpudentia confutatur quos cum professio
redarguat venditoris scelerati tamen sibi vindicat iura contractus et
exortes reatus esse se credunt dum dicunt quid ad nos tu videris. Amen-
tes plane qui putent solvi se magis auctoris scelere quam teneri.

II

Si nosse cupimus quę peccata maiora sint et graviora, id ex magnitudine pęnarum et suppliciorum gravitate facile perpendere possumus.
Nam quę maioribus pęnis et gravioribus a Deo puniuntur suppliciis, ea
necesse est esse maiora et graviora peccata. Neque enim maiora essent
et graviora, nisi maiores pęnas et graviora mererentur supplicia. Quoniam et nullum peccatum magnum esset et grave nisi magnam pęnam et
grave mereretur supplicium. Et nullum peccatum esset noxium nisi
aliquam pęnam et aliquid mereretur supplicium. Cęterum cum Deus sit
iustus iudex et reddat unicuique secundum opera sua, non maioribus et
gravioribus peccatis minores pęnas et leviora irrogat supplicia, et minoribus et levioribus peccatis maiores et graviora infert supplicia. Alioquin
nec iustus esset, nec unicuique secundum opera sua redderet. Sed quoniam iustus est et unicuique reddit secundum opera sua, necesse est ea
esse maiora et graviora peccata quibus maiores pęnas reinstituit et
graviora supplicia irrogat. Quę autem sint necesse est ut videamus.

(P. 19) Procul dubio Adę inprimis peccatum est, id est inobedientia
qua contra pręceptum Dei de ligno quod erat in medio paradisi comedit.
Huic peccato irrogata est mors omnium hominum, non solum corporis

[684] Ps. 29:6 f.
[685] Matt. 27:4.

verum etiam animę et ęternitatis amissio et exilium a paradiso, et im-
mortalitatis expoliatio, et omniformium labor et dolor miseriarum. Quibus nulla maior pęna, nullumque supplicium gravius cogitari potest. Et
quidem hoc quantum ad humanę opinionis iudicium non nimis magnum
non multum grave, non adeo turpe videtur vel horrendum, nec magnum
Deo intulit dampnum si unum comedit pomum. Sed non respexit Deus
ad dampnum pomi sed ad contemptum sui et ad pręcepti sui inobedien-
tiam, quę dissolvit obedientiam et illi omnino est contraria. Ac pro hoc
maximum est et gravissimum peccatum quoniam contrarium suum obedientia maximum est et precellentissimum bonum. Ut enim ait Samuel:
Melior est sapientia quam victimę et ascultare magis quam offerre adipem
arietum, quoniam quasi peccatum arriolandi est repugnare et quasi scelus
idolatrię nolle adquiescere.[686] Si ergo melior est sapientia quam victimę
et inobedientia peccato idolatrię et arriolandi comparatur et hoc non
humano sed divino iudicio, perspicuum est ut quanto melior est obedientia tanto deterior sit inobedientia. Illa enim prima et maxima est omnium virtutum, ista primum et maximum est omnium viciorum ac per
hoc ex merito maxima pęna et gravissimo supplicio est multatum.

Post hoc Cain peccatum considerandum est, id est fratricidium. Hoc
humano iudicio maius et (p. 20) gravius estimatur quam est peccatum
Adę, sed non est tam magna pęna tamque gravi supplicio punitum.
Neque enim mors huic peccato illata est, sed stupor mentis et corporis
tremor, et cordis gemitus. Et hoc non in perpetuum sed in septem gen-
erationes. In septima enim generatione interfectus legitur et peccatum
eius dissolutum est ut Hieronimus asserit in epistola de septem vindictis
Cain.[687] Unde et in Genesi legitur: *Quia*, inquit Lamech, *occidi virum*
in ira mea et adolescentulum in livore meo, septies ultio dabitur de Cain,
de Lamech vero septuagies septies.[688] Quia ergo iste Lamech ut Iudei
autumant occidit Cain adhuc in septima generatione viventem, septuagies
septies ultio data est de Lamech iuxta hoc quod dictum erat. Omnis qui
occiderit Cain septuplum punietur, subaudis quam Cain, quia Cain punitus est usque ad septimam generationem, Lamech vero usque ad septu-
agesimam septimam, id est usque ad Salvatoris adventum cuius morte
peccatum ipsius dissolutum est, secundum sancti Hieronimi sententiam.
Sed tamen et ultio de Cain septies data et ultio de Lamech septuagies
septies minoris est penę et levioris supplicii quam ultio quę data est de
Adam, inmo de omni homine quia hęc finita est et ad tempus, et duabus
tantum irrogata personis illa infinita et sine termino et omnibus illata

---

[686] I Sam. 15:22 f.
[687] Migne, P. L., XXII, ep. xxxvi, coll. 452 ff.
[688] Gen. 4:24 f.

hominibus. Sine termino, dico, quantum ad illos qui in Christum credere noluerunt. Nam credentes Christi morte liberati sunt ab ęterna morte, quanvis nullus a morte corporis liber esse potuerit. Unde maius et gravius videtur esse peccatum (p. 21) Adę quam Cain et Lamech. Similiter et peccatum Lamech maius et gravius videtur esse quam peccatum Cain, quia maiori pęna et graviori supplicio punitum est. Sed hoc divino iudicio non humano. Nam humano iudicio maior et gravior est fratris occisio quam homicidium alieni et homicidium maius et gravius quam inobedientia.

Considerandum etiam nunc est peccatum illud propter quod factum est diluvium, de quo scriptura loquitur ita: *Noe vero cum quingentorum esset annorum, genuit Sem, Cham, et Iafeth. Cumque cepissent homines multiplicari super terram et filias procreassent, videntes filii Dei filias hominum quod essent pulcrę, acceperunt sibi uxores ex omnibus quas elegerant. Dixitque Deus: Non permanebit spiritus meus in homine in ęternum, quia caro est.* Et paucis interpositis, *Videns autem Deus quod multa malicia hominum esset in terra et cuncta cogitatio cordis intenta esset ad malum omni tempore, penituit eum quod hominem fecisset in terra* et precavens in futurum *et tactus dolore cordis intrinsecus, Delebo, inquit, hominem quem creavi a facie terrę ab homine usque ad animantia, a reptili usque ad volucres cęli. Penitet enim me fecisse eos.*[689] Et hęc quidem in Genesi referuntur. Delevit ergo Deus hominem et omnia animantia terrę et volucres cęli aquis diluvii, exceptis his quę in arca reservata sunt. Sed videte quantum peccatum sit quod Deum fecit penitere se fecisse hominem, quod spiritum Dei abstulit ab homine, quo ipse Deus tactus est dolore cordis intrinsecus, quo delevit hominem et omnes bestias terrę et volucres cęli et quo totus mundus vindice (p. 22) aqua periit. Hęc de nullo alio peccato contigisse leguntur, nec etiam de Sodomitico de quo hoc tantum legitur: *Dixit Dominus: Clamor Sodomorum et Gomorrę multiplicatus est et peccatum earum aggravatum est nimis. Descendam et videbo utrum clamorem qui venit ad me, opere esset ad malum omni tempore, penituit eum quod homines fecisset in terra* et precavens in futurum *et tactus cordis intrinsecus, Delebo, inquit, conpleverint, an non est ita ut sciam.* Non dicit quod tactus sit dolore cordis intrinsecus et quod peniteat eum fecisse homines et animantia terrę et volucres cęli, sed dicit *descendam et videbo utrum clamorem qui venit ad me opere conpleverint, an non,*[690] quasi adhuc ignorans et dubitans immo per misericordiam dissimulans et omni illi loco dimittere cupiens si decem iustos inveniat in medio civitatis. Descendit itaque et

[689] Gen. 5:31–6:7.
[690] Gen. 18:20 f.

venit Sodomam et vidit clamorem quia verus erat. Nam etiam duobus angelis in quibus descenderat abuti voluerunt et eos violenter opprimere. Propter quod percussit eos cecitate et nullo iusto invento, excepto Loth quem egredi fecit cum uxore et duabus filiabus suis, subvertit eos ignis et sulphuris exterminio. Verumtamen sine dolore cordis et poenitentia. Et quia incomparabiliter minori pęna et leviori supplicio punitum est hoc peccatum quam peccatum illud propter quod aquis diluvii totus periit mundus, manifestum est quod incomparabiliter minus et levius est hoc peccatum quam illud.

Repperiuntur etiam in divinis litteris et alia peccata Sodomorum peccatis adeo maiora et graviora ut si ad illa comparentur Sodomorum peccata iusticia reputentur. Ut per Iezechielem prophetam de peccatis suis ad Iherusalem dicitur: *Vivo ego, dicit Dominus Deus, quia non fecit (p. 23) Sodoma, soror tua, ipsa et filię eius sicut fecisti tu et filię tue.* . . .[691] Et hęc quidem per prophetam loquitur Dominus. Ex quo perpenditur quia gravius et sceleratius peccavit Hierusalem quam Sodoma. Iusticia sunt peccata Sodomorum non quidem per se set ad comparationem scelerum Hierusalem, sed scelerum omnium Hierusalem maximum et gravissimum est quod Salvatorem occiderunt. Nam ex huic peccato si cętera conferantur, iusticia reputabuntur. Hoc autem remissibile fuit et veniale. Alioquin pendens in cruce non precaretur Patrem [Deum] dicens: *Pater dimitte illis*; (p. 24) *quia nesciunt quid faciunt.*[692] Iuxta quod et multis legitur esse remissum hoc peccatum. Nam ab apostolis postea baptizati sunt et ad predicationem illorum egerunt poenitentiam et sic remissionem consecuti sunt ne inanis et cassa esset Christi oratio. Verum si hoc peccatum est remissibile et veniale multo magis et alia quę minora sunt et leviora remissibilia sunt et venialia. Multo magis etiam et Sodomorum peccata quę illis comparata iusticia reputantur remissibilia sunt et venialia. Et ne humanis coniecturis id adstruere videamur, auctoritate divina probemus peccata Sodomorum esse remissibilia, quia vel iam remissa vel in futuro sunt remittenda. Unde et per prophetam loquitur Dominus: *Convertam Sodomam restituens eam.*[693] *Et Sodoma et filię eius revertentur ad antiquitatem suam,*[694] id est ad antiquum vitę incontaminabilis statum, quo erat sicut paradysus Dei. Antequam enim peccaret Sodoma cum adhuc simplicitatem vitę incontaminabilis custodiret erat sicut paradisus Dei. Ubi vero decolorari cepit et peccatorum maculis obscurari sicut Egiptus facta

[691] Ez. 16:48–55.
[692] Cf. Luke 23:34.
[693] Ez. 16:53.
[694] Ez. 16:55.

est. Sed convertente et restituente eam Deo revertetur in antiquum statum ut sit sicut paradisus Dei. Hinc et Hieronimus [695] in primo libro super Naum prophetam loquitur adversus hereticos qui *arguunt legis Deum* [696] *quasi crudelitatis, quod multos puniat et pro peccatis irroget cruciatus. Quid ergo, ait, contra Dominum cogitatis? ipse qui creavit mundum et consummationem faciet. Quod si videtur vobis crudelis rigidus et cruentus, quod in diluvio genus delevit humanum, super Sodomam et Gomorram ignem et sulphurem pluit, Ęgip* (p. 25) *tios submersit fluctibus, et Israhelitarum cadavera prostravit in heremo: scitote eum ideo ad pręsens reddidisse supplicia, ne in ęternum puniret. Certe aut vera sunt quę prophetę loquntur aut falsa. Si vera sunt, qui de severitate eius videntur dicere; ipsi dixerunt, Non vindicabit Dominus bis in id ipsum in tribulatione. Sin autem falsa sunt, falsum erit et hoc quod dicitur non consurget duplex tribulatio; falsa est ergo et crudelitas quę in lege descripta est. Quod si verum est quod negare non poterit, dicente propheta: Non vindicabit Dominus bis in id ipsum in tribulatione; ergo qui puniti sunt, postea non punientur. Sin autem illi postea punientur, scriptura mentitur, quod dicere nefas est. Receperunt ergo et qui in diluvio perierant et Sodomitę et Egiptii et Israelitę in solitudine mala sua in vita sua. Querat hic aliquis, si fidelis deprehensus in adulterio decolletur, quid de eo postea fiet? Aut enim punietur, et falsum est hoc quod dicitur: Non vindicabit Dominus bis in id ipsum in tribulatione. Aut non punietur, et optandum est adulteris ut in presentiarum brevi et cita pęna cruciatus frustrentur ęternos. Ad quos* [quod, in Migne], *respondebimus, Deum ut omnium rerum* [ita et, in Migne] *suppliciorum quoque mensuras scire, et non prevenire sententiam iudicis, nec illi in peccatorem exercendę hic* [dehinc, in Migne] *penę auferre potestatem, et magnum peccatum magnis diurnisque elui cruciatibus. Si quis autem punitus sit ut ille in lege qui Israelitis maledixerat et qui in sabbato ligna collegerat, tales postea non puniri quia culpa levis presenti supplicio conpensata sit.* Et hec quidem Hieronimus. Quod autem non solum peccata Sodomorum verum etiam omnia alia peccata et blasphemię remit (p.26) tantur filiis hominum excepta blasphemia Spiritus sancti affirmat ipse Christus in evangelio. Dicit enim secundum Mattheum: *Omne peccatum et blasphemia remittetur hominibus, Spiritus autem blasphemia non remittetur. Et quicunque dixerit verbum contra Filium hominis remittetur ei. Qui autem dixerit contra Spiritum sanctum, non remittetur ei neque in hoc seculo neque in futuro.* [697] Secundum Marcum vero dicit cum iuramento:

[695] Migne, P. L., XXV, coll. 1267 f. on Nahum 1:9.
[696] In marg.: legis Deum.
[697] Matt. 12:31 f.

Amen dico vobis, quoniam omnia dimittentur filiis hominum peccata et blasphemię quibus blasphemaverint. Qui autem blasphemaverit in Spiritum sanctum, non habet remissionem in ęternum sed reus erit ęterni delicti. Quoniam dicebant spiritum inmundum habet.*[698]* Quoniam ergo veritas hęc loquitur, Sodomorum peccata et blasphemię eis remittentur. Hinc et iam ad Capharnaum loquitur Dominus: *Quia si in Sodomis factę fuissent virtutes quę facte sunt in te, forte mansissent usque in hanc diem. Veruntamen dico vobis, quia terrę Sodomorum remissius erit in die iudicii quam tibi.*[699] Per quod etiam ostenditur quia sceleratius et gravius peccavit Capharnaum quam Sodoma, quia si factę fuissent virtutes in Sodomis que factę sunt in Capharnaum *in cinere et cilitio penitentiam egissent* [700] et mansissent. Capharnaum autem secundum duriciam suam et cor inpęnitens thesaurizavit sibi iram in die irę et ideo peccavit inremissibiliter. *Illud autem sciendum est quia peccatum hoc quod dicimus Sodomorum non tantum peccatum est sed etiam pęna peccati.

In hoc quod peccatum est et turpe est et execrandum. In hoc vero quod pęna peccati est, divinę iusticię prefert pulchritudinem. Punit enim Deus iusto iudicio peccata (p. 27) peccatis et hoc pulchrum est quod iuste facit. **Quod autem hoc peccatum sit pęna alterius peccati testatur Gregorius in xi. omelia super Ezechielem,[701] ex testimonio apostoli de quibusdam Deum intelligentibus sed non honorantibus dicentis: *"Cum cognovissent Deum non sicut Deum glorificaverunt, aut gratias egerunt; sed evanuerunt in cogitationibus suis.*[702] Ecce est peccatum et causa peccati. Ex qua causa quid sequatur adiungit: *Et obscuratum est insipiens cor eorum; dicentes enim se esse sapientes stulti facti sunt. Et mutaverunt gloriam suam* [Dei, in Rom.] *in similitudinem imaginis corruptibilis hominis et volucrum et quadrupedum et serpentum.*[703] *Ecce est peccatum et pęna peccati. Sed peccatum solummodo et pęna peccati esset, si non adhuc ex hoc peccato et aliud sequeretur.** Nam post infidelitatem eorum subditur: *Propter quod tradidit illos Deus in desideria cordis eorum in inmundiciam, ut contumeliis afficiant corpora sua in semetipsis.*[704] Qui igitur cognoscentes Deum non sicut Deum glorificaverunt, ex eo peccato et causa peccati ad hoc quoque perducti sunt, ut ad cultum serpentium et volucrum laberentur. Sed quia per hanc

[698] Mark 3:28 ff.
[699] Matt. 11:23 f.
[700] Matt. 11:21.
[701] Migne, P. L., LXXVI, coll. 915 f., quoted verbatim to the end of the paragraph.
[702] Rom. 1:21.
[703] Rom. 1:21 ff.
[704] Rom. 1:24.

etiam cęcitatem usque ad inmundiciam et carnis contumelias ceciderunt, ipsa infidelitatis eorum cęcitas precedenti intellectui et peccatum est et pęna peccati. Subsequenti vero inmundicię peccatum factum est et causa peccati."

Sed veniamus nunc ad vetus testamentum et videamus quę peccata morte puniri iussa sunt et quę non. Nam ea quę morte puniebantur ex pari pena paria esse probantur. Hęc autem sunt quę morte puniebantur: *Qui superbierit nolens obedire sacerdotis imperio, qui eo tempore ministrat Domino Deo tuo et decreto iudicis morietur homo ille, et auferes malum de medio Israhel.*[705] *Qui maledixerit patri suo et matri morte moriatur. Qui patri matrique maledixerit sanguis eius sit super eum. . . .*[706] Hęc omnia pari pena puniuntur, scilicet superbia non obediendi sacerdotis imperio et decreto iudicis, maledictio patris et matris, coitus alterius uxoris, coitus novercę, coitus masculi, coitus iumenti, coitus mulieris menstruatę, et stuprum filię sacerdotis. Hęc igitur quoniam pari pena puniuntur, paria esse monstrantur. Sed de his quę morte non punituntur quid dicemus? Erunt maiora (p. 29) an minora, an paria? Sed sunt quidam qui ea maiora esse et graviora probare nituntur divina auctoritate qua in veteri lege dicitur. *Homo si maledixerit Deum peccatum* accipiet, vel *portabit,* ut in alia translatione legitur. *Qui* autem *nominat* [blasphemaverit, in Levit.] *nomen Domini morte* [morte] [707] *moriatur.*[708] Quid est hoc? Qui maledixerit Deum non habet pęnam mortis, sed qui nominaverit nomen Domini? Nonne multo gravius est maledicere Deum quam nominare, quanvis in vanum nominasse dicatur? Et quomodo qui maledicit Deum peccatum suscipit tantum, qui autem nominat morte multatur? Hęc ergo sunt quę in hoc loco solent questionem movere quę ignorantibus sensum scripturarum inconsequenter dicta videntur et incongrue. Putant enim quod qui maledicit nomen Dei statim puniri debeat, illi vero qui nominaverit nomen Domini, hoc est superfluo et in vanum nominaverit, sufficiat accepisse peccatum. Sed non consequentia sermonis talis videtur, ut temptemus aperire maius esse peccatum in quo maledicitur Deus quam in quo nominatur. Sed quia hęc dubitare nunc possumus, restat ut ostendamus multo esse gravius aliquem accipere peccatum et habere secum quam morte multari. Mors quę penę causa infertur pro peccato purgatio est peccati ipsius, pro quo iubetur inferri. Absolvitur ergo peccatum per penam mortis, nec superest aliquid quod pro hoc crimine iudicii dies et pęna ęterni

---

[705] Deut. 17:12.
[706] Exod. 21:17; Levit. 20:9–16, 18; 21:9.
[707] Underscored for deletion.
[708] Levit. 24:15 f.

ignis inveniat. Ubi vero quis accipit peccatum et habet illud secum, ac permanet cum ipso nec aliquo supplicio penaque diluitur, transit cum ipso etiam post mortem. Et quia temporalia hic persolvit, ibi expendit ęterna supplicia. Vides ergo quanto gravius sit accipere peccatum quam mor-(p. 30)te multari? Hic enim mors pro vindicta datur, et apud iustum iudicem Dominum non vindicatur bis in id ipsum sicut propheta dixit.[709] Ubi autem non est soluta vindicta, peccatum manet illis ęternis ignibus exigendum. Quia autem hęc ita se habeant, possum tibi testes ex divinis voluminibus adhibere: Ruben et Iudas patriarchas loquentes ad patrem suum Iacob cum vellent assumere secum Beniamin et ducere in Egiptum propter sponsiones quas cum Ioseph fratre pepigerant ibi.   Ergo Ruben quidem ita dicit ad patrem: *Ambos filios meos occide, nisi reduxero ad te Beniamin.*[710] Iudas vero ait: *Peccator ero in te nisi reduxero eum tibi.*[711] Iacob ergo pater ipsorum sciens multo esse gravius quod promiserat Iudas qui dixerat, Peccator ero in te, ab eo qui dixerat, Filios meos occide· Ruben quidem non credidit filium tanquam qui leviorem elegerit pęnam, Iudę vero tradidit sciens gravius esse quod elegerat. Hoc ergo modo convenienter aptavit scriptura divina ei quidem qui maledixerit Deum, ut peccatum sumat ei vero qui levius delinquit quod morte moriatur. Vis autem et de evangeliis noscere quod qui receperit in hac vita mala sua, ibi iam non recipiat; qui autem non receperit, ibi [ei][712] serventur ei omnia? Docet nos exemplum Lazari pauperis et illius divitis ad quem dicitur in infernis a patriarcha Abraham: *Memento, fili, quia recepisti bona tua in vita tua et Lazarus similiter mala; nunc vero tu quidem cruciaris; hic vero requiescit.*[713] Et solent homines ignorantes iudicia Dei quę sunt abissus multa conqueri adversus Deum et dicere cur homines iniqui et iniusti, raptores, impii, scelesti in hac vita nichil patiantur adversi, sed cuncta eis prosperis successibus cedant, honores, divitię, potentia, sanitas quoque eis ipsa (p. 31) et corporis habitudo famuletur. *Econtra innocentibus ac piis et colentibus Deum innumerabiles erumnę [714] superveniant, abjecti humiles contempti et sub colaphis potentium vivant, non nunquam etiam sevius eis morbi quoque ipsi corporis dominentur.** Sed hęc ut dixi conqueruntur ignorantes qui sit ordo in divinis iudiciis. Quanto enim gravius eos puniri volunt tanto necessarium est differri penas quę differentur. Temporales utique leviores essent, quia finem cum morte

[709] Cf. Nahum 1:9.
[710] Cf. Gen. 42:37.
[711] Cf. Gen. 44:32.
[712] Underscored for deletion.
[713] Cf. Luke 16:25.
[714] In c.: erunę.

reciperent. Nunc vero quia differuntur certum est quia ęternę erunt et cum seculis extendentur. Contra igitur si velint iustis et innocentibus in pręsenti seculo bona reddi, essent etiam ipsa bona temporalia et celeri termino concludenda. Quanto autem magis differuntur in futurum, tanto erunt perpetua et nescientia finem. Hoc est ergo quod nos scripturę huius locus paucis sermonibus comprehensus edocuit, ut sciamus multo esse gravius quenquam accipere peccatum et habere ac secum ad inferna deferre, quam in presenti dare penam commissi. Et ideo hęc sciens expedire fidelibus apostolus, dicit de eo qui peccaverit: Quem *tradidi*, inquit, *Sathanę in interitum carnis*,[715] hoc est morte multasse. Qui autem sit fructus mortis huius ostendit in sequentibus dicens: *Ut spiritus salvus fiat in die Domini nostri Ihesu Christi*.[716] Vides ergo quomodo aperte apostolus utilitatem mortis exposuit? Quod enim dicit, Tradidi in interitum carnis, hoc est in afflictionem corporis quę solet a pęnitentibus expendi eumque carnis interitum nominavit. Qui tamen carnis interitum vitam spiritui conferat. Et nunc si qui[s] forte nostrum recordatur in semetipso alicuius peccati conscientiam, si quis se obnoxium novit esse delicto, confugiat ad poenitentiam et spontaneum suscipiat carnis interitum, ut expurgatur in presenti vita spiritus eius mundus et purus pergat ad Christum Dominum nostrum. (P. 32) Iisdem etiam alibi de utroque genere peccatorum magnifice disseruit, exponens illud preceptum quod in lege scriptum est: *Homo si maledixerit patrem aut matrem suam morte moriatur*.[706] Et post multa quę pręcepit quibus etiam pęnas prevaricationis asscripsit, addidit in clausula: *Et servate omnia pręcepta mea et iustificationes meas et iudicia mea*.[717] Unde consequens mihi videtur requirere quid in his singulis indicetur. Et quidem secundum quod observare potui, pręceptum est sive mandatum illud quod verbi gratia in decalogo dicitur: Non occides, non adulterabis. Hoc enim solum precipitur et non ascribitur pęna commissi. Nunc autem iterantur quidem eadem sed additis pęnis. Dicitur enim: *Homo quicunque adulteraverit uxorem viri et uxorem proximi sui morte moriantur; ambo rei sunt*.[718] De his autem in prioribus iam data fuerant precepta, sed non observantem quę maneret pęna non fuerat ascriptum. Nunc ergo eadem repetuntur et uniuscuiusque pęna peccati decernitur. Et ideo recte hęc iustificationes et iudicia appellantur, quibus quod iustum est recipere iudicatur ille qui peccat. Sed intuere divinę sapientię ordinem. Non continuo pęnas cum primis statuit praeceptis. Vult enim ut non

[715] I Cor. 5:5.
[716] Ibid.
[717] Cf. Levit. 25:18.
[718] Cf. Levit. 20:10.

metu penę sed amore pietatis Patris precepta custodias. Sed si con-
tempseris non tam homini iam quam contemptori pęna mandatur. Primo
ergo benignitate provocaris ut filius. *Ego enim dixi dii estis et filii Excelsi
omnes.*[719] Quod si filius esse obediens non vis, contemptor plecteris ut
servus. Post hęc dicit: Et *si quis dormierit cum nuru sua, moriantur
ambo.*[720] Impietatem fecerunt, rei sunt. Et has leges, vel hęc precepta
absque penis superius dederat; dixerat enim: *Turpitudinem nurus tuę
non revelabis, quoniam uxor filii tui est* (p. 33) *non revelabis turpitudinem eius* [721] et omnia quę subsequentur. Et hunc locum simili modo ibi
absque suppliciis, hic vero cum diversis suppliciorum generibus ascribit.
Quo in loco recordor sermonis illius quem beatus apostolus ad Hebreos
scribens dicit: *Irritam quis faciens legem Moysi, sine ulla miseratione
duobus aut tribus testibus moritur; quanto maioribus suppliciis dignus
putabitur qui filium Dei conculcaverit et sanguinem testamenti pollutum
duxerit, in quo sanctificatus est, et spiritui gratię contumeliam fecerit?* [722]
Sed quam ob causam mentionem fecerim scripturę huius tusculatę? Secundum legem adulter vel adultera morte moriebantur, nec poterant
dicere: poenitentiam petimus et veniam deprecamus. Non enim erat
lacrimis locus nec emendationis ulla concedebatur facultas, sed omni-
modis puniri eos necesse erat, qui incurrissent in legem. Hoc autem
servabatur et in singulis quibusque criminibus quibus erat pęna mortis
ascripta. *Apud christianos vero, si adulterium fuerit admissum; non est
pręceptum ut adulter vel adultera corporali interitu puniantur nec potestas data est episcopo ecclesię adulterum praesenti morte dampnare, sicut
tunc secundum legem fiebat a presbyteris populi.** *Quid igitur doce-
bimus? Quod lex Moysi crudelis est que iubet puniri adulterum vel
adulteram et evangelium Christi per indulgentiam resolvit auditores in
deterius? Non ita est.** Propterea enim sermonem Pauli protulimus in
superioribus dicentis: *quanto magis deterioribus suppliciis dignus est qui
filium Dei conculcaverit* [723] et cetera. Audi ergo quomodo neque tunc
crudelis lex neque nunc dissolutum videatur evangelium propter venię
largitatem sed in utroque Dei benignitas diversa dispensatione teneatur,
propter hoc quod secundum legem verbi causa adulter vel adultera presenti morte puniebatur, propter hoc ipsum quod peccati sui pertulit
pęnam (p. 34) et commissi sceleris exsoluit digna supplicia, quid erit post
hęc quod animabus eorum ultionis immineat? Si nichil aliud deliquirunt,

---

[719] Ps. 81:6.
[720] Cf. Levit. 20:11.
[721] Levit. 18:15.
[722] Hebr. 10:28 f.
[723] Cf. Hebr. 10:29.

si aliud peccatum non est quod condempnet eos, sed hoc solum commiserunt et tunc tantum cum puniti sunt et legis pro hoc supplicium
pertulerunt; non vindicabit Dominus bis in id ipsum. Receperunt enim
peccatum suum et consumpta est criminis pęna. *Et ideo invenitur hoc
genus pręcepti non crudele sicut heretici asserunt accusantes legem Dei
et negantes in ea humanitatis aliquid contineri quod sit plenum misericordia; iccirco quod per hoc purgaretur ex peccatis populus magis quam
condempnantur. Nunc vero non infertur pęna corpori, nec purgatio
peccati per corporale supplicium constat, sed per pęnitentiam.** Quam
utrum quis digne gerat, ita ut mereri pro ea veniam possit videte. Multi
sunt qui nec ad hoc inclinantur nec penitentię refugium querunt, sed cum
ceciderint surgere ultra nolunt. Delectantur enim in eo luto quo [cui,
supersc.] heserint volutari. Nos tamen non obliviscamus precepti illius
quod dicitur: *Qua mensura mensi fueritis, eadem remetietur vobis.*[724]
Dicimus enim et ad Deum *quoniam dedisti nobis panem lacrimarum et
potasti nos in lacrimis in mensura.*[725] Sunt ergo ista peccata quę dicuntur
ad mortem. Unde et consequens est ut quotiens commiserit quis tale peccatum totiens moriatur. Multas enim esse peccati mortes, significat etiam
apostolus cum dicit: *Qui de tantis mortibus* [periculis, II Cor.] *eripuit
nos et eripit in quo speramus, quia et adhuc eripiet.*[726] Quas ergo hic
mortes plures commemorat, nisi peccatorum? Si enim hęc non diceret
de mortibus peccatorum videretur Paulus secundum sententiam suam
immortalis esse mansurus ab hac communi morte qui dixit quia *de tantis
mortibus eripuit nos et eripit, in quo speramus, quia et adhuc eripiet.*
Si enim et eripuit et eripiet, nunquam (p. 35) erit quando moriatur quem
Dominus semper eripiet. Et ideo secundum ea quę discussimus, videndum est ne forte aliquando etiam gravius sit nobis qui pro peccato communi hac morte minime punimus, quam illis quos legis sententia
corporaliter condempnabat. Quia nobis ultio reponitur in futurum, illos
absolvebant commissi sui per soluta supplicia. Quod si et aliquis est
qui forte preventus sit in huiusce modi peccatis admonitus nunc verbo
Dei ad auxilium confugiat poenitentię, ut si semel admisit, secundo non
faciat. Aut si et secundo preventus iam, aut tercio etiam est, ultra non
addat. Est enim apud iudicem iustum penę moderatio, non solum pro
qualitate, verum etiam pro quantitate.

Inter cetera ergo peccata quę morte puniuntur refert divina lex, quod
et qui maledicerit patri aut matri morte moriatur. Nomen patris grande
misterium est et nomen matris archana reverentia est. Pater tibi secun-

---

[724] Matt. 7:2; Mark 4:24.
[725] Cf. Ps. 78:6.
[726] Cf. II Cor. 1:10.

dum spiritum Deus est, mater Hierusalem celestis est. Pro propheticis
hęc et apostolicis testimoniis disce. Hic ipse pater tuus adquisivit te et
possedit te. Apostolus vero dicit de *Hierusalem celesti quia libera est*.[727]
Quę est inquit *mater omnium nostrum*. Primo ergo tibi pater Deus est,
qui genuit spiritum tuum qui et dixit: *Filios genui et exaltavi*.[728] Sed
et Iacobus apostolus dicit: *Obtemperemus patri spirituum et vivemus*.[729]
Secundo tibi pater est carnis pater, cuius ministerio in carne natus es,
atque in hunc mundum venisti. Qui te portavit in lumbis, sicut dicitur
de Levi, quia in lumbis erat adhuc Abrahę quando occurrit ei Melchisedech regresso a cede regum et benedixit eum et decimas accepit ab eo.
Quia igitur tam sacratum nomen est patris et tam venerabile, iccirco qui
maledixerit patri aut matri morte morietur. Similia etiam de matre esti-
manda sunt, cuius labore, cuius cura, cuius ministerio et natus es et
nutritus. Et oportet te secundum (p. 36) apostolum parem gratiam
referre parentibus. Si enim dehonoraveris patrem carnalem, huius con-
tumelia ad patrem spiritualem redit. Et si iniuriam feceris matri carnali,
ad illam matrem Hierusalem cęlestem redundat iniuria. *Sic et servus si
domino inreverens sit, per hunc corporalem dominum in Dominum
maiestatis contumeliam iactat.** Et ideo nullo genere adversus patrem
aut matrem ne verbi quidem habendum certamen est aut movenda
contradictio. Pater est, mater est, ut ipsis videtur sic agant, faciant,
dicant, ipsi noverint, viderint. Quantumcunque detulerimus obsequii
nondum vicem gratię qua geniti sumus, qua portati hausimus lucem, qua
nutriti sumus, fortassis et eruditi, et honestis artibus instituti. Et ipsis
fortasse auctoribus agnovimus Deum, et ad ęcclesiam Dei venimus et
sermonem divinę legis audivimus. Propter hęc ergo omnia quicunque
maledixerit patri aut matri morte morietur. Quod si hęc de corporalibus
parentibus decernuntur quid illis fiet qui Deum patrem maledicis vocibus
lacessunt, qui eum negant conditorem esse mundi, aut qui celestem
Hierusalem quę est mater omnium nostrum indignis sensibus intelligentes dicta prophetica ad conditionem terrenę alicuius urbis adducunt?
Bonum ergo est observare nequando aut carnalem patrem aut cęlestem
minus digna honorificentia veneremur. Similiter et matris observare
etiam omne mandatum quod nobis pudicitiam castitatemque commendet,
ut neque in presenti vita secundum legem obnoxii simus morti, neque
secundum spiritualem legem futura nos pęna maneat ignis ęterni. Ex quo
effugere et evadere omnibus nobis concedat Dominus noster Ihesus

---

[727] Cf. Galat. 4:26.
Cf. Pseudo-Isidore, Hinschius, ed., Anacletus xiv, p. 73; Lucius, vii, p. 178.
[728] Cf. Isai. 1:2.
[729] Cf. Hebr. 12:9.

Christus. His itaque dictis veniamus et ad novum testamentum et videamus quę peccata excludunt homines a regno Dei et ignem merentur ęternum, ut cognita paritate (p. 37) pęnarum, cognoscamus et paritatem peccatorem. Hęc *autem* sunt *fornicatio et omnis inmundatia, aut avaritia,* quę *nec nominanda sunt in nobis sicut decet sanctos.*[730] Nam et apostolus dicit: *Hoc autem scitote intelligentes quod omnis fornicator aut inmundus aut avarus quod est ydolorum servitus non habet hereditatem in regno Christi et Dei.*[731] Hinc etiam in epistola ad Galatas: *Manifesta,* inquit, *sunt opera carnis, quę sunt fornicatio, immundicia, luxuria, avaritia, inpudicitia, ydolorum servitus, veneficia, inimicitię, contentiones, emulationes, irę, rixę, dissensiones,* hereses, *sectę, invidię, homicidia, ebrietates, commessationes, et his similia quę predico vobis sicut predixi, quoniam qui talia agunt regnum Dei non consequentur.*[732] Hęc igitur omnia excludunt homines a regno Dei. Quę sunt autem quę ignem merentur ęternum? Dicat nunc ipse Christus: *Qui dixerit fratri suo fatue, reus erit gehennę ignis.*[733] *Sed et in iudicio veniens dicet iis qui a sinistris eius erunt: Discedite a me maledicti in ignem ęternum qui preparatus est diabolo et angelis eius. Esurivi enim et non dedistis mihi manducare; sitivi et non dedistis mihi potum; hospes eram et non collegistis me; nudus et non operuistis me; infirmus et in carcere et non visitastis me. Tunc respondebunt et ipsi dicentes: Domine, quando te vidimus esurientem aut sitientem aut hospitem aut nudum aut infirmum vel in carcere et non ministravimus tibi? Tunc respondebit illis dicens: Amen dico vobis, quamdiu non fecistis uni de minoribus his nec michi fecistis. Et ibunt hii in supplicium ęternum.*[734] Sed et homicide et adulteri et fornicatores ibunt in supplicium ęternum. Similiter diabolus et angeli eius ibunt in sup-(p. 38)plicium ęternum, id est in ignem ęternum. Hic ignis omnis hos torquebit et puniet. Ac per hoc una et eadem erit pena omnium, idemque supplicium. Unde et omnium horum peccata aestimantur esse paria. Sed illud videtur esse contrarium quod superius dictum est omnia peccata et blasphemię remittentur filiis hominum excepta blasphemia Spiritus et hoc quod isti ibunt in supplicium ęternum. Si enim eterno supplicio puniendi sunt, numquam remittentur eorum peccata. Quod contra si eorum peccata remittentur eterno supplicio minime punientur. *Remittentur autem omnia eorum peccata, sicut ipsa testatur veritas excepta Spiritus sancti blasphemia, quę neque in

---

[730] Eph. 5:3.
[731] Eph. 5:5.
[732] Galat. 5:19 ff.
[733] Matt. 5:22.
[734] Matt. 25:41 ff.

hoc seculo remittetur neque in futuro. Hoc igitur solum peccatum ęterno supplicio est puniendum.** Sed fortasse huic contrarietati, talis potest adhiberi solutio. Nam ubicumque fuerit Spiritus sancti blasphemia quę est *inpęnitentia [734a] sive desperatio* qua Spiritus sanctus desperatur non posse remittere peccata vel non postulatur ab eo venia per penitentiam cordis, nulla ibi remittuntur peccata. Ubi autem non fuerit, omnia remittentur peccata. Et sic utrunque non erit contrarium, quod omnia videlicet peccata et blasphemię remittentur filiis hominum et quod isti ibunt in supplicium ęternum quoniam de iis quę male gesserunt non egerunt pęnitentiam sed usque ad mortem in peccatis permanserunt et secundum duriciam suam et cor inpenitens thesaurizaverunt sibi iram in die ire et revelationis Christi, qui reddet unicuique iuxta opera sua aut de misericordia Dei desperaverunt et remissionem peccatorum quę est in Spiritu sancto mente obstinata minime quesierunt. Hec de magnitudine peccatorum et de qualitate eorum et de penis et suppliciis quibus vel iam punita sunt vel in futuro punienda reservantur a nobis in presentiarum dicta sint, sed utrum recte an perperam sapientium iudicio derelinquimus.

TRACTATE J7
ON FORGIVENESS AND PENITENCE

(P. 55) Cum aliquis in iudicio de crimine reus convincitur, tunc a iudice investigandum est, utrum inde confessus fuerit et pęnitentiam acceperit, quoniam post confessionem et penitentiam, a nullo debet iudicari, dicente apostolo. *Si nosmet ipsos diiudicaremus, non utique* iudicare *iudicaremur*.[735] Neque enim Deus iudicat eos (p. 56) qui se iudicant. Nec homo iudicare debet, quos Deus non iudicat, nec exigere pęnas de peccatis quę Deus condonat. Sed necque aliud iudicare debet homo quam Deus iudicat. Nam cum Deus verum iudicat, si aliud quam Deus iudicat homo, non est verum sed falsum quod iudicat. Propter hoc dicit apostolus: *Nolite ante tempus iudicare, quoadusque veniat Dominus, qui illuminabit abscondita tenebrarum et manifestabit consilia cordium.*[736] Pernitiosum quippe est ante tempus iudicare, et pernitiosius non secundum Deum iudicare sed secundum hominem. Verum ut ad propositum revertamur, inquirendum est de eo qui criminis reus esse convincitur, utrum id semel tantum perpetraverit, an etiam ussum eius fecerit. Nam de usu, austerius et districtius est iudicandus. De semel

---

[734a] The identification of blasphemy against the Holy Spirit as impenitence goes back to Augustine. Cf. Sermo LXXI, 20; Migne, P. L., xxxviii, col. 455.

[735] I Cor. 11:31; iudicare underscored for omission.

[736] I Cor. 4:5.

vero perpetrato mitius est corrigendus. Verum si usum eius fecit, tunc de ceteris eius operibus inquirendum est: utrum bona an mala fuerint. Si mala, dampnationi est proximus, et maxime, si incorrigibilis extiterit. Nam utrum possit corrigi, taemptandum est et elaborandum per misericordiam et caritatis compassionem, ne habundantiori tristicia absorbeatur * frater.* Quod si bona fuerint cetera ipsius opera, veniam de uno debet consequi, quia iniustum est, ut de malo tantum recipiat talionem et de bonis minime, cum bona magis retribuenda sint per iusticiam et mala dimittenda per misericordiam.

TRACTATE J10
DE POTESTATE SACERDOTALI ET REGIA

(P. 85) *Duo sunt quibus hic mundus principaliter regitur, sacerdotalis auctoritas et regalis potestas.*[737] Sed sacerdotalis auctoritas potestate regali maius habet privilegium atque prestantius, tanto siquidem quanto terrenis celestia et corporibus anime et divina prestant humanis. Eius namque privilegium est celeste atque divinum et attingens usque ad animas. Cuius virtus est ea que ratione exigente cum semper terram, tum etiam in celo ligare potest et solvere, non solum illam eandem regalem potestatem, verum etiam omnem terrene celsitudinis dignitatem. Potest quippe omnium peccata remittere, potest et retinere, potest celum aperire, potest et claudere, potest inferni portas irrumpere, potest et paradisi ianuam penetrare. Ineffabili autem misterio panem et vinum in Christi corpus et sanguinem mutare potest, et omnia sacramentorum genera, cooperante Dei verbo, perficere potest. In vasa misericordie vasa ire apta in interitum promovere potest, filios perditionis in filios adoptionis provehere potest. Vere autem et universaliter dicendum quia sine sacerdotali privilegio nulla de peccatis remissio, nulla de divina ira propitiatio, nulla de per(p. 86)ditione liberatio, nulla de morte perpetua resurrectio, nulla de perhempni[738] captivitate redemptio, nulla de originali vetustate reparatio, nulla est de novitate eterne felicitatis comparatio. Verum autem et hoc privilegio sacerdos omnis angelus Domini dicitur, hoc etiam *christus* esse perhibitur, hoc communicato[739] cum Deo nomine, spretu et honore gloriatur.

At vero regalis potestatis privilegium privilegium sola est publicarum rerum administratione contemptum, neque est usque ad praedictam divini privilegii virtutem extentum. Neque enim eorum que prediximus

[737] Gelasius, ep. 12 c.2.
[738] A rare mid-eleventh-century form of *perennis*. Du Cange, V. Found in Nicholas II, 1061, Jaffé-Löwenfeld, No. 4456.
[739] Crossed out space after *t*.

ab eadem virtute fieri, quicquam a regali [740] potestate praevalet adimpleri, licet pro tuenda sacerdotali auctoritate instituta sit in his quę sunt ad seculum; sicut et sacerdotalis auctoritas pro iuvanda regali potestate constituta est in his quę sunt ad Deum. Ut igitur esset divina, sic regalem potestatem componit et sanctificat, animarumque et corporum dominatur et in omni cęlo omnique inferno et universo orbe potenter operatur. Regalis vero potestas ut terrena est et corporalis in corpora tantum dominatur et hoc inperfecte, nihil in omnino cęlo, parum autem in angustissima quadam terreni orbis potenter operatur. *Quod si hanc [potestatem] sacerdotali privilegio conferre voluerimus livens plumbum fulgenti auro erit comparatum.** Sed et hoc dicendum quia sanctę ęcclesię rex filius est non presul, discipulus non magister, subditus, non.[741]

TRACTATE J21/S:149 f.

On Evil as the Absence of Being

Nichil enim aliud esse dicuntur quam iniusticia [to this point, Scherrinsky] quę nichil aliud est quam absentia iusticię, id est rectitudinis voluntatis propter se conservate. Hęc autem omnino nichil aliud est, sicut cecitas. Non enim est aliud cęcitas quam absentia visus ubi debet esse, quę non magis est aliquid [741a] in oculo ubi debet esse visus quam in ligno ubi non debet esse. Non enim est iniusticia talis res qua inficitur et corrumpatur anima velut corpus veneno et quę faciat aliquid, sicut videtur quando malitiosus homo mala facit opera. Nam quem admodo cum indomita fera ruptis vinculis discurrendo sevit et cum navis si gubernatur dimisso gubernaculo dimittat eam ventis et motis maris vagatur invehitur in quęlibet pericula, dicimus quia hoc facit absentia catenę aut gubernaculi, non quod absentia earum aliquid sit aut quicquam faciat, sed quoniam si adessent facerent ne fera seviret aut navis periret, ita cum malus homo sevit et in quęlibet animę suę, pericula quę sunt mala opera impellitur, clamamus quia hęc operatur iniusticia, non quod ipsa ulla essentia sit aut faciat aliquid. Sed quoniam volunter cui subditi sunt omnes voluntarii motus totius hominis, absente iusticia, diversis appetibus impulsa se et omnia sibi subdita in multimoda mala levis et effrenata et sine rectore praecipitat, quod totum iusticia si adesset prohiberet ne fieret. Ex his ergo facile cognoscitur quia [in]iusticia

---

[740] In c., quisquam aregari.

[741] Breaks off with a period, though the sentence and the line are unfinished. On the next line begins the late title for the following Tractate, "De canonibus et decretis."

[741a] In c., ab quid.

(p. 123) nulla habeat essentiam, quamvis iniustę voluntatis affectus et iustos [742] actus, qui per se considerati aliquid sunt, usus iniusticiam vocet. Hac ipsa ratione intelligimus malum esse nichil. Sicut iniusticia non est aliud quam absentia debitę iusticię, ita malum non est aliud quam absentia debiti boni. Nulla autem essentia quam illi esse aliquid. Nulli enim essentię est aliud malam esse quam deesse illi bonum quod debet habere. Deesse vero bonum quod habet adesse, non est aliquid esse. Quare malam esse non est illi essentię aliquid esse. Si ergo malum nichil est et nusquam est, et si nusquam est, nec in hominibus, nec in angelis, nec in alia creatura est. Sunt ergo sine malo omnia ac per hoc nulla res mala est, sed bona sunt omnia. Omnis enim res est essentia. Essentię autem nichil est contrarium, ni non essentia, quę nichil omnino est, id est quę non est aliquid. Quare cum omnis essentia bonum sit, huic bono nichil est contrarium. Et hęc quidem vera sunt de hoc [quod] simpliciter malum dicitur. Nam sunt quędam quę dicuntur mala, sed non simpliciter sed quia quibusdam nocere videntur, dicuntur mala. Sed ipsis quibus nocere videntur et quia videntur iuvare quosdam sunt bona et quia sibi ipsis non nocent, sibi ipsi sunt bona et quia universitatis ordinem complent, *in universitate sunt valde bona.*[743] A[-b hac] *summa* (enim essentia quę) *in*(com)*mutabiliter bona* [Trinitate] (est) *creata sunt omnia,* (nec) *summe, nec ęqualiter* [nec immutabiliter] *bona, sed tamen bona etiam singula. Simul vero universa valde bona qui(a) ex omnibus consistit universitatis admirabilis pulchritudo.*[744]

The remainder of the Tractate to the point where it is taken up again by Scherrinsky is copied from Augustine's Enchiridion, chs. 11–14.[745]

TRACTATE J24A/(L4)

Magna digressio de voce "sanctus" a Boehmer omissa [746]

Ideo igitur consecrantur et benedicuntur sacerdotes et reges, ut sanctę gentis et seminis benedicti, sancti sint rectores et benedicti et sanctę potestati (p. 153) sanctoque regimini sancti cohereant, et ministri et sanctorum decens sit copula et in glutino Dei unita conventio.[747] *Sancti* inquit *estote quia ego sanctus sum Dominus Deus noster.*[748] Nomen hoc "sanctus" quid sibi velit quidve significet in scripturis divinis diligentius

---

[742] In c., iustus.

[743] Cf. Gen. 1:31.

[744] Augustine, Enchiridion, 10, modified. Brackets indicate material in the Enchiridion only; parentheses, words limited to the Anonymous.

[745] Migne, P. L., XL, coll, 256–38.

[746] Contents summarized above, n. 541.

[747] J24/L4: 669, 7.

[748] Levit. 11:44; noster, sic.

sicut Origenes dicit requirendum est, ut cum vim verbi didiceremus, etiam opus eius possimus implere. Congregemus ergo de scripturis divinis super quibus sanctum dici invenimus et deprehendemus non solum homines sed etiam animalia sancta appellata. Invenimus et vasa ministerii sancta vocitata et vestimenta sancta dici et loca nichilominus quę in urbibus vel suburbibus posita sunt sacerdotibus deputata. Ex mutis quidem animalibus primogenita bovum[749] vel pecorum sanctificari per legem divino iubentur et dicuntur. Ne facias, inquit, in eis opus ullum, quoniam Domino sanctificata sunt.[750] Super vasis vero cum in tabernaculo testimonii vasa ministerii turibula vel phialę vel cetera huiusmodi vasa sancta appellantur. Super vestimentis etiam cum stola pontificis Aaron et tunica linea et cętera huiusmodi vasa sancta dicuntur. Si ergo intueamur quo sensu hęc omnia sancta nominata sunt, adverteamus quomodo etiam nos dare operam debeamus, ut sancti esse possimus. *Natus est mihi primo primogenitus bos, non mihi licet occupare eum ad opus commune. Est enim Domino consecratus et ideo dicitur sanctus.*[751] Intelligimus ergo ex hoc muto animali quomodo lex quod sanctum vult esse nulli alii id deservire iubet nisi Domino soli. Iterum patere vel fialę quas dicit sanctas ille sunt quę numquam iubentur exire de templo sed esse in sanctis nec vult penitus humanis usibus ministrare. Similiter et vestimenta quę sancta nominantur non iubentur intra domum usui deservire pontificis, sed in templo esse et inde omnino numquam efferri sed ad hoc (p. 154) tantum consecrata esse ut his Deo ministrans pontifex induatur et sint semper in templo. Ad ceteros vero usus communes utatur communibus indumentis. Similiter et pateris et fialis his quę sancta appellantur ad humanos et communes usus uti non licet, sed tantum ad divina ministeria. Quod si intellexisti quomodo vel animalia vel vasa vel vestimenta sancta appellat, consequenter intellige quod his observationibus et legibus etiam homo sanctus appellatur. Si quis enim seipsum devoverit Deo, siquis nullis negotiis sęcularibus se implicuerit ut ei placeat cui se probavit, siquis separatus est et segregatus a reliquis hominibus carnaliter viventibus et mundanis negotiis obligatis, non quęrens ea quę super terram sed quę in cęlis sanctis sunt, iste merito sanctus appellatur. Donec enim permixtus est turbis et in multitudine fluctuantium voluptatum nec vacat soli Domino, segregatus a vulgo, non potest esse sanctus. Nam de his quid dicemus qui cum gentilium turbis ad spectacula maturant et conspectus suos atque auditus inpudicis verbis et actibus fędant? Non est verum pronunciare de talibus. Ipsi enim sentire et

---

[749] In c., bonum.
[750] Cf. Num. 18:17.
[751] Num. 18:17.

videre possunt quam sibi deligerint partem. Tu ergo qui hęc audis, cui hęc divina recitantur, quem ipsius etiam sermo Dei convenit dicens: *Sancti estote quia et ego sanctus sum Dominus Deus vester*,[752] sapienter intellige quę dicuntur, ut sis beatus cum feceris ea, hoc est, enim quod dicitur tibi: *Separate ab omni non solum homine sed et fratre inquiete ambulante et non secundum traditiones apostolicas*.[753] *Separamini et enim qui portatis*, inquit, *vasa Domini et exite de medio eorum, dicit Dominus*.[754] Separate a terrenis actibus, separate a concupiscentia mundi. *Omne enim quod in mundo est*, secundum Apostolum, *concupiscentia est carnis et concupiscentia oculorum quę non* (p. 155) *est a Deo*.[755] Cum ergo separaveris te ab iis omnibus, devovete Deo tanquam primogenitum vitulum. Non operetur pro te peccatum nec iugum tibi inponat malicia, sed esto semotum et segregatum usibus tanquam sacerdotalibus tanquam primogenitum animal mancipatum. Segregare et secernere tanquam fialę sanctę et sancta turibula, solis templi usibus. Et Dei ministerio vacans, separate et semove ab omni pollutione peccati et esto semotus et segregatus intra templum Domini tanquam sancta indumenta pontificis. In templum namque Dei est segregatus et separatus ille *qui in lege Dei meditatur die ac nocte et qui in mandatis eius cupit nimis*.[756] *Sancti ergo estote* dicit Dominus *quia et ego sanctus sum*.[757] Quid est quia et ego sanctus sum? Sicut ego, inquit, segregatus sum et longe separatus ab omnibus quę adorantur et coluntur sive in cęlo sive in terra, sicut excedo omnem creaturam atque ab universis qui a me facta sunt segregor, ita et vos segregati estote ab omnibus qui non sunt sancti, nec Deo dicati. Segregari autem dicimus non locis, sed actibus nec regionibus, sed conversationibus. Denique et ipse sermo in Greca lingua quod dicitur "hagios" [758] quasi extra terram esse significat. Quicumque enim segregavit se Deo merito extra terram et extra mundum videbitur. Potest enim et ipse dicere: *Super terram ambulantes conversationem in celis habemus*.[759] Salomon quoque in Proverbiis dicit: *Laqueus est viro forti cito aliquid de suis sanctificare*.[760] Postea enim qua voverit evenit pęnitentere. Et hoc est utique quod dicitur: Ne forte qui cum fructus ex area *aut vinum ex torcularibus colligit* [761] et dixerit: *Volo

[752] Levit. 11:44.
[753] Cf. II Thes. 3:6.
[754] Cf. II Cor. 6:17.
[755] I Joh. 2:16.
[756] Cf. Ps. 76:7, 118:47.
[757] Levit. 11:44.
[758] In c., aGjoc. Isidore.
[759] Phil. 3:20.
[760] Prov. 29:6.
[761] Cf. Jer. 48:33.

tantum offerre ęcclesię vel in usus pauperum aut peregrinorum tantum
prebere.** Si per ea ex hoc quod vovet aliquid ad usus proprios pręsumat
iam (p. 156) non de suis fructibus presumpsit, sed sancta Dei violavit.
Et ideo laqueus fortis est sanctificare aliquid. Hoc est vovere Deo et
post modum pęnitentia ductus ad usus proprios ea quę consecraverat
revocare. Sed et si nos ipsos consecramus et offerimus Deo aut etiam si
aliud vovemus, observemus hunc laqueum ne forte per ea qui nos Deo
vovimus iterum humanis usibus vel actibus subiugemus. Vovet autem
se unusquisque verbi gratia sicut Nazarei faciebant tribus aut iiii aut v.
placuisset annis in templo se consecrantes Dei, ut ibi semper vacarent,
observantes illa quę de Nazareis scripta sunt ut comam capitis nutrirent,
nec ascenderet ferrum super caput eorum toto vitę suę tempore aut
vinum non continerent, neque aliquid ex vitę et cętera, quęcunque com-
plexa fuisset, voti professio. Sed et alium quis ita vovet Deo sicut Anna
fecit Samuelem? Ante enim qui nasceretur obtulit eum Deo dicens: et
dabo eum Domino datun omnibus diebus vitę suę.[762] *Ex quibus omnibus clarum est quomodo unusquisque nostrum qui vult esse sanctus
consecrare se debeat Deo et nullis preter ea negotiis vel actibus qui ad
Deum minime pertinent occupare.**

Ideo [763] igitur consecrantur sacerdotes et reges et sanctificantur ut
nullis negotiis vel actibus qui ad Deum minime pertinent occupentur, sed
sancti sint, id est extra mundum segregati inter Deum et populum mediatores effecti et in cęlis conversentur et in terris subditos moderentur.

[762] Cf. I Sam. 1:11.
[763] L4: 669, 8.

THE APPENDIX: A DESCRIPTION OF ITS CONTENTS WITH SELECTED
PORTIONS GIVEN IN FULL [764]

Parts	Page in Codex	Correspondence [765]	Remarks
I. [Consecratio sacerdotis = Ordinatio episcopi.]			
Talis quippe est pontificis consecratio.	164		Begins at top of p.
1. [Domine sancte pater omnipotens ęternę] deus honorum omnium. deus	164	R4	Opening phrase in c. different from R. Begins with only ordinary capitalization and not with initial.
2. Hoc domine copiose in eius caput influat.	165	R5	For the original rubric the A. gives another which is similar to that [765a] added in the margin of R.
3. Ungantur manus iste et sanctificentur.	166	R8	
4. Deus et pater domini nostri ihesu christi.	166	Rf	
5. Deus totius creaturę principum.	166	Rh	
6. Accipe anulum discretionis	166	R13	
7. Omnipotens et misericors deus	167	Rg	
8. Accipe baculum sacri regiminis signum.[766]	167	R12	
9. Accipe baculum pastoralis officij signum.	167	R11	
10. Accipe euangelium et uade prodica populo tibi commisso. potens est enim deus tibi augere gratiam qui uiuit et regnat in secula seculorum. Amen.	167		Wanting in R.
11. Populus te honoret. adiuuet te dominus.	167 f.	R17	
12. Omnipotens sempiterne deus qui distinctis ordinibus	168	Ri	

---

[764] Since an exact transcript of the documents copied out in the Appendix is of especial value in textual comparisons, I have here reproduced the text without any alteration of spelling, capitalization, or punctuation.

[765] The references under this heading are the following:

R = Archbishop Robert's Benedictional. The numbers refer to the formularies of the original *Ordinatio episcopi*; the letters, to the formularies of the Rouen Supplement. See above, p. 40.

H = S. Hellmann, who has edited and numbered the nine Greek Proverbs of our Codex. Op. cit., pp. 121 ff.

W = H. Wasserschleben, op. cit. The numbers refer to chapters of liber xxv.

[765a] Op. cit., p. 126, n. 3. The A. reads: Hic mutet vocem et dicat · quasi orationem ponens olevm in capite mixtum cum crismate. Unguatur. et consecratur caput. . . .

[766] In full above, n. 114.

TRACTATE J24A/(L4) (*continued*)
THE APPENDIX: A DESCRIPTION OF ITS CONTENTS WITH SELECTED PORTIONS GIVEN IN FULL

Parts	Page in Codex	Corre-spondence	Remarks
13. Omnipotens pater sanctę deus ęternę	168 f.	R15	Rubric hereto unique to the A.[766a]
14. Domine ihesu christe. tu pręelegisti apostolos tuos.	169	R16	
II. [Consecratio regis]	169–172;	Rpp. 140–7	No indication that episcopal *ordo* is completed and that the royal Ordo has begun. The misplaced quire of the Codex affects the pagination of the royal Ordo. Robert is reproduced almost exactly, formulary by formulary (1–24).
1. Hęc tria populo christiano	189–194		
24. Benedic domine fortitudinem principis . . . quia ascensor Cęli auxiliator suus in sempiternum fiat .;.			
III. [Hibernensis, lib. xxv+Proverbia Graecorum]			
1. DE NOMINE REGNI.	194 f.		Cap. 2 in Hibernensis No. 9.

Isidorus ait. Regnum a regibus dictum est. Nam sicut reges a regenda uocantur. ita regnum a regibus uocatum est. Non autem regit qui non corrigit. Recte igitur faciendo nomen regis teneretur. peccando amittitur. Vnde et apud ueteres tale erat prouerbium. Rex eris si recte facias. si non facias non eris. Rex tribus modis dicitur. Primo eo quod frangit inimicos. Secundo eo quod armat exercitum. Tercio eo quod exigit tributum.

Item ysidorus. Regię potestatis apud grecos basilici uocantur. Quia tanquam basses populum sustineat. unde et baseas coronas habent. Quanto enim magis quisque proponitur. tanto amplius pondere laborum grauatur.

2. De quinque temporibus regni in prouerbijs grecorum legitur.[767] Quinque tempora regni sunt apud romanos	195	H1	Cap. 1 in Hibernensis No. 9; found also in No. 6.
3. Octo columnę sunt quę fortiter	195	H2	
4. Septem speciosiora sunt alijs	195	H3	
5. Rex pacificus lęta facię	196	H4	
6. De septem moribus omni regni conuenientibus hieronimus ait. Sunt septem	196	W15ab[768]	Adds to . . . in bello: aquileię uiros.

[766a] Finita benedictione cathedrę ij episcopi Benedictum eposcopum in cathedram episcopalem mittant · quorum unus subscriptas orationes dicat.

[767] Except for this one introductory phrase, I am giving the opening phrase of the Proverb itself and not the introductory wording of the Anonymous which Hellmann gives with each Proverb.

[768] Lower case letters refer to the subsections of the Wasserschleben edition. The Anonymous often gives only some of these, perhaps adding others (x, y, z) or adding to the Wasserschleben subsections (+). Only the supplementary material is here reproduced. Only the most notable variant readings are indicated under Remarks.

Tractate J24A/(L4) (*continued*)

The Appendix: A Description of its Contents with Selected Portions Given in Full

Parts	Page in Codex	Correspondence	Remarks
7. Tria sunt quę in regalibus moribus	196 f.	H5	Unique to MS 415 according to H.
8. Paradisus in prope rex iustus et pacificus.	197	H6	
9. De eo quod malorum regum opera suum destruumt regnum patricius ait.	197	W3	
10. Septem ora sunt	197 f.	H7	
11. De increptatione regum in libro sapientię scriptum est.	198		In Hibernensis No. 6 (= Wisdom, 6:2–7 with minor variations from Vulgate).
12. Rex impius leonis personam habere	198	H8	
13. De non adulando regi uel peccatori regi [c] Item paulus pandit. Quicunque adulari uoluerit. aut pro necessitate aut pro adulatione benigne reuelat. Item paulus. si hominibus placuissem seruus dei non essem.	198 f.	W19ab	
14. Mendacium regis multi affirmant.	199	H9	
15. De eo quod bonorum regum opera ędificant patricius palat.	199	W4abc	
16. De rege Non habente uxores plurimas in deuteronomo dicitur.	200	W6ab	W. has: in Regum libris.
17. De non custodiente regem.	200	W8	
18. De censu regi dando christus in euangelio ait.	200	W9a	
19. De utrisque hieronimus ait [x] Item augustinus. Quę sunt cesaris? id est nummus argentum. Quę sunt dei? id est homo cuius imago est in uerbo.	200 f.	W9b x	Minus last sentence.

Tractate J24A/(L4) (*continued*)
The Appendix: A Description of its Contents with Selected Portions Given in Full

Parts	Page in Codex	Correspond-ence	Remarks
		c	
		d	
[f+] . . . Hęc descriptio prima facta est a praeside syrie cirino. Et ibant omnes ut profiterentur singuli in suam ciuitatem.		f+	
[y] Item christus reddit pro se et petro dicens. Redde pro me et te.		y	
		g	Anonymous ascribes to Orosius.
		e	Anonymous adds: uel hieronimus.
20. De censu regi non dando super ęcclesiam mundialibus rebus liberam christus ait.	201	W10ab+, xe	

[b+] . . . Augustinus hunc sermonem tractat inquiens. Intellegendum est liberos esse id est non esse uictigales. Multo ergo liberiores esse debent quolibet regno terreno filij regni illius sub quo sunt omnia regna terrena. [x] Item hieronimus in tractatu mathei manifestat. Dominus noster et secundum carnem et secundum spiritum filius regis erat. uel ex stirpe dauid generatus. uel omnipotentis uerbum patris est. Ergo tributa quasi regis filius non debebat. sed qui humilitatem assumpserat debuit adimplere omnem iusticiam. Ille pro nobis crucem sustinuit et tributa reddedit. sed nos pro illius honore tributa non reddimus quasi filij regis a uectigalibus inmunes sumus.

| 21. De rebus pauperum in censum non dans hieronimus in | 201 f. | W(11) | Corresponds to W11 but wording quite different. |

tractatu mathei manifestat. sed simpliciter intellectus ędificat auditorem dum tantę dominus pauperitatis est: ut unde tributa apostolus redderet non habuerit. Quod siquis obicere uoluerit. quomodo iudas in loculis portabat pecuniam. respondebimus. Quod res pauperum in usus suos uertere nefas putauit. nobis quidem tribuit exemplum.

| 22. De Grauitate imperij regis samuel narrauit | 202 | W12 | |
| 23. De ordinatio regis cum oleo | 202 f. | W1+ | |

[1+] . . . in principem et insiliet in te spiritus domini et prophetabis et mutaberis in uirum alium [I Sam. 10:6]. Item. Tulit samuel cornu olei et uncxit dauid in medio fratrum eius et directus est spiritus domini in dauid a die illa [I Sam. 16:13] et uncxerunt salomonem nathan propheta et sadoch sacerdos regem in gyon et exclamantes leti dixerunt. Viuat rex salomon [I Kings 1:39 & 45 conflated].

Tractate J24A/(L4) (*continued*)

The Appendix: A Description of its Contents with Selected Portions Given in Full

Parts	Page in Codex	Corre-spondence	Remarks
24. De inobedientibus regum legibus aperte puniendis	203	Wab	
25. De sermone regis occidente inimicum et quod loca sancta non defendunt reos. licet aliquanto tempore peracto.	203 f.	W17a+, cde	
26. De sermone regis aut ducis protegente inimicum aut uin[c]tum sed tantum misericordię gratia.	203 f.	W18abd	Ends with (.;.).
IV. [The "Exordium" of "De consecratione," Version B] Sancta ęcclesia sponsa christi est.	204 ff.	Böhmer	J24/L4: 662 ff. Begins with a normal capital. No initial as in the foregoing items from the Hibernensis. Moreover, there is no space between it and item 26.

TRACTATE J24c

On the Laity and Baptism

(P. 235) Laicus et christianus hęc duo nomina, aut equalia sunt in dignitate aut alterus altero est dignius. Sed non sunt ęqualia in dignitate. Alterum igitur altero est dignius. Christianus quippe hoc nomen dignius est quia sanctum nomen est et a sancto sanctorum, id est Christo, denominatum. Christus enim nomen illud est *quod est super omne nomen quod Pater dedit filio ut in nomine eius omne genuflectatur,* usque, *in gloria Dei Patris.*[769] *Ab hoc nomine denominatur christianus, ut sicut Dei filius hoc homen quod est Christus accepit propter gratię et totius sanctitatis plenitudinem, ita et adoptionis fiilius eiusdem nominis participationem accipiat, ut a Christo christianus denominetur propter eiusdem gratię et sanctitatis participationem, per quam fit ut etiam glorię Christi assequatur communionem et divinitatis adeptionem.** *At vero hoc nomen quod est laicus non ad aliquam gratiam potest referri, non ad gloriam, non ad participationem divinitatis Christi, sed sumptum est a Greco lai quod interpretur populus et sonat popularis sive (p. 236)

[769] Phil. 2: 9 ff.

publicanus, quod magis ad ignominiam refertur quam ad gloriam, ad vitę immundaciam quam ad sanctimoniam.** Quia et nomen istud commune est et omnibus, non baptizatis et baptizatis etiam qui non vivunt secundum formam et rationem sacri baptismatis. Nam quicunque vivunt secundum formam et rationem sacri baptismatis, quę est sacrosancta christianitas, quia sancti sunt et participes gratię Christi, improprie immo iniuste vocantur laici. *Magna quippe est sanctitas baptismi, divinumque sacramentum et tantę magnitudinis ut cętera omnia in se contineat sacramenta et ex eo cuncta dependeant sacerdotium videlicet et cętera quę sacerdotis inferiora sunt, unde et sanctius et praestantius his omnibus probatur esse baptismatis et christianitatis sacramentum.** Quod ex eorum effectibus, facile potest agnosci. Baptismum quippe efficit christianum, id est participem Christi et coheredem. Coheres autem Christi filius est et heres Dei, quo nichil sublimius nihil sanctius divina gratia confert homini. *Facit etiam baptismum ut homo fiat hęreditas Domini, sors Dei et quia sortitur a Deo sine visibile signo in spiritu et unitate clericus est Domini.** Quia de numero illorum est quibus Petrus loquitur dicens: *Vos genus electum, regale sacerdotium, gens sancta, populus adquisitionis.*[770] Facit propterea baptismum ut corpus regenerati fiat caro crucifixi, fiat etiam templum sanctum Dei, fiat et habitaculum Spiritus sancti ut in [771] ara cordis offerat sacrificium iusticię, *hostiam vivam Deo placentem et sacrificium spiritus,*[772] quia et sacerdos in spiritu. *Nam et qui baptizatur summum sacerdotem induit, id est Iesum Christum, et stolam primam recipit et anulum fidei sanctitatis quoque amictu et vestimento salutis induitur.*[773] ** Quę omnia praestantiora et sanctiora esse omnibus nemo negat ni imperitur. Effectus autem sacerdotii ad horum ministerium intendit, et ad expianda commissa hominum institutum esse videtur. Sed tamen utriusque effectus et sacerdotii et baptismi sanctus est atque divinus, ideoque nec sacerdos nec christianus iuste et proprie dicti potest laicus, id est popularis sive publicanus. Alterum enim sicut dictum est, nomen est glorię, id est christianus, alterum ignominię, id est laicus.

TRACTATE J24D

ON EXCOMMUNICATION

(P. 237) Dominus noster Iesus Christus si Petro soli contulit claves regni cęlorum, id est potestatem ligandi atque solvendi, constat profecto

---

[770] I Petr. 2:9.
[771] Blurred in c.
[772] Cf. Rom. 12:1.
[773] Cf. J22(26)/L2: 655, 1 ff.

quia aliis apostolis eandem potestatem minime contulit. Sed sicut evangelica usitate didicimus, contulit illam et aliis apostolis. Secundum Matheum enim omnibus dixisse legitur: *Quęcunque alligaveritis super terram usque soluta erit et in cęlis.*[774] Secundum Iohannem vero post resurrectionem apparens, insufflavit eis et dixit: *Accipite Spiritum sanctum* usque *retenta sunt.*[775] Hanc igitur potestatem ęqualiter omnibus tribuit, et in hac ęquales eos exhibuit. Nam et quod soli Petro dixisse videtur: *Tibi dabo claves [claves] regni cęlorum* [776] et cętera, non Petro soli, sed in Petro omnibus promissit, qui pro omnibus ei respondit: *Tu es Christus filius Dei vivi.*[777] Non tamen a Petro hanc potestatem acceperunt alii, sed a Christo pariter et Petrus et alii apostoli. Sed querendum nobis est, utrum idem Dominus hanc potestatem et aliis contulerit quam apostolis. Nam si contulit, equales illos fecit apostolis. Sed non legitur quod eius temporis aliquos fecerit ęquales apostolis. Non ergo aliis hanc potestatem contulit quam apostolis. Sed neque post apostolos hoc alicui fecisse legitur. Unde ergo episcopi hanc potestatem acceperunt. Si ab apostolis, quomodo eam potuerunt in alios transfundere apostoli? Deditne eis potestatem qua possent transfundere in alios hanc potestatem? Si non dedit, non potuerunt, si dedit, utique potuerunt, quod tamen in usitate evangelii minime potest repperiri. Verum si apostoli in alios transfuderunt, in illos videlicet transfuderunt quos episcopos ordinaverunt et non in alios. De quibus rursus quęrendum est, utrum et ipsi acceperint ab apostolis potestatem qua in alios transfunderent hanc potestatem. Nan si acceperunt, transfundere utique potuerunt. Si non acceperunt, non potuerunt. *Sed fortasse aliquis dicat: Quia non apostolis tantum non episcopis, sed sanctę et universali ęcclesię hęc potestas collata est a Christo. Sancta autem et universalis ęcclesia omnium fidelium est congregatio in Christo. Omnium igitur fidelium congregationi in Christo collata est hęc potestas, si ecclesię collata est, in qua et apostolorum (p. 238) et episcoporum constat eam esse consortem.** Sed episcopus et ecclesia magnam adhibere captelam ligandis atque absolvendis hominibus. Nam omnium hominum alii sunt membra Christi, praeelecti et praedestinati ad vitam, benedicti a Patre, et quibus regnum Dei paratum est a constitutione mundi; alii membra diaboli, ab ęterno dampnati in mortem et maledicti ituri in ignem ęternum qui paratus est diabolo et angelis eius. Horum igitur si quemlibet episcopus absolverit non propter hoc salvus erit, nec membrum Christi poterit fieri, talemque excommuni-

---

[774] Matt. 18:18.
[775] John 20:23.
[776] Matt. 16:19.
[777] Matt. 16:16.

care superfluum esse videtur, ni ut gravius dampnetur et deterior efficiatur. Quod contra si membrum Christi electum et praedestinatum ad
vitam et benedictum a Deo Patre omni benedictione spirituali in cęlesti-
bus in Christo ligaverit, id est, excommunicaverit, non propter hoc
poterit dampnari et diaboli membrum fieri; eoque talem excommunicare
excommunicanti periculosum est atque dampnabile. Quapropter episcopus omnis sive ęcclesia his excommunicandis maximam debet adhibere
cautelam. His autem qui excommunicatur diligenti sciscitatione debet
inquiere utrum sit pastor qui excommunicat an mercennarius vel latro.
Si pastor est, timeat propter reverentiam. Si mercennarius vel latro non
timeat propter homorem Dei et gloriam. *Nam qui talibus irrogat contumelias honorem Deo tribut et gloriam.** Tales enim *non intrant per
hostium in ovile ovium sed ascendit aliunde*[778] et non veniunt ni ut
furentur et mactent perdant. Fures enim sunt et latrones quia non intrant per Christum, qui est hostium *quod sibi proprie retinuit et nulli
alii concessit*, sicut Augustinus in libro super Iohannem asserit: *Christus,*
inquiens, *et pastor est et hostium, quod pastor est aliis concessit. Nam
Petrus pastor est et Paulus pastor est et ceteri apostoli et episcopi pastores sunt.*[779] Hostium vero nec Petrus est nec Paulus nec aliquis alius
ni solus Christus. Quapropter qui non intrant per Christum ni intrant
per hostium etiam si per Petrum intraient[780] et Paulum ni per apostolorum quemlibet alium. Non autem intrant per Christum qui non divina
electione vel iudicio intrant sed humano intuitu et preconio intruduntur.

[778] John 10:1.
[779] Tract. 47, c., § 3, but not exactly; Migne, P. L., XXXV, col. 1734.
[780] Sic in c.